Contents

Foreword

Has the pen or pencil dipped so deep in the blood of the human race as the needle?' asked the writer Olive Schreiner. The answer is, quite simply, *no*. The art of embroidery has been the means of educating women into the feminine ideal, and of proving that they have attained it, but it has also provided a weapon of resistance to the constraints of femininity.

In this book I examine the historical processes by which embroidery became identified with a particular set of characteristics, and consigned to women's hands. By mapping the relationship between the history of embroidery and changing notions of what constituted feminine behaviour from the Middle Ages to the twentieth century, we can see how the art became implicated in the creation of femininity across classes, and that the development of ideals of feminine behaviour determined the style and iconography of needlework. To know the history of embroidery is to know the history of women.

London 1982

1 : The Creation of Femininity

Needlework is the favourite hobby of two percent of British males, about equal to the number who go to church regularly. Nearly one man in three fills in football coupons, in an average month, or has a bet. [1]

The *Guardian* was no doubt confident that its coverage of a Government survey of changing trends in leisure activities was eye-catching, and that this opening sentence was guaranteed to amuse by its incongruity. The unspoken assumption implied by the juxtaposition of male needleworkers and churchgoers is that these men are pious, prim and conformist. Real men gamble and fill in football coupons; only sissies and women sew and swell congregations.

The sexual division that assigns women to sewing is inscribed in our social institutions, fostered by school curricula which still direct boys to carpentry and girls to needlework. Even in today's progressive schools the assumptions and divisions remain intact. An enthusiastic report on a large suburban primary school praised the diligent, pioneering teaching practised by the staff.

Two photographs illustrated science teaching methods: in one, a small group of boys were shown unselfconsciously engrossed in a 'wave power machine'; in the other, two smiling girls displayed copper atoms embroidered in silk.[2]

The role of embroidery in advertising and commercial design also endorses the notion that a man who practises embroidery is imperilling his sexual identity. Embroidery is invariably employed to evoke the home. The cover of a brochure produced by a British home removal firm illustrates an embroidery of a house, the stock motif of so many samplers, and bears the embroidered words 'Home Moving Guide'. Embroidery connotes not only home but a socially advantaged home, securely placed in the upper reaches of the class structure. An advertisement for embroidery patterns promises that 'the tapestries are a pleasure to make and once completed will elegantly grace any home and become much valued family heirlooms'.

It is not only home and family that embroidery signifies but, specifically, mothers and daughters. Heinz based an advertising campaign for tomato ketchup on a picture of a sampler stitched with the words, 'If other ketchups were as rich, then I'd say so stitch by stitch. Ann and Lucy James (but mostly Lucy)'. The sampler associates tomato ketchup with the ideal of childhood as sincere, innocent and pure.

Embroidery also evokes the stereotype of the virgin in opposition to the whore, an infantilising representation of women's sexuality. Thus Lil-lets the menstrual tampons were recently packed in a box masquerading as fabric, embroidered with pastel flowers to represent menstruation as natural and entirely nonthreatening. The conflation of embroidery and female sexuality, both innately virginal and available for consumption, is blatantly expressed in the title bestowed on a porn magazine, the *Rustler Sampler*, which offered 'nearly two hundred, yes, two hundred juicy, picture-packed pages'. The word 'Sampler' evokes an image of innumerable passive, powerless women just waiting to be selected and roped in by the 'Rustler'. Embroidery has become indelibly associated with stereotypes of femininity.

I shall define briefly what I mean by femininity. In *The Second Sex*, 1949, Simone de Beauvoir wrote: 'It is evident that woman's "character" – her convictions, her values, her wisdom, her morality, her tastes, her behaviour – are to be explained by her situation.'[3] In other words, femininity, the behaviour expected and encouraged in women, though obviously related to the biological sex of the individual, is shaped by society. The changes in ideas about feminity that can be seen reflected in the history of embroidery are striking confirmation that femininity is a social and psychosocial product.

Nevertheless, the conviction that femininity is natural to women (and unnatural in men) is tenacious. It is a crucial aspect of patriarchal ideology, sanctioning a rigid and oppressive division of labour. Thus women active in the upsurge of feminism which began in the 1960s set out to challenge accepted definitions of the innate differences between the sexes, and to provide a new understanding of the creation of femininity. In consciousness-raising groups and campaigns we compared our experiences at work, at school, at home, in relationships, as mothers, as daughters and sisters. The workings of sexism were scrutinised in the division of labour in and out of the home, in sexuality, the family, health care, child care, language, the law, education, the arts, the media and government policy. How race, class and sex intersect to shape women's lives became clearer.

Institutional discrimination co-exists and interacts with the mechanisms and effects of psychic subordination, though obviously rigid divisions cannot be drawn between internal and external oppression. The complex of emotional attitudes of passivity, submission and masochism which guarantee the subordination of women cannot simply be shrugged off or discounted. Juliet Mitchell, in *Psychoanalysis and Feminism*, 1974, observed that:

> . . . the status of woman is held in the heart and the head as well as in the home: oppression has not been trivial or historically transitory – to maintain itself so efficiently it courses through the mental and emotional bloodstream. To think that this should not be so does not necessitate pretending it is already not so.[4]

Many feminists have looked to psychoanalysis and Marxist theory to provide an account of how masculinity and femininity are constructed and reproduced historically. The family was identified as the place where the 'inferiorised psychology'[5] of women was reproduced and the social and economic exploitation of women as wives and mothers legitimised. Writing of the construction of femininity in the family, anthropologist Gayle

Rubin in an essay in *Towards an Anthropology of Women*, 1975, commented: 'One can read Freud's essay on femininity as a description of how a group is prepared to live with oppression', and she makes clear how painful the process is. 'It is certainly plausible to argue that the creation of "femininity" in a woman in the course of socialisation is an act of psychic brutality.'[6]

It is, however, important to distinguish between the construction of femininity, lived femininity, the feminine ideal and the feminine stereotype. The construction of femininity refers to the psychoanalytic and social account of sexual differentiation. Femininity is a lived identity for women either embraced or resisted. The feminine ideal is an historically changing concept of what women should be, while the feminine stereotype is a collection of attributes which is imputed to women and against which their every concern is measured. Millicent Fawcett, the nineteenth-century British feminist, declared, 'We talk about "women and women's suffrage", we do not talk about Woman with a capital W. That we leave to our enemies.'[7]

In other words, there is a significant difference between acknowledging the construction of femininity in the family and its maintenance in social institutions, and accepting the cultural representation of women imposed upon us. The feminine stereotype categorises everything women are and everything we do as entirely, essentially and eternally feminine, denying differences between women according to our economic and social position, or our geographical and historical place. In fact, what Gayle Rubin termed 'the act of psychic brutality' meets with resistance at all levels, in different ways at different historical moments.

What, then, is the purpose of the feminine stereotype? In *Old Mistresses: Women, Art and Ideology*, 1981, Griselda Pollock and I looked at the role of the feminine stereotype in the writing of art history. We asked why painting by women has been set apart from painting by men and why women's art, in all its diversity, has been described as homogeneous. We revealed the feminine stereotype to be one of the major elements in the construction of the current view of the history of art.[8] The particular way women's work is presented – the constant assertion of the feminine weakness of women's art – sustains the dominance of masculinity and male art.

The situation of embroidery is more elusive. When women paint, their work is categorised as homogeneously feminine – but it is acknowledged to be art. When women embroider, it is seen not as art, but entirely as the expression of femininity. And, crucially, it is categorised as craft. The division of art forms into a hierarchical classification of arts and crafts is usually ascribed to factors of class within the economic and social system, separating artist from artisan. The fine arts – painting and sculpture – are considered the proper sphere of the privileged classes while craft or the applied arts – like furniture-making or silver-smithery – are associated with the working class. However there is an important connection between the hierarchy of the arts and the sexual categories male/female. The development of an ideology of femininity coincided historically with the emergence of a clearly defined separation of art and craft. This division emerged in the Renaissance at the time when embroidery was increasingly becoming the province of women amateurs, working for the home without pay. Still later the split between art and craft was reflected in the changes in art education from craft-based workshops to academies at precisely the time – the eighteenth century – when an ideology of femininity as natural to women was evolving.

The art/craft hierarchy suggests that art made with thread and art made with paint are intrinsically unequal: that the former is artistically less significant. But the real differences between the two are in terms of *where* they are made and *who* makes them. Embroidery, by the time of the art/craft divide, was made in the domestic sphere, usually by women, for 'love'. Painting was produced predominantly, though not only, by men, in the public sphere, for money. The professional branch of embroidery, unlike that of painting, was, from the end of the seventeenth century to the end of the nineteenth century, largely in the hands of working-class women, or disadvantaged middle-class women. Clearly there are huge differences between painting and embroidery; different conditions of production and different conditions of reception. But rather than acknowledging that needlework and painting are different but equal arts, embroidery and crafts associated with 'the second sex' or the working class are accorded lesser artistic value.

The classification of embroidery is a difficult task. To term it 'art' raises special problems. Moving embroidery several rungs up the ladder of art forms could be interpreted as simply affirming the hierarchical categorisations, rather than deconstructing them. Moreover, to describe embroidery as 'art' is to fail to distinguish it

5

from painting, concealing the profound differences that have developed historically between the two media. However, to call it 'craft' is no solution. Embroidery fails to comply with the utilitarian imperative that defines craft – because much of it is purely pictorial. Traditionally, women have called embroidery 'work'. Although to some extent an appropriate term, it tends to confirm the stereotypical notion that patience and perseverance go into embroidery – but little else. Moreover, the term was engendered by an ideology of femininity as service and selflessness and the insistence that women work for others, not for themselves. I have decided to call embroidery art because it is, undoubtedly, a cultural practice involving iconography, style and a social function.

That embroiderers do transform materials to produce sense – whole ranges of meanings – is invariably entirely overlooked. Instead embroidery and a stereotype of femininity have become collapsed into one another, characterised as mindless, decorative and delicate; like the icing on the cake, good to look at, adding taste and status, but devoid of significant content.

The association between women and embroidery, craft and femininity, has meant that writers concerned with the status of women have often turned their attention towards this tangled, puzzling relationship. Feminists who have scorned embroidery tend to blame it for whatever constraint on women's lives they are committed to combat. Thus, for example, eighteenth-century critical commentators held embroidery responsible for the ill health which was claimed as evidence of women's natural weakness and inferiority. In the nineteenth century, women wanting to be taken seriously in supposedly 'male' spheres deliberately declared their rejection of embroidery to distance themselves from the feminine ideal. In Helen Black's late nineteenth-century publication, *Notable Authors of The Day*, 1893, consisting of interviews with novelists, Adeline Sargeant stated, 'I have done some elaborate embroidery in my time but now I never use the needle for amusement, only for necessity.'[9] She asserts her seriousness and her disdain for feminine frivolity. The majority of interviewees, however, stress their needlework. For although writing novels was, by then, an acceptable activity for women, professionalism was frowned upon. Women therefore covered themselves with their amateur 'work'. Mrs L. B. Walford, for example, is described as 'wearing a pretty blue tea gown richly

1 *Madame de Pompadour,* Francois-Hubert Drouais (French, 1727–1775),
National Gallery, London. Oil on canvas, 2.17 × 1.56 m.
In the eighteenth century, embroidery signified a leisured, aristocratic life-style.

2 Frontispiece, *Needlecraft: Artistic and Practical*, Butterick, New York, 1889. Readers are told that this book describes skills which will assure the class standing of their household: 'It covers a range of subjects extending from the simplest towel-making to the making of the various decorative adjuncts which impart an air of refinement, and without which the most sumptuously furnished apartment is never quite satisfying.'

3 Nineteenth-century print of a mother and daughter. Published in *Gay Left*, 1980. Embroidery as a tool for transmitting feminine behaviour from mother to daughter created both a bond between women and a focus for mutual resentment.

4 *The Lion in Love*, Abraham Solomon (British 1824–1862), Christies, London. 71.1 × 88.9 cm.

5 *In Love*, Marcus Stone (British, 1840–1921), Castle Museum, Nottingham, 1888. Oil on canvas, 118.8 × 167.8 cm. Eyes lowered, head bent, the embroiderer's pose signifies subjugation, submission and modesty, yet her silence also suggests self-containment. The silent embroiderer has, however, become implicated in a stereotype of femininity in which the self-containment of the woman sewing is represented as seductiveness.

7 Anonymous sampler, English, Victoria and Albert Museum, London. Second half of the seventeenth century. Silk on linen, 68.6 × 19.8 cm.

6 Anonymous mourning picture, private collection, London. Late eighteenth century. Silk, chenille and water colour.
There were several different forms of embroidered mourning pictures and samplers: historical, allegorical, personal, and public.

embroidered in silk by her own hand',[10] and Helen Mather is offered as a 'great needlewoman, not only are the long satin curtains by her own hand but the pillows, cushions and dainty lampshade.'[11]

To reject embroidery, as Adeline Sargeant did, was to run the risk of appearing to disparage other women, or to endorse the stereotypical view of the art propounded by a male-dominated society. For purely tactical reasons therefore, women who might have been critical of embroidery praised it. Thus the more enlightened seventeenth-century women educationalists had included needlework in their curriculum largely to provide an acceptable face for women's education. Nineteenth-century writers defended embroidery, claiming it as an unappreciated art form. Some believed in raising the status of women, not by dismissing women's traditional creative activity, but by demanding that its true worth be recognised. In her novel *The Beth Book*, 1897, Sarah Grand offers embroidery as evidence of women's superiority. Beth embroiders, selling her work secretly through the discreet commercial outlets provided by the Arts and Crafts Movement to market 'ladies' work'. For Sarah Grand embroidery represents the beauty of the female imagination, its spiritual clarity in contrast to male pedestrian rationalism. But this attempt to validate women's work ultimately reinforces the rigid sexual categorisation and justifies the separate spheres.

Novels like *The Beth Book* are a rich source of information on attitudes towards embroidery, which is, from the eighteenth century onwards, repeatedly used to signify femininity. Through the work of four novelists I shall show briefly how each employs embroidery to comment on the position of women in society. May Sinclair takes the identification between embroidery and feminine purity to suggest that women's sexuality is innately pure and innocent, but corrupted by men. Nevertheless women's purity as embodied in embroidery has the potential power to transform patriarchal corruption. Walter Majendie in *The Helpmate*, 1907, is unfaithful to his wife with an embroiderer called Maggie, and the delicacy of her work signifies that Maggie is the seduced not the seducer. Finally her embroidery draws Majendie's family's attention to her existence; she is 'tracked down by the long trail of her beautiful embroidery'.[12] The work is ultimately responsible for revealing to the man the errors of his ways: 'He hated to see his innocent child dressed in the garment which was the token and memorial of his sin.'[13]

May Sinclair and Sarah Grand represent that tendency in nineteenth-century feminism which, by positing women's essential spiritual superiority, inadvertently confirmed the oppressive Victorian stereotype of 'The Angel in the House'. Twentieth-century novelists largely write about embroidery and femininity not as a superior essence of women, but as the product of sexual difference, of family life, and the mother/daughter relationship in particular.

Edith Wharton in *The Age of Innocence*, 1920, conjures the archetypal scene in which a mother and daughter embroider together for Newland Archer, the son of the family:

> After dinner, according to immemorial custom, Mrs Archer and Janey trailed their long silk draperies up to the drawing room where, while the gentlemen smoked below stairs, they sat beside a Carcel lamp with an engraved globe, facing each other across a rosewood work-table with a green silk bag under it, and stitched at two ends of a tapestry band of field flowers destined to adorn an 'occasional' chair in the drawing room of young Mrs Newland Archer [the son's future wife].[14]

Economically and ideologically, Janey – the unmarried, upper middle-class daughter – is destined to remain at home, locked into 'genteel' pursuits with her mother. Young Mrs Newland Archer, on the other hand, has escaped through marriage, but her own mother's influence, encapsulated in embroidery, follows her and, with peer-group pressure, ensures that she reproduces the sexual hierarchy of her own family:

> She was not a clever needle-woman: her large capable hands were made for riding, rowing and open-air activities; but since other wives embroidered cushions for their husbands she did not wish to omit this last link in her devotion . . . she was simply ripening into a copy of her mother, and, mysteriously, by the very process, trying to turn him into a Mr Welland [her father].[15]

Edith Wharton exemplifies two common uses of embroidery in women's novels. First, the image of the woman who is clumsy with the needle is repeatedly employed to counter the feminine stereotype and to combat the way in which embroidering was used to justify the sexual division of labour. Women are so nimble-fingered, it's claimed, but women's embroidery has everything to do with their place in society and nothing to do with the size of their fingers. At the same time Edith Wharton, through embroidery, demonstrates the extraordinary power of social ideology.

Colette similarly employs embroidery to undermine the stereotype and to illuminate femininity. She, however, is less fatalistic than Edith Wharton. Demonstrating a different dynamic, she suggests that the construction of femininity is rarely complete and that it can be ruptured; and that, moreover, femininity contains its own curious power.

When her daughter Bel-Gazou was nine, Colette's friends expressed their surprise and disapproval that the child was unable to sew. Anxious not to fail as a mother, and concerned that her child fulfil the social expectations that confront her, she urges Bel-Gazou to take up needlework. She remembers, however, the way her own mother had reacted when she had embroidered as a child: 'When I was a young girl, if I ever happened to occupy myself with needlework, Sido always shook her soothsayer's head and commented "you will never look like anything but a boy who is sewing".'[16] It was her mother's attitude that enabled Colette to practise embroidery and to insist that other areas of creative work were as appropriate for women.

She does, however, have mixed feelings when her own daughter embroiders. Her women friends applaud: 'Just look at her, isn't she good,' but secretly Colette disagrees:

> I shall speak the truth: I don't much like my daughter sewing. When she reads, she returns all bewildered and with flaming cheeks from the island where the chestful of precious stones is hidden, from the dismal castle where a fair-haired orphan child is persecuted. She is soaking up a tested and time-honoured poison whose effects have long been familiar. If she draws, or colours pictures, a semi-articulate song issues from her, unceasing as the hum of bees around the privet. It is the same as the buzzing of flies as they work, the slow waltz of the house painter, the refrain of the spinner at her wheel. But Bel-Gazou is silent when she sews, silent for hours on end, with her mouth firmly closed, concealing her large, new-cut incisors that bite

into the moist heart of a fruit like little saw-edged blades. She is silent, and she – why not write down the word that frightens me – she is thinking.[17]

The child's silence, her thoughts kept to herself, signify her separateness from her mother. Colette conjures up an ideal past when embroidery maintained the mother-child bond rather than underlining separation and the child's approaching adulthood. She thinks of

young embroiderers of bygone days, sitting on hard little stools in the shelter of their mother's ample skirts! Maternal authority kept them there for years and years, never rising except to change the skein of silk, or to elope with a stranger. . . What are you thinking about, Bel-Gazou?
Nothing, Mother, I'm counting my stitches.[18]

Colette's sense of anxiety when faced with her silent stitching child conveys the two sides of embroidery. Eyes lowered, head bent, shoulders hunched – the position signifies repression and subjugation, yet the embroiderer's silence, her concentration also suggests a self-containment, a kind of autonomy.

The silent embroiderer has, however, become a part of a stereotype of femininity in which the self-containment of the woman sewing is interpreted as seductiveness. The following scene from a ¬tory in *Cosmopolitan* magazine can also be found in innumerable romantic novels:

you never saw a woman sit so still. Her stillness seemed part and cause of that still summer. Day after day she sat in a basket chair on the stones beneath the pretty white iron spiral stair-case, sewing among her roses . . . Rose's hands seemed usually to be still, though the needle was always threaded. She drove men demented.[19]

In fiction the silence and stillness of the sewer can mean many things from serious concentration to a silent cry for attention, but in terms of the stereotype it is a sexual ploy. If a woman sits silently sewing she is silently asking for the silence to be broken. The stereotype denies that there is anything subversive in her silence by asserting that it is maintained for men. Yet the way the intimations of autonomy are so resolutely quashed by the stereotype suggests that there is something disturbing in the image of the embroiderer deep in her work.

The manner in which embroidery signifies both self-containment and submission is the key to understanding women's relation to the art. Embroidery has provided a source of pleasure and power for women, while being indissolubly linked to their powerlessness. Paradoxically, while embroidery was employed to inculcate femininity in women, it also enabled them to negotiate the constraints of femininity. Observing the covert ways embroidery has provided a source of support and satisfaction for women leads us out of the impasse created by outright condemnation or uncritical celebration of the art. Nevertheless, it would be a mistake to underestimate the importance of the role played by embroidery in the maintenance and creation of the feminine ideal. During the seventeenth century the art was used to inculcate femininity from such an early age that the girl's ensuing behaviour appeared innate. By the eighteenth century embroidery was beginning to signify a leisured, aristocratic life style – not working was becoming the hallmark of femininity. Embroidery with its royal and noble associations was perfect proof of gentility, providing concrete evidence that a man was able to support a leisured woman. Moreover, because embroidery was supposed to signify femininity – docility, obedience, love of home, and a life without work – it showed the embroiderer to be a deserving, worthy wife and mother. Thus the art played a crucial part in maintaining the class position of the household, displaying the value of a man's wife and the condition of his economic circumstances. Finally, in the nineteenth century, embroidery and femininity were entired fused, and the connection was deemed to be natural. Women embroidered because they were naturally feminine and were feminine because they naturally embroidered. Then embroidery was blamed for the conflicts provoked in women by the femininity the art fostered. By the end of the century, Freud was to decide that constant needlework was one of the factors that 'rendered women particularly prone to hysteria' because day-dreaming over embroidery induced 'dispositional hypnoid states'.[20]

The subject matter of a woman's embroidery during the eighteenth and nineteenth centuries was as important as its execution in affirming her femininity (and thus her worth and worthlessness in the world's eyes). It was expected to reflect the current feminine ideal, which was held to be the highest, yet paradoxically most natural, achievement of women. If the content conformed to the ideal it supposedly won the needlewoman love, admiration and support. By examining the content of embroidery throughout this book, we will see how women responded to the current ideologies of femininity from the Renaissance onwards, how they used these ideologies and were used by them.

The iconography of women's work is rarely given the serious consideration it deserves. Embroidery is all too often treated only in terms of technical developments. One reason why the subject matter of embroidery is summarily dismissed is that embroiderers employ patterns. The interpretation, adaptation and variation of pattern is an integral aspect of the activity and it is therefore assumed that stylistic and technical properties are all that concern the embroiderer. However, needlewomen chose particular patterns, selecting those images which had meaning for them. The enormous popularity of certain images at different moments indicates that they had specific importance and powerful resonance for the women who chose to stitch them. Where embroiderers have actually employed contemporary paintings as patterns, we can perceive what could or could not be stitched by women, and how they were able to make meanings of their own, by observing which they selected and where they departed from their models. Nevertheless, the meanings of any embroidered picture have to be carefully considered within their historical, artistic and class context. What a picture conveys often relates to the needs of a woman's class as much as to her experience as a woman at that time, as well as to the dominant concerns of contemporary paintings and to the history of embroidery.

Sometimes embroiderers reinforced the feminine ideal in their work, comfortingly concealing the disjunctures between the 'ideal' and the 'real' by the words and images they stitched – 'Home Sweet Home'. At other times they resisted or questioned the emerging ideology of feminine obedience and subjugation, as in the following seventeenth-century sampler verse:

> When I was young I little thought
> That wit must be so dearly bought
> But now experience tells me how
> If I would thrive then I must bow

And bend unto another's will
That I might learn both care and skill
To Get My Living with My Hands
That So I Might Be Free From Band
And My Own Dame that I may be
And free from all such slavery.
Avoid vaine pastime fle youthful pleasure
Let moderation allways be thy measure
And so prosed unto the heavenly treasure.

The verse is a curious mixture of piety and rebellion, resentment and acquiescence. Because samplers were becoming the place where moral sentiments were impressed upon young girls, they were sometimes also the place where conflicts underlying the ideology were expressed.

Such overt recognition of the clash between individual ambition and the ideology of femininity is rare indeed. More often the embroiderers' desire was to achieve exactly what was expected of them, developing satisfying and praiseworthy levels of skill. From our vantage point, it is all too easy to sneer at the Victorian embroiderer completing yet another pair of slippers stitched with a fox head, or at the eighteenth-century embroiderer reproducing in thread the moralising, sentimental domestic genre paintings of her time. But rather than ridiculing them, or turning embarrassed from our history, we should ask why they selected such subjects, what secondary gains they accrued from absolute conformity to the feminine ideal, and how they were able to make meanings of their own while overtly living up to the oppressive stereotype.

Sometimes the secondary gains, or the ways women made meanings of their own, are covert indeed. The ubiquitous late eighteenth-century mourning pictures, for example, overtly conform to the ideology of wifely obedience and fidelity. Whatever the complexity and ambivalence of a woman's personal response to bereavement, embroidering conventional memorial pictures provided the security of social approval. Women are depicted in silk tending the family tomb. In Chapter Six I describe how these pictures related both to the expansion of domestic mourning ritual and to contemporary attitudes to death represented in neo-classical art. But a comparison between paintings by men of mourning women and embroidered mourning pictures by women reveals significant differences. Embroiderers endow their *mourners* with particular prominence and power, even as they manifest their allegiance to the ideology of the 'virtuous widow'.

While recognising the varied ways in which women have conformed to and resisted the dictates of femininity in their work, it is important to remember that embroidery has been and is a source of artistic pleasure to many women. Olive Schreiner, in her novel *From Man to Man*, 1927, evoked the satisfaction of needlework, particularly the narcissistic pleasures it provided:

> All her life she had dreamed of having a dress made of thick black silk, with large blue daisies with white centres embroidered in raised silk work all over it at intervals. Her mother had had such a bit of silk in a patchwork quilt she had brought from England with her.[21]

Embroidery summons up both 'advanced' civilisation and very early childhood when a primal, unproblematic unity with the mother still existed. However, the work provides narcissistic pleasure not only because it evokes the love and unity of early childhood; but also because women were taught to embroider as an extension of themselves; and quite crudely because embroidery is used on clothing where it provokes admiration. Urged to embroider clothing and furniture, encouraged to see it as the natural expression of their nature, women were still accused of vanity when they embroidered for themselves. The stereotype of embroidery as a vain and frivolous occupation, like the stereotype of the silent, seductive needlewoman, controls and undermines the power and pleasure women have found in embroidery, representing it to us negatively.

Nevertheless, women have found gratification in the activity. Olive Schreiner conveys the immense creative satisfaction it provides:

> Slowly the scores of little tucks and fine embroidery shaped themselves. At the end of the week there were two tiny armholes. At the end of a fortnight the long white rope with its delicate invisible stitching was also complete. . .[22]

She also perceived the bond that embroidery forged between women; sewing allowed women to sit together without feeling they were neglecting their families, wasting time or betraying their husbands by maintaining independent social bonds:

> They were unalike physically and mentally but they had tastes which harmonised. While Veronica sat upright on a high-backed chair knitting heavy squares for a bed quilt, Mrs Drummond, on a low settee, with her head a little on one side, chose carefully the shades of silk for an altarcloth which she was making.[23]

The women's choice of work indicates the different personalities; that they both engaged in domestic art reveals what they share as women in society.

After placing embroidery at the centre of women's lives, Olive Schreiner makes a plea that it be recognised as art, as a creative expressive activity, but nevertheless betrays her kinship to the attitude towards needlework manifested by the contemporary novelists Sarah Grand and May Sinclair:

> The poet, when his heart is weighted, writes a sonnet, and the painter paints a picture, and the thinker throws himself into the world of action; but the woman who is only a woman, what has she but her needle? In that torn bit of brown leather brace worked through and through with yellow silk, in that bit of white rag with the invisible stitching, lying among fallen leaves and rubbish that the wind has blown into the gutter or street corner, lies all the passion of some woman's soul finding voiceless expression. Has the pen or pencil dipped so deep in the blood of the human race as the needle?[24]

While placing embroidery as an art like poetry and painting, Olive Schreiner reasserts its association with femininity. It is the bearer of women's soul. The images of the white rag with the invisible stitching, the yellow silk besmirched and trodden underfoot silently suggest a comparison with women's fate in the streets. Olive Schreiner maintains the link betwen embroidery and feminine purity, thus presenting it as a sexual characteristic, and failing to establish it as an art form equal to painting and poetry. In part this reflects Olive Schreiner's own ambivalence towards the domestic labour she describes: 'The worst of this book of mine is that it's so womanly. I think it's the most womanly book that ever was written, and God knows I've willed it otherwise.'[25] But the effect of the passage is largely determined by the hierarchical categorisation of art forms in our culture. By claiming that embroidery should be valued because of its intimate associations with women's lives and domestic tradition, Olive Schreiner inevitably though unwittingly discounted it as art.

The extraordinary intractability of embroidery, its resistance to re-definition, is the result of its role in the creation of femininity during the past five hundred years.

2: Eternalising the Feminine

Embroidery and Victorian mediaevalism
1840–1905

The Victorians re-discovered mediaeval embroidery, wrote the first histories of the craft in Britain, and produced embroidery based on mediaeval models.

Mediaeval embroidery production and the place of the art in society demonstrated dramatically different conditions from those that later prevailed. Both men and women embroidered in guild workshops, or workshops attached to noble households, in monasteries and nunneries. Embroidery was considered the equal of painting and sculpture.

Victorian historians of embroidery obscured its past and instead suggested that embroidery had always been an inherently female activity, a quintessentially feminine craft. However, the central importance of mediaeval embroidery to the Victorians and the mythic history they constructed for it has crucially shaped twentieth-century attitudes to the art. Amongst the most popular of contemporary commercial canvas patterns are mediaeval scenes with castle and stitching damsel, and twentieth-century historical accounts of the history of embroidery still contain information accepted unquestioningly from nineteenth-century sources.

The tenacity of the Victorian reading of this history is largely due to the way it meshed with nineteenth-century ideologies of femininity. Twentieth-century concepts of femininity are still deeply imbued with Victorianism. Throughout the nineteenth century there was an elaboration of femininity – a rigid definition of women and their role. Amongst the cluster of characteristics which constituted the feminine ideal was included a natural propensity to embroider. The rediscovery of mediaeval embroidery was coloured by the nineteenth-century notions of women's essential nature and embroidery as essential to women. By contrasting Victorian accounts of mediaeval embroidery production with the evidence gleaned from such sources as royal records, judicial records and the history of the guilds, I hope to demonstrate how ideologies about women determine both the writing of history and the stitching of images.

Among all the contradictions that besieged the Victorian middle class, the place of women was one of the most irreconcilable. With the growing power of middle-class men in nineteenth-century society the material circumstances of middle-class women improved, yet their legal and financial dependence deepened. The pressure for young girls to remain at home and gain accomplishments had taken hold, and that the women of the family were not wage-earners was an important indication of class status. Women were, on the one hand, the frail sex, untouched by intellect, at the mercy of physical weakness and volatile feelings, and on the other hand they were to provide the spiritual face of their class, occupying a higher, purer sphere than men – the possessors of animal drives chained to the corrupt world of commerce. During the 1840s, the time that mediaeval embroidery began to assume some importance in Victorian culture, women were increasingly voicing resentment at the contradictions that bound their lives. Mrs Hugo Reed, for example, in *A Plea for Women*, 1843, commented witheringly that, 'Woman is taught to believe, that for one half of the human race, the highest end of civilisation is to cling upon the other, like a weed upon a wall.'[1]

As Cora Kaplan in her introduction to *Aurora Leigh* pointed out in 1978:

the 'woman question' should not be seen as marginal to a

8 *The Talisman* (from the novel by Sir Walter Scott), Mrs Billyard, Victoria and Albert Museum, London. c 1860. Berlin woolwork.
The Victorians invoked mediaeval chivalry to secure both the class structure and relations between the sexes. Images of the middle ages appeared to confirm the naturalness and rightness of separate spheres. And the Victorian embroiderer found a reassuring representation of her own power and powerlessness in the lady of courtly romance.

9 Altar frontal, Ladies' Ecclesiastical Society, designed by George Street, St James-the-Less Church, Westminster, London. 1861. Photo: Victoria and Albert Museum.
An example of church embroidery produced under the impetus of the Gothic revival.

10 Unfinished piece of Berlin woolwork. Mid-
nineteenth century. Photo: Norfolk Museums
Service.
This was the type of embroidery that became the
focus of attacks by theorists of the Gothic revival.

11 *Mariana*, Sir Frederick Millais (British,
1829–1896), collection Lord Sherfield, 1853.
Oil on canvas.

male-dominated ruling class, increasingly threatened from below by an organising proletariat. Caught between this and the need to accommodate a limited demand for equity from the informed women of their own class, they were equally committed to the absolute necessity of maintaining social control over females, and its corollary, the sexual division of labour. [2]

The middle ages constituted an era that *appeared* to provide historical confirmation for the naturalness and rightness of the doctrine of separate spheres for the sexes. In her study of the mediaeval ideal in nineteenth-century literature, *A Dream of Order*, 1971, Alice Chandler usefully identifies two major aspects of mediaevalism linked by the ideal of chivalry:

> One is its naturalism – its identification with nature and the past and thus with simpler and truer modes of feeling and expression and nobler more heroic codes of action. The other its feudalism – its harmonious and stable social structure which reconciled freedom and order by giving each man an allotted place in society and an alloted leader to follow. The bridge between these two aspects of mediaevalism is chivalry, which made the spontaneous generosity of the natural man the guiding principle of man in society which compensated for human frailty by having the strong protect the weak. [3]

Not only did chivalry sanction and secure the hierarchical Victorian class structure, but it was also a weapon of cultural resistance[4] in the face of women's growing restlessness and rebellion – an attempt to still the doubts of both the powerful and the powerless.

Articles on the 'woman question' occupied considerable space in British magazines and constantly invoked the spirit of chivalry. But a profound sense of unease echoes through these protestations of chivalry. Take for example, the following observation from an article by T. H. Lister in the *Edinburgh Review* of 1841:

> In all modern civilized communities, and especially in the most refined and cultivated portions of these communities, women are treated by men with peculiar deference, tenderness, and courtesy. Do they owe this treatment to their strength or to their weakness? Undoubtedly to the latter. The deference, the

19

tenderness, the courtesy of man towards the other sex, are founded principally on the feeling that they need his protection, and can never question his power. . . But let man be made to feel that he must stand on the defensive – and the spirit of chivalry will speedily cease.[5]

Mediaevalism permeated every aspect of Victorian culture, but in particular, mid-century religious revivals. Writings on mediaeval embroidery, begun in the late 1830s, called for the revival of embroidery based on a prototype from the middle ages to furnish the Gothic revival churches. Both the Anglican and Roman Catholic churches were consciously concerned with embroidery. The British Catholic architect, Augustus Welby Pugin, wrote in 1843, 'We must earnestly impress on all those who work in any way for the decoration of the altar that the only hope for reviving the perfect style is by strictly adhering to *ancient authorities*.'[6]

Mediaevalism had different primary connotations for the various architects and craftworkers who turned to it. For some it suggested spirituality and piety which they believed would create the coherence and clarity of style felt to be lacking in nineteenth-century art. For others it evoked security and solidity in a time of disturbing, rapid change. For William Morris it represented a dream of pre-capitalist production in which designer and executor were one, and production and consumption not separated. Clearly all these Victorian concerns were interrelated.

In the 1840s, however, a quite specific attitude informed writings on mediaeval embroidery and instructions for church furnishings. In the hands of male theorists, awareness of 'the woman question' fused with religious fervour. A curious mixture of chivalry, piety and misogyny appears in the texts, expressing women's traditional association with embroidery and their particular place in Christianity. Within Christian doctrine women both provoked the Fall and produced the Saviour, providing the major source of sin and the primary symbol of purity. Writers who called for a revival of mediaeval-style embroidery for the church, blamed the present state of the art on the depravity of women. For them mediaeval work represented a kind of pre-Fall holiness. 'From the accession of William III may be traced the rapid downfall of both church principle and church feeling. The ladies worked still, but, as at present, for the drawing room and not for the church,'[7] wrote C.E.M. in *Hints on Ornamental Needlework as applied to Ecclesiastical Purposes* in 1843.

A. W. Pugin felt that the Gothic style was needed to cleanse British embroidery of secular femininity:

> Well meaning ladies transfer all the nicknackery of the work-room, the toilette-table, and the bazaar to the altar of God. The result is pitiable . . . pretty ribbons, china pots, darling little gimcracks, artificial flowers, all sorts of trumpery are suffered to be intruded.[8]

Like all crude stereotypes, Pugin's characterisation of mid-nineteenth-century embroidery contained a grain of accurate observation, and the demand for embroidered furnishings for Gothic revival churches did provide women with a chance to change and vindicate embroidery – and themselves.

Large numbers of women were involved in both the Evangelical Movement and the high-church Oxford Movement which re-instituted lavish church hangings and vestments. Women's religiosity was a complex phenomenon. Sarah Stickney Ellis in *Women of England* expressed the contemporary view that it was at times motivated 'more by the excitement it produced and the exemption it afforded from domestic duties than from a true spirit of Religious goodness'.[9] Behind Sarah Ellis's criticism lies the fact that religious observance was part of the middle-class cult of the family; less a question of belief than a standard of moral behaviour and a code of conduct.

Embroidering for the church in the drawing room combined domesticity and piety, making it a highly acceptable activity for ladies. Providing church furnishings and writing books on the history and practice of the art also gave a public voice to women who would otherwise not have been heard outside the home. The importance of the mid-nineteenth-century written histories of embroidery and instruction manuals by women cannot be over-emphasised. They illustrate attitudes among women who, though in no way radical, were aware that all was not well with their sex – and were offering their particular solution. Their histories set out to combat the denigration of embroidery; to claim Gothic revival embroidery as women's particular province, and to assert the artistic value of embroidery and thus the worth of women's work in the home.

The *Handbook of Needlework*, 1842, and *Church Needlework*, 1844, were among the first to appear. Their author, Miss Lambert, begins by thanking her husband for allowing her to use her maiden name. But however self-effacing the presentation, and however archaic the language may appear to us, Miss Lambert was taken seriously by her contemporaries. Her books received good reviews with only a hint of chivalrous jocularity from such magazines as the *Spectator*, the *Athenaeum*, *Atlas*, *Literary Gazette* and the *Polytechnic*. She considered that her books, with their mixture of historical material and practical advice, directly contributed to the Gothic revival:

> With the revival of a more correct taste in Ecclesiastical Architecture the interior decorations of the sacred edifice, other than those which fall within the province of the architect and sculptor, naturally claim attention, to the consideration of one branch of these – belonging by right to women – it is intended to devote the following pages. [10]

She emphasises that embroidery is women's particular sphere and insists that embroidery be recognised as an art and not relegated to the status of craft: 'My aim has been to view the subject, both in its historical and practical bearings, in one light only – that of art.' [11] Ironically her very insistence that embroidery was naturally and by right women's work discounted it as art. For by the nineteenth century, what women did was identified with nature and nurture as opposed to culture. Women's creative work was conflated with their procreative capacity; their painting, embroidery and sculpture were considered an extension of their womanliness.

Elizabeth Stone, however, in her *Art of Needlework*, 1840, published under the name of its editor Viscountess Wilton, [12] attempts to validate embroidery as art by pleading that the cultural worth of *embroiderers* be recognised. A highly romantic account of the history of needlework from biblical times, the book was in its third edition by 1844. The author makes no secret of her resentment at the treatment of women:

> Women are courted, flattered, caressed, extolled; but still the difference is there, and the 'lords of the creation' take care that it shall be understood. Their own pursuits – public, are the

theme of the historian – private, of the biographer; nay, the every-day circumstances of life – their dinners – their speeches – their toasts – and their *post coena* eloquence, are noted down for immortality: whilst a woman with as much sense, with more eloquence, with lofty principles, enthusiastic feelings, and pure conduct – with sterling virtue to command respect, and the self-denying conduct of a martyr – steals noiselessly through her appointed path in life . . . And this is but as it should be.[13]

Stone's apparent *volte face*, her descent from a crescendo of outrage to meek support for the status quo was a symptom of the particular relationship writers on embroidery had to the 'woman question'. They wished to transform courtesy into real regard and deference into genuine respect. But they wanted a solution which maintained yet dignified the separate spheres, and looked to the history of embroidery to confer a sense of importance and purpose to the activity that absorbed so much of middle-class women's time. Male writers, on the other hand, looked to the past for confirmation that the present order of things was immutable and inevitable. It would be an error to assume that historians deliberately distorted the past; rather they read it through the filter of nineteenth-century ideologies.

The first book published to concentrate entirely on *mediaeval* embroidery was *English Mediaeval Embroidery*, C. H. Hartshorne, 1848. The image he created of the mediaeval embroiderer is not significantly different from that of the women historians, although his reading of the past betrays other needs, expectations and desires. His book became the source material for future histories, initiating a chain of illusions that carry through to the present day. He constructed an imaginary division of labour for the mediaeval embroidery workshops:

Doubtlessly these labours were . . . pursued by females, both for their amusement as well as their profit, and there exists [an] entry on the Liberate Rolls in proof of it, authorizing a payment to Adam de Bakering of 6s and 8d for 'a cloth of silk and a fringe purchased by our command, to embroider a certain embroidered chasuble which Mabilia of St Edmund's made for us'. It seems most reasonable therefore to conclude that the men travailed at the orfevrie [gold embroidery, and goldsmithery] department whilst the women undertook the needle-work. [14]

While acknowledging that women worked professionally, Hartshorne nevertheless emphasises that females laboured primarily for amusement and, more importantly, he makes the strange statement that men were responsible for the beaten gold embellishments and gold thread that characterised mediaeval embroidery while women 'undertook the needlework' – the embroidery in silk. He offers no proof and provides no explanation as to why such a hypothesis should 'seem reasonable'.

Despite this, his theory was taken up by Frances and Hugh Marshall in *Old English Embroidery*, 1894. 'Ladies at this time were not above pursuing the craft of embroidery for profit as well as amusement. The men, it appears from an old close roll of the time of Henry III, usually "travailed" at the orfevrie department while the women did the more elaborate needlework.' [15] Ostensibly quoting primary sources, this is taken directly from Hartshorne. The only difference is that fifty years of Victorian femininity had transformed Hartshorne's 'needlework' into 'elaborate' work, suitable for nimble-fingered ladies.

Not only was Hartshorne responsible for perpetuating the myth of a mediaeval sexual division of labour, he also provided an image of the mediaeval noblewoman embroiderer which has since ossified into a stereotype.

> Shut up in her lofty chamber. Within the massive walls of a castle or immured in the restricted walls of a convent, the needle alone supplied an unceasing source of amusement; with this she might enliven her tedious hours, and depicting the heroic deeds of her absent lord, as it were visibly hastening his return; or on the other hand, softened by the influence of pious contemplation, she might use this pliant instrument to bring vividly before her mind the mysteries of that faith to which she clung. [16]

In a passage which is an amalgam of fantasy and research, Hartshorne transforms the mediaeval noblewoman into a blue-print for the middle-class Victorian wife: pious, secluded, faithful and dutiful. Even the sharp needle becomes a pliant instrument.

Evidence does suggest that embroidery was part of a noble

girl's education in mediaeval Britain, but there is nothing to indicate that adult women worked in pious, interesting isolation. Quite the contrary, noble households maintained embroidery workshops employing female and male embroiderers in which the lady of the household could have joined. The Domesday Book, recording that King Canute's daughter Aelthelswitha set up an embroidery workshop near the monastry of Ely, considered it noteworthy that she did actually participate in the work: 'With her own hands, being extremely skilled in the craft she made a white chasuble.'[17]

Hartshorne's image, however, had enormous resonance for the Victorians. The same elements – incarceration, the slow passage of time, embroidery as compensation for male absence – appear in Alfred, Lord Tennyson's poem 'Mariana' and inspired John Everett Millais' painting *Mariana*. Drawn from Shakespeare's *Measure for Measure*, the poem describes 'Mariana in the moated grange' waiting for her lover:

> She only said, 'My life is dreary,
> He cometh not,' she said;
> She said, 'I am aweary, aweary,
> I would that I were dead!'

Millais portrays Mariana standing over her unfinished embroidery to signify her confinement in the moated grange, her long wait and her nobility. But Mariana has abandoned her 'work'; driven by frustration and desire she has put down her needle and disorder has entered the house. Dead leaves have drifted in, a mouse creeps undisturbed across the floor and an altar lies unattended in the background. Mariana's pose has been described as just 'awkwardly langorous' and the result of 'Millais' resolve to paint someone stretching with boredom'.[18] But the pose surely suggests something other than boredom. The whole angle of the body, the position of the arms and the gaze indicate a sexual provocativeness, an element of rebelliousness, that could only be held in check by embroidery frames, stained glass windows, the restricted limits of a convent and the massive walls of a castle conjured up by Hartshorne.

The image of the embroidering lady was not offered simply to negate or contain fears that women might put down their needles and 'break out': it acted as both an acknowledgement and a denial of that 'curse of middle-class existence, the death in life, ennui' as the *English Woman's Journal* put it in 1858. And *ennui* was not simply boredom but a manifestation of more profound distress echoed in the psychosomatic weariness constantly represented in women's poetry. Christina Rossetti wrote:

> It's a weary life, it is, she said:–
> Doubly blank in a woman's lot:
> I wish and I wish I were a man:
> Or, better than any being, were not:[19]

When women writers presented their picture of the noble embroiderer, they were, in their own way, redressing their sex's dissatisfaction and unhappiness. Elizabeth Stone, for example, describing the Bayeux Tapestry, completed by c. 1086, wrote:

> This Herculean labour has a halo of deep interest thrown around it from the circumstances of its being the proud tribute of a fond and affectionate wife, glorifying in her husband's glory, and proud of emblazoning his deeds . . . Little did the affectionate wife think whilst employed over this task, that her domestic tribute of regard should become an historical memento of her country, and blazon forth his illustrious deeds and her own *unwearying* affection.[20]

The affectionate wife was William the Conqueror's Queen Mathilda, supposed author of the Tapestry. Stone offered Mathilda as a source of inspiration and fantasy for all those weary women whose embroidery was belittled rather than respected. She presented Mathilda as a pattern of perfect Victorian femininity, who worked for love, in private, her glory a reflection of her husband's, her reward coming after death. 'The astonishing labours of Mathilda, consort of William the Conqueror' are also mentioned in Miss Lambert's chapter titled 'Needlework of the English Queens and Princesses'. In conferring aristocratic associations on the art practised by thousands of middle-class women, she revealed another reason why the image of the noble embroiderer was so popular in the nineteenth century. 'In past ages the higher or picturesque gradations of it were confined to the delicate fingers of Queens and court ladies', confidently stated Mrs Warren and Mrs Pullan in *Treasures of Needlework*, 1855.[21]

12 *Queen Mathilda with her Women and Saxon Maidens with the Bayeux Tapestry*,
George Elgar Hicks (British 1824–1914), Christies, 1899. Oil on canvas, 88.9 ×
180.2 cm.
Although the Bayeux Tapestry was a professional workshop production,
throughout the nineteenth century it was attributed to Queen Mathilda, wife of
William the Conqueror. The queen was presented as an exemplary embroiderer,
working with other women, in private, and for her husband's glory, not her own.

13 *The Bayeux Tapestry*, Ville de Bayeux, Normandy, France. c 1080.
Embroidered wool on linen, 50 cm × 70.4 m. The 'tapestry' records events from
the accession of Edward the Confessor to the defeat of Harold at Hastings.

17 *Banner of St Margaret*, Ladies' Ecclesiastical Society, designed by G F Bodley, Wicken Bonhunt Church, Essex. c 1860. Photo: Laurie Sparham.
Compared with the mediaeval St Margaret, the nineteenth-century St Margaret, a product of the Gothic revival, reveals the transformation effected by Victorian ideologies about women upon mediaeval iconography.

14 (top left) Altar frontal detail, Domina Johanna Beverley, Victoria and Albert Museum, London. c 1300.
The altar frontal bears the signature of the nun who embroidered it.

15 (centre left) Altar frontal design, Miss Lambert, *Church Needlework*, London. 1844.
'The aim of the needlewoman is not to imitate either painting, sculpture, carving or goldsmiths' work; but to produce an effective piece of needlework, that shall be strictly in accordance with the laws of good taste and the harmony of colours.'
Theorists of the Gothic revival wanted embroidery recognised as an art in its own right. But in their anxiety to prove embroidery worthy of a place among the arts, they denied needlewomen any artistic independence.

16 (bottom left) *The Butler-Bowden Cope*, detail, Victoria and Albert Museum, London. 1330–1350. Velvet embroidered with coloured silks, silver-gilt and silver thread, pearls, green beads and small gold rings. Full dimensions 167.6 × 345.5 cm. A detail from the cope shows St Margaret, patron saint of childbirth. With St Catherine, St Margaret was the most frequently embroidered female saint during the middle ages.

18 *The Girlhood of Mary Virgin*, Dante Gabriel Rossetti (British, 1828–1882),
Tate Gallery, London. 1848–9. Oil on canvas.
The nineteenth-century feminine ideal, represented by Mary embroidering a lily,
shows the extent to which embroidery has become associated with the concept of
femininity as purity and submissiveness. By contrast a mediaeval prototype
illustrates Anna, the Virgin's mother, instructing her daughter from a book.

19 Chasuble orphrey, a detail from *The Nativity of the Virgin*, Victoria and Albert Museum, London. 1390–1420. Linen embroidered with silks, silver-gilt and silver thread.

20 *Banner of the Virgin of the Annunciation*, School of Mediaeval embroidery, from an engraving reproduced in the *Magazine of Art*, 1880. Photo: Anthea Callen.

21 Alms pouch, Cathedral treasury, Sens, France. Mid-fourteenth century.
Taken from the poem of the Châtelaine de Vergy, the embroidery depicts a lady
receiving a ring from her lover. These small, richly embroidered bags for money,
gloves and prayer books were hung from the belt.

Had Mathilda stitched all 270 feet by 20 inches of embroidered linen known misleadingly as the Bayeux *Tapestry*, the generic name for woven textile, it would have been truly a Herculean task. The embroidery records events from the accession of Edward the Confessor to the defeat of Harold at Hastings. Although it is the only surviving example of Romanesque political embroidery, descriptions of similar work exist. In 1070 the Abbot of Bourguoil described an embroidery on the same subject worked in gold, silver and jewels, hanging in an alcove around the bed of Adela, daughter of William the Conqueror.

In 1900 Mathilda was still named as creator of the tapestry. However, the embroidery has been the subject of intensive research prompted partly by nationalism. The problem that absorbed historians was not so much who made it, as where it was made. Even Victorian historians were torn between patriotism and the desire to celebrate Mathilda as an example of wifely excellence. Miss Lambert added the footnote: 'Though Queen Mathilda directed the working of the Bayeux Tapestry, yet the greater part of it was most probably executed by *English* ladies, who were at this period, as we have stated before, celebrated for their needlework.'[22]

Later historians in part agree with her.[23] Today it is considered to have been commissioned by the French from an English workshop. Bishop Odo, half-brother of William the Conqueror, is believed to have ordered it to be hung in the Cathedral at Bayeux. Judging from the style and technique, it is English, and there was a school of embroidery known for the type of work at Canterbury.

Nevertheless, the French continued to call it 'Queen Mathilda's Tapestry' and images of the stitching queen still cling to it, so powerful was the nineteenth-century presentation of its history. They wrote of it as an individual effort rather than a workshop production, as an aristocratic activity rather than a professional art work, as an all-female undertaking rather than the creation of men and women. They neither could nor would disentangle the work's history from the way the art was practised by nineteenth-century upper- and middle-class women.

The tapestry's association with aristocratic femininity has shaped its treatment by twentieth-century writers, who tend to refer to its 'perennial charm' and fail to consider the embroidery in the light of developments in mediaeval art, or of what it teaches us about mediaeval craft practice. There are of course exceptions. Arnold Hauser in *The Social History of Art*, 1938, analyses it in the context of art history, calling it 'The most important monument of secular art of the middle ages' and pointing out that it anticipates the cyclical narratives of Gothic art. His dismissal of Mathilda's authorship is nevertheless somewhat ambiguous: 'Contrary to the legend this is obviously in no sense the work of a dilettante.'[24]

Victorian historians were confident of their image of the lone noble embroiderer because of the use they made of the literature of courtly love as a source of information on mediaeval secular embroidery. Courtly love, with its idealisation of women and view of love as an ennobling passion, developed at the end of the eleventh century and flourished until the thirteenth century. Emerging in the courts of the nobility in Southern France, it spread throughout Europe. Although it affected the lives of a very narrow stratum of women, it left a highly influential body of literature.

In *Art of Needlework* Elizabeth Stone defended her use of courtly love as a source of information, claiming that mediaeval chronicles and histories provided nothing on needlework:

'The costly and delicate needlework' is here, as elsewhere, passed over with merely a mention. It is, naturally, too insignificant a subject to task the attention of those whose energies are devoted to describing warfare and welfare of kingdoms and thrones . . . but as the 'novel' now describes those minutiae of everyday life which we would think it ridiculous to look for in the writings of politicians and historians, so the romances of the days of chivalry present us with descriptions which, if they be somewhat redundant in ornament, are still correct in groundwork . . .[25]

What courtly literature actually provided was groundwork for the fantasies of Victorian needlewomen. Describing the accoutrements of mediaeval knights, Stone writes that they were, 'varied in form but mostly made of rich silk, lined or trimmed with choice or expensive furs, and usually, also, having the armorial bearings of the family richly embroidered. *Thus were women even the heralds of those times.'*[26] (my italics)

Leonore Davidoff's 1973 study of the Victorian Season[27] suggests that women of the privileged classes were the heraldic reflection of their *own* time. She describes the key role they played in organising the social rituals of society in which the problems of social definition were becoming more and more acute. The Victorian lady found a reassuring representation of her own curious power and powerlessness in the mediaeval lady of courtly love.

Embroidery did indeed play an important part in the stories of adulterous love that dominate the literature of courtly love. In the *Lay of The Nightingale* by Marie de France, the lady and her lover would meet nightly at her window until her husband became suspicious. The lady, to allay his fears, says she is unable to sleep because a nightingale singing outside her window enchants her. The husband has the bird killed. The lady then 'took a piece of white samite bordered with gold, and wrought thereon the whole story of this adventure. In this silken cloth she wrapped the little body of the bird, and calling to her trusted servant of her house, charged him with the message and bade him bear it to her friend.'

The most popular nineteenth-century image from courtly romances was that of the knight wearing the lady's embroidery and defending it with his life. 'It is recorded in "Perceforest",' writes Elizabeth Stone, 'that at the end of one tournament ladies were so stripped of their head attire, that the greatest part of them were quite bareheaded . . . their robes also were without sleeves; for all had been given to adorn the knights; hoods, cloaks, kerchiefs and mantuas . . .'[28] The self-forgetfulness, abandon and excitement so forbidden to Victorian ladies is represented in the context of embroidery, but safely distanced by hundreds of years, and dignified by the morality and nobility associated with the middle ages in Victorian minds.

Elizabeth Stone quotes poetry which referred to embroidered bags hung at the waist for money, papers, prayer books or gloves:

> She seyde, Syr Knight, gentyl and hende,
> I wot thy stat, ord and ende,
> Be naught aschamed of me;
> If thou wylt truly to me take,
> And alle women for me forsake,
> Ryche i wyll make the.

> I wyll the geve an alner,
> Imad of Sylk and of gold cler
> With fayr ymages thre;
> As oft thou puttest the hond therinne,
> A mark of gold thou schalt wynne,
> In wat place that thou be.

Plate 21 shows such a mediaeval bag from France embroidered in the fourteenth century with figures from the *Roman de la Rose*. Etienne Boileau's book of crafts names a maker of such pouches as 'Margaret the Emblazoner' for they were usually stitched with the owner's coat of arms. Elizabeth Stone, referring to the poem, comments, 'The labours of those days were not confined to merely good appearing garments; the skill of the needlewoman, for doubtless it was attributable to that – could imbue them with value far beyond that of mere outward garnish.'[29] With laboured humour she pursues her goal – the validation of women and their work.

It is easy to see why the Victorians considered that the literature of courtly love proved that embroidery and embroiderers were once highly valued (and thus should be again in the nineteenth century). What they failed to grasp was that the standing of embroidery in courtly society did not indicate that women were valued as embroiderers, but rather it signified social place and allegiance. Wills, funeral effigies, illuminated manuscripts and paintings all testified to the power of embroidery as a distinguishing mark of rank.

The centrality of embroidery in courtly literature indicated the jostling for place among *men* rather than the power of women. There is anyway considerable disagreement over the effect of courtly love on women's lives, the cause and content of courtly love verse and fables. Was the love celebrated sexual or platonic? Did the honour and worship accorded women reflect the power of women as landowners, or was it simply compensation for their total subordination to the men of their class? Did it ameliorate the position of women or, as Eileen Power comments in *Mediaeval Women*, 1975, 'How often in real life must the lady of chivalry have been not romantically unhappy but simply bored?'[30] Did courtly love undermine marriage or shore up a system of economic alliances? Meg Bogin in *The Women Troubadors*, 1976, has argued convincingly that the rituals of courtly love served to buttress the identity of the feudal male, that the landless courted the ladies to reach their men. The lady was mediator in a symbolic transference of status between men of different classes.[31]

Whatever the social reality behind the literature of courtly love, the early Victorians saw the middle ages as a time when embroidery and embroiderers were accorded the value which Victorian women themselves desired. And in contrast to their own lives mediaeval embroiderers appeared to have enjoyed an unthinkable freedom: 'So highly valued was a facility in the use of the needle prized in these "ould ancient times",' wrote Elizabeth Stone, 'that a wandering damsel is not merely *tolerated* but *cherished* in a family in which she is a perfect stranger solely for her skill in this much loved art.'[32]

During the latter half of the nineteenth century, writers on embroidery became less interested in chivalry and courtly love. Lady Marion Alford's *Needlework as Art*, 1886, had little of Elizabeth Stone's delight in tournaments. Lady Marion retires her mediaeval embroiderer from the lists to the hearth. Sir Walter Scott's romantic novels, with their jousts and hawking parties, were cast out in favour of the utopian view of the fourteenth century of the art theorists John Ruskin and William Morris. Ruskin's lady buckles on her knight's armour rather than tossing him her embroidered clothing:

> You cannot think that the buckling on of the knight's armour was a mere caprice of fashion. It is the type of an eternal truth – that the soul's armour is never well set to the heart unless a woman's hand has braced [it] . . . But how, you will ask, is the idea of this guiding function of the woman reconcilable with a true wifely subjection? Simply in that it is a guiding not a determining function.[33]

Alford transforms the earlier image of the romantic mediaeval embroiderer into the domestic and maternal preceptor: 'In mediaeval homes lessons of morality and religion, and the love and fame of noble deeds, were taught by the painting of the needle to the minds of young men who would have scorned more direct teaching.'[34]

By reproducing Ruskinian ideology, Lady Marion Alford accommodated the contradictions in nineteenth-century middle-class women's lives. She attempted to dignify the very work that signified their lack of public importance. Like earlier historians of embroidery she wanted to suggest that women and their embroidery did exercise an influence over their society. But to Alford the power of women lay not in being the 'heralds' of society, the people who ordered social hierarchies, but in exemplary morality and purity. Influenced by William Morris and the Arts and Crafts Movement she believed that art had an inherently beneficial, elevating effect on all who came into contact with it. 'The history of domestic embroidery', she wrote, 'ought to be looked upon as an important factor in the humanising effect of aesthetic culture.'[35]

Mediaeval ecclesiastical embroidery was evoked by Victorian historians to justify their claims that embroidery was innately pious, pure and spiritualising. Lady Marion Alford offered her ideal of monastic embroidery:

> In the dark and mediaeval ages, time was of no account. Skilled labour, such as was needed for carving, illuminations, and embroideries, was freely given as the duty of a life, for one particular object, the good of a man's soul. The cloistered men and women worked for no wages; neither to benefit themselves nor their descendants; hardly for fame – that was given to the convent which had the credit of patronising and producing art, while the very name of the artist was forgotten. It was from pure love of the art as a craft, and the belief that it was a good work in which they were engaged, and from their abundant leisure, that they were enabled to evolve the lovely creations which delight and astonish us . . . Like the silkworm they spent themselves; and by their industrious lives were surrounded in their living graves by the elaborated essence of their own natures, a joy and consolation to themselves, and a legacy to all time. To them, also, art appeared as the consoler.[36]

This is of course less a description of a mediaeval nun than a prescription (and consolation) for ideal Victorian womanhood; dutiful, pious, wageless and modest. The image is belied by surviving embroidery signed by one of Alford's 'anonymous nuns'. An altar frontlet of the early fourteenth century is signed 'Donna Ionna Beverlai Monaca Fecit'.

Contrary to the impression provided by Alford and others, mediaeval women were often drawn to the cloistered life for social and political reasons, not simply out of piety. The surviving words of mediaeval women themselves indicate the danger of generalising about them. The following twelfth-century poem relates to the decision to enter holy orders, and provides a corrective to the Victorian stereotype.

> Lady Carenza of the lovely, gracious body,
> give some advice to us two sisters,
> and since you know best how to tell what's best,
> counsel me according to your experience:
> Shall I marry someone we both know?
> or shall I stay unwed? that would please me,
> for making babies doesn't seem good,
> and it's too anguishing to be a wife.
>
> Lady Carenza, I'd like to have a husband,
> but making babies is a huge penitence:
> your breasts hang way down
> and it's too anguishing to be a wife.
>
> Lady Alais and Lady Iselda,
> you have learning, merit, beauty, youth, fresh
> colour, courtly manners and distinction
> more than all the other women I know;
> I therefore advise you, if you want to plant good seed,
> to take as a husband Coronat de Scienza,
> saved is the chastity of her who marries him.[37]

The poem belongs to the development of the courtly lyric in Provence during the twelfth century. Nothing is known about the three women. Meg Bogin, who translated their verses, has pointed out that the poem is a strange mixture of colloquial and religious language; Coronat de Scienza is a Cathar or Gnostic name for God.

Written histories of mediaeval embroidery were only one aspect of Victorian mediaevalism. As important was the revival of embroidery in the mediaeval style. And just as the written histories were determined by Victorian attitudes to women, so contemporary ideologies about women affected the theory, style and iconography of the mediaeval embroidery revival which began in the 1840s.

The style was instigated by men and produced by women. As mentioned above, writers who called for a return to mediaeval models blamed what they considered the decadence of contemporary church needlework on 'the ladies', and aimed as much at reforming the ladies as their work. A curious mixture of anxiety, bombast and ridicule informs their texts. A.W. Pugin's treatise on ecclesiastical embroidery reads like a sermon on chaste conduct. He demanded that church embroidery 'strictly adhere' to mediaeval models, with 'proper observation' of the 'heraldic laws of colour'. C.E.M. confessed how 'inexpressibly painful' he found it to observe some pattern on an altarcloth one day which had been seen in the 'drawing room the day before'. Gilbert French considered contemporary haloes to be 'unhappily suggestive of the metal plates of the Sun Fire Insurance Company'.[38]

Another tactic employed was to ridicule implicitly the embroiderer's femininity. The Reverend T. James insinuated that contemporary embroidery reflected a femininity that had become blowzy and overblown. In *Church Work for Ladies* he characterised Victorian canvas work as '. . . gigantic flowers, pansies big as peonies; cabbage roses which deserve the name, suggesting pickle rather than perfume; gracefully falling fuchsias big as handbells.'[39] Mortified, women replaced the cabbage rose with the Tudor rose.

The male theorists may have mocked embroidery but they nevertheless offered new possibilities for women embroiderers by allowing embroidery an important place in the Gothic revival. In 1848 the Ecclesiological Society published twelve plates of working patterns of flowers drawn from mediaeval embroideries by Agnes Blencowe. Seven years later she co-founded the Ladies Ecclesiastical Society. The members embroidered church furnishings free of charge, asking only that the churches supply the cost of the materials. Promising to honour and obey the theorists of the Gothic revival, they declared that their aim was 'to supply altarcloths of strictly ecclesiastical design either by reproducing ancient examples or by working under the supervision of a competent architect.'[40]

There was no shortage of competent church architects willing to supply patterns. George Frederick Bodley, J.D. Sedding and

Edmund Street all designed embroideries. Street assured the embroiderers of the benefits they would gain from working his designs, of 'the happiness which must result from employing their fingers and their eyes on something fair and beautiful to behold instead of upon horrid and hideous patterns in cross stitch, for foot-stools, slippers, chair covers, and the like too common objects'.[41]

The prototype embroideries can be roughly divided into two phases: those produced before 1860 and those stitched under the influence of the Arts and Crafts Movement. The first phase was dominated by religious revival and the insistence that church work (and church workers) should display piety, purity, taste and restraint. Miss Lambert's *Church Needlework* belongs to this phase. She reminds her readers repeatedly of the need for spirituality and taste. The chapter providing instructions for altarcloths ends with the warning that 'he (sic) must have fixt aims and strong hand who hits decency and misseth sluttery'.[42] The patterns she offers tend to be restrained to the point of dullness with repeated representations of the cross and holy monogram, and border patterns drawn from church cornices rather than from the lively and elaborate embroidery of the middle ages.

'Care and neatness are the only requisites for success,' Miss Lambert assured her readers. But as the embroidery revival continued embroiderers became more ambitious. Schools and teaching organisations spread, instructing embroiderers in large figurative work. In 1863 the Ladies Ecclesiastical Embroidery Society merged with the Wantage Needlework Association. The Church Extension Society formed in 1871, and the School of Mediaeval Embroidery was organised by the Sisters of St Catherine in Queens Square, Bloomsbury, to provide church embroideries and to teach mediaeval work.

St Margaret was among the most frequently embroidered of all saints and martyrs during the late middle ages and thus a candidate for nineteenth-century figurative work. Two depictions of St Margaret, one from the middle ages and the other from the nineteenth century, reveal the transformations effected by Victorian ideologies about women upon mediaeval iconography. Plate 16 is taken from the Butler Bowden Cope and shows the saint spearing the dragon. Plate 17 is a banner of St Margaret designed by the architect G.F. Bodley for the Ladies Ecclesiastical Society.

The myth of St Margaret recounts how a Christian living in Antioch during the third century caught the eye of the Governor, who was not a Christian. He wanted to marry her and demanded that she renounce her religion. Margaret refused, insisting that she was dedicated to Christ. The Governor repeatedly tortured the young woman to make her change her mind, but her resistance never wavered. When she was locked in a dungeon, the devil appeared to her disguised as a dragon. Margaret fell to her knees and made the sign of the cross but the dragon was undeterred and swallowed the saint. Within the beast's body the cross that Margaret had made took shape, expanded and finally split the dragon open, allowing Margaret to escape unharmed. Her courage and miraculous escape provoked mass conversion to Christianity so the Governor decided to execute her. On her way to her death the saint prayed that the memory of her escape from the dragon might support women in childbirth. She thus became the intercessor for women in labour. During the middle ages liturgical invocations and hymns celebrated her protective powers. In art, she is shown spearing the dragon or bursting from his body as in the Steeple Aston Cope, Plate 32. Bodley's saint, on the other hand, raises her eyes to heaven in passive, mute supplication while the dragon catches her robe in his teeth.

By the nineteenth century St Margaret had been transformed from dragon slayer to victim. The Victorians even rewrote her legend as part of changing ideologies of childbirth. In Mrs Jameson's popular study, *Sacred and Legendary Art*, 1848, the saint simply holds up the crucifix and the dragon flees in abject terror, and her role as patron saint of childbirth is attributed as much to her acute suffering as to her escape from the devil. 'Her story is singularly wild,' writes Mrs Jameson, but reminds her readers reassuringly that the saint's name has been bestowed on 'that little lowly flower we call the daisy'.

St Margaret's passivity and helplessness related to women's loss of control of childbirth through the intervening centuries. Henceforward childbirth was to be managed by men. The whole of women's reproductive capacity – menstruation and parturition – was seen as evidence of women's inherent weakness – sickness even. 'Labour [is] a series of convulsions [which are] indistinguishable from epilepsy,' confidently stated Dr Robert Barnes in the *Lancet* of 1873.[43]

In her essay 'Wisewomen and Medicine Men: Changes in the

Management of Childbirth', 1976, Anne Oakley sets out two models of childbirth, one of which demonstrates management by women and the other by men:

> [When] the control of reproduction – contraception, abortion, pregnancy, and parturition – lies with the female community, men are not polluted because they are not involved. Alternatively, the control of reproductive care is in men's hands, and through the creation of rules and rituals which define women as passive objects vis à vis their reproductive fate, men are able to confine and limit and curb the creativity and potentially polluting power of female procreation – and also, incidentally, the threat of female sexuality.[44]

The rules and rituals which characterised the nineteenth-century management of childbirth by men had their counterpart in embroidery production as yet another manifestation of the controls society placed upon women's creativity. 'Ancient authorities' had to be 'strictly adhered to', rules of colour properly observed, the patterns of architects obediently followed. And women, fearful that their femininity would be impugned if they deviated from prescribed models, conformed.

Another pattern of passivity provided for embroiderers to work in thread (and to emulate in life) was the Virgin of the Annunciation embroidered by the School of Mediaeval Embroidery. Like the St Margaret banner, it demonstrates how the iconography of ecclesiastical embroidery changed before and after childbirth was taken out of the hands of women. The nineteenth-century virgin, her eyes cast humbly downwards, crosses her hands meekly over her breast. In the narrative cycles of mediaeval embroidery, the Annunciation was immediately followed by the Visitation, in which Mary and her cousin Elizabeth, mother of John the Baptist, are shown embracing. The two scenes are among many mediaeval images recounting and celebrating the miracle of Mary's fertility connoted by the lily of the Annunciation; Christ was 'The flower willed to be born of the flower, at the time of flowers'.[45] By the nineteenth century the lily no longer connoted spring flowering and fertility, but only purity and asceticism.

The extent to which embroidery had become associated with feminity as purity and submissiveness can be gauged from a painting by Dante Gabriel Rossetti. He depicts the Virgin Mary with her mother. The work relates to a scene from the apocryphal Life of Mary – a popular narrative sequence in mediaeval art. In this same art the Virgin's mother, Anna, is shown teaching her daughter from a book. But in Rossetti's painting, books merely provide a pedestal for a lily, which the Virgin reproduces in thread. In fact the painting delineates an absolute sexual division of labour. The two women are ensconced with embroidery in the domestic sphere; outside Joachim, Anna's husband, labours in the vineyard.

Exceptionally pale, delicate and ethereal, Mary presents the middle-class ideal of femininity, and the physical justification for the confinement of her sex within the home – middle-class women were considered by the Victorians to be 'pure but sick; working-class women outside the home able-bodied but contaminated and sickening'.[46]

The sex and class connotations of embroidery – its associations with goodness and domesticity – were not invented by the theorists of the embroidery revival. They did however emphasise the spiritual associations of the art, and laid down the conditions under which women could embroider for the public sphere – obedience to the church and a reflection of a pious passivity in the depiction of religious subject matter.

A large exhibition of mediaeval embroidery opened in London in 1905. Despite the presence of many impressive examples of the finest period of mediaeval embroidery, a reviewer, May Morris, noted a certain ambiguity in the attitude of visitors to the exhibition. Writing in the *Burlington Magazine* she commented:

> I gather it has come as a surprise to many people that work so distinguished, so highly developed and so varied, should have been produced at this early date. The surprise surprises me, for they accept without exclamation the font of Wells Cathedral, illuminated books from Winchester, and so forth, and this is but part of the same story.[47]

May Morris was well qualified to review the exhibition. Her father, William Morris, key figure in the nineteenth-century Arts and Crafts Movement, had encouraged May to begin embroidering by the time she was seven years old. Since 1885 she had been in charge of the Morris, Marshall and Faulkner embroidery workshop. She had written on embroidery history and practice, and directed the embroidery class at the Central School of Art and Design in London. In this review, with somewhat elusive irony, she rebuked visitors for carrying their prejudices with them. But her analysis of the situation is primarily socialist, not feminist. She suggested that people were amazed at the achievements of embroiderers only because they had unquestioningly accepted the division of art forms into Fine or High art, practised by the privileged classes, and Craft or Applied Art, practised by anyone else. They could accept the excellence of mediaeval painting and sculpture but could not believe that embroidery, a so-called craft, could attain such heights.

The situation of embroidery is however, significantly different from that of other crafts. The crucial factor determining the reception of the exhibition was not simply embroidery's association with craft as opposed to art. Rather it was the total identification that had been effected between embroidery and the Victorian feminine ideal. By the time the 1905 exhibition was mounted publications on mediaeval embroidery had been devoted to propagating a particular reading of history, and producing a specific image of the mediaeval embroiderer for more than fifty years. The historians had provided women's work with a heritage they believed would win it the respect and recognition it truly deserved – and women needed. In doing so they concealed the professional production of embroidery by women and men behind an image of the solitary stitching queen. They reduced the heterogenous character of ecclesiastical work to the modest undertakings of self-denying nuns. And the character of mediaeval embroidery itself was pruned and tamed in Victorian prototypes to affirm contemporary notions of femininity. Far from fulfilling their intentions to validate embroidery, the Victorian historians devalued it in the eyes of a society which equated great art with masculinity, the public sphere and professional practice.

3: Fertility, Chastity and Power

The Victorian imposition of their feminine ideal on to mediaeval embroidery conceals a complex set of relationships between the art's patrons – the church and the nobility – and the content of ecclesiastical embroidery; between the church's denigration of women and women's central place in society and within mediaeval craft production.

Opus Anglicanum is the generic name for ecclesiastical embroidery produced in England from approximately 900 to 1500. The embroidery is on linen or velvet with silk and metal threads, pearls, jewels and beaten gold. Split stitch was employed for the figures and the background was worked with underside couching. Technically superb and extraordinarily expressive, embroidery was not considered a lesser art form than painting and sculpture. The dividing of media into crafts and fine art only commenced at the Renaissance.

Opus Anglicanum was exported all over the continent; the name is derived from entries in European inventories of the time. The inventory of the Holy See, 1295, mentions Opus Anglicanum more frequently than any other embroidery. Pope Innocent IV had letters written to the abbots of the English Cistercian orders during 1246 demanding quantities of embroidery. He commented 'England is our garden of delight; truly it is a well inexhaustible, and from where there is great abundance, from thence much more may be extracted.' Recording the Pope's words, Matthew Paris, the thirteenth-century chronicler, wrote, 'This command of my Lord Pope did not displease the London Merchants who sold them at their own price.'[1]

With property obtained through huge benefactions and endowments, the church was becoming increasingly wealthy. Ecclesiastical power was consolidating and centering upon a revived papacy. The new authoritarian, militant spirit of the church needed art to reflect, assert and impress its power on the people. The magnificent vestments of Opus Anglicanum, the richness of the materials used in their creation – gold, silver gilt, silk, velvet and seed pearls – associated the trappings of earthly power with heavenly power.

Embroidery was, of course, also applied to secular objects and purposes. The wills and inventories of the wealthy disclose a formidable use of embroidery. The inventory of Thomas Woodstock, Earl of Gloucester, made in 1397 lists his embroidered beds. He owned a large bed of blue baudekyn, [silk woven with threads of gold for royalty, nobility and the church] embroidered with silver owls and fleurs de lys; a bed of black baudekyn powdered with white roses; a great bed of gold with coverlet, tester and valance in fine blue satin worked with gold garters and curtains to match; a large bed of white satin embroidered with his arms and helm in cyprus gold; an old bed of blue worsted embroidered with a stag; a red bed of worsted embroidered with a crowned lion, two griffins and chaplets and roses; a bed of blue worsted embroidered with white eagles; a coverlet and tester of red worsted embroidered with a white lion crouched under a tree.[2]

In dress too, from the eleventh century onwards, embroidery became increasingly prominent. Women wore a shirt embroidered at the neck, described by Chaucer in *The Miller's Tale*.

> Whyt was her smock and brouded all before
> And eek behind, on her coller aboute
> Of col-blak silk, with-inne and eek with-oute.

Over the shirt a long, wide, upper garment was gathered at the belt where a richly embroidered bag hung. Some indication of the magnificence of embroidered clothes among the nobility in the later middle ages can be gleaned from royal household accounts. Edward III for example, on one occasion ordered a white doublet with green borders covered in clouds and vines in gold with the King's motto 'It is as it is' and a green robe embroidered with pheasant's feathers.[3]

Heraldry also increased the demand for embroidery as a means of identification on the battlefield. A reconstruction of the Black Prince's jupon hangs in his tomb at Canterbury. The royal arms of England stitched in gold are appliquéed to a quilted background. By the fourteenth century a man not only displayed his political allegiance through embroidered garments, but his wife could also have her garments embroidered with her own coat of arms impaled with her husband's.

Embroidery was thus politically and artistically a leading English art, sharing with painting and sculpture the task of affirming the power of the church, the crown and the nobility. But who were the embroiderers at this time of extraordinary expansion?

Embroidery was produced in both secular workshops and in religious houses. Convents were centres of embroidery production. The majority of cloistered nuns were drawn from the nobility. Six hours of a nun's day were devoted to labour, and nunneries employed people to perform the mundane tasks of the establishment, leaving embroidery as one of the few acceptable forms of work for the nuns. But the church had reservations about convent embroidery. In the sixth century an edict had been issued forbidding nuns to work with precious stones and depict flowers. In 747 the time nuns spent embroidering was limited, and in 1314 an injunction was sent to the English convents of Nunkeeling, Yedingham and Wykeham that no nun should absent herself from divine service 'on account of being occupied with silk work'.[4] The edicts were prompted both by the church's view of women and by the conditions within convents.[5] Embroidery was deeply associated with self adornment as a mark of social power; in relation to women this spelled vanity. The concepts of chastity as a virtue, and vanity as a vice, were both employed as mechanisms of control over women who were dubbed by the church as more dangerous to men than 'the poison of asps and dragons.'[6] There is, though, no doubt that convent embroidery was not always dedicated to the church. When the writer and politician Christine de Pisan visited her daughter at the Dominican Abbey of Poissey in the fifteenth century, the nuns presented their visitors with decidedly secular embroideries: belts and purses worked in silk and gold thread.[7] *The Ancren Riwle* (rules for anchoresses) frowned on this practice, ordering women to 'make no purses to gain friends therewith. . . but shape and sew and mend church vestments and poor people's clothes.'[8]

Eileen Power in her study of English nuns surmises that nuns eked out their income by doing fine needlework for ladies of the world.

However, a group of religious women, known to be embroiderers, cut across the image of the worldly embroidering nun. Women shared the prevailing religious enthusiasm of the late middle ages. They were not only involved in the religious poverty movements – the new mendicant orders founded by St Dominic and St Francis in the thirteenth century – but also founded their own movements. Among them were the Beguines, a non-establishment reform movement that originated in Liège at the end of the twelfth century. Theirs was an organisation with no hierarchy, with no system of permanent vows and no rigid structure. They sometimes lived in groups in a house inherited by one of their number, and slowly set up convents.

Members were required to give up all their possessions and, instead of begging, to live by the labour of their hands. Drawn initially from the nobility, the work they knew was embroidery. The movement spread quickly through France and Germany. Matthew Paris commented in 1243 that 'they have so multiplied within a short time that two thousand of them have been reported in Cologne and neighbouring cities.'[9] However, the embroidering Beguines were to be a short-lived movement: 'I would have them married or thrust into an approved order', wrote the Bishop of Olmutz to the Pope in 1273.[10] The women were condemned by the Church Council of 1312 at Vienne with a document which revealingly began, 'Since these women promise no obedience to anyone . . .' Finally the Archbishop of Cologne ordered the association to be dissolved.[11]

Although nuns and holy women were known for their embroidery, the art was not restricted to one sex alone. Monks too embroidered. For example, Thomas Selmiston, a monk who died in 1419, was remembered as an outstanding embroiderer: 'For he was in the art of embroidery a most cunning artificier having none like him.'[12]

Similarly, in secular workshops both sexes embroidered. These gained importance over ecclesiastical workshops from the thirteenth century onwards when increased demand for embroidery necessitated greater capitalisation.

Twentieth-century historians believe that women disappeared from professional production at the time when workshops became more highly organised and capitalised. W.R. Lethaby, in the proceedings of the Society of Antiquarians in 1907 observes that 'down to the mid-thirteenth century we hear of women in connection with the production of such works, after that I only know of men who are named as embroiderers.'[13] Seventy years later Mary Gostelow was of much the same opinion, 'Opus Anglicanum was produced particularly from the middle of the thirteenth century to the end of the fourteenth century. Famous throughout Europe, it was executed generally in workshops in London, by professional embroiderers, mostly men.'[14] Grace Christie, in her thorough study *Medieval Embroidery*, 1938, wrote: 'From the middle of the thirteenth century the demand for embroideries had become so great that the craft, at first perhaps mainly in the hands of individual workers scattered in different places, became an organised commercial activity located in definite centres. . . Before this time the names of the executants noted were mostly those of women . . . but afterwards, with few exceptions, they are those of men living in or near London.'[15]

It seems highly unlikely that women disappeared from production just when the craft expanded. They clearly were active as professionals immediately before the major period of the production of Opus Anglicanum. At the time of the Norman conquest, William of Poitiers, chaplain and chronicler to King William, had praised the gold embroidery the French found in England, attributing it to 'the women of England [who] are very skilful with the needle'.[16] In the Domesday Book reference is made to Leviet who worked for the King and Queen and to Alwid the Maiden who held two hides of land in Buckinghamshire in return for teaching Count Goderic's daughter to embroider. The chasuble which Queen Mathilda bequeathed to the Church of the Holy Trinity at Caen is described as the work of Alderet's wife in Winchester.[17]

Once again it was the Victorian historians who were largely responsible for providing the impression that Opus Anglicanum was mostly the work of men. They imposed their ideal sexual division of labour on to mediaeval embroidery production. Chapter Two traced the process by which the mediaeval woman embroiderer was represented as incarcerated nun or solitary noble lady. The image was maintained by attributing professional work to men. Historians fastened eagerly on to the names of men listed in royal records in connection with embroidery commissions and claimed they were the professional producers of Opus Aglicanum. G.H. Hartshorne lists Adam de Basinges, Adam de Bakering, John de Colonia, Thomas Cheiner, John Blaton, William Courtnay, Stephen Vyne, Thomas Carleton, William Sanston, Robert de Asshecombe and William of Gloucester as embroiderers.[18] Later historians unquestioningly accept the list. Even a recent, carefully researched article by M. Fitch on the numbers and geographical location in London of the embroiderers of Opus Anglicanum describes embroiderers as 'craftsmen sitting cross-legged at work'.[19] Some men named by Hartshorne were, indeed, embroiderers. Stephen Vyne was embroiderer to Richard II and Henry IV, William Courtnay was named as embroiderer of London when he was paid by Edward III for a velvet vest worked with tabernacles and images of gold. But amongst the men named as embroiderers were merchants, goldsmiths or clerks to the king who simply *received* the commissions. Adam de Basing, for example, is always cited as an embroiderer although he was, in fact, a merchant who worked for Henry III.[20] Three agents were involved in the King's commission: the merchant supplier, the producing artist and the royal clerk or administrator. Henry III's major project was Westminster Abbey: rebuilding it, furnishing it and constructing a shrine for Edward The Confessor. Embroidery was commissioned for the abbey and for the King to offer as donations to other churches and monasteries, or to dispense as marks of favour to individuals and visiting foreign dignitaries.

De Basing, like others who acted as merchant suppliers to the king, was a wealthy Londoner. By 1240 he appears to have had a workshop of embroiderers who carried out substantial commissions. On the marriage of the King's daughter, Margaret, to Alexander III of Scotland, de Basing was paid more than £87 for three chasubles, six copes, three sets of tunics and dalmatics with stoles, amices, cuffs, and collars, an altar border of orphreys, albs, surplices and other church fittings. In December 1243 he was paid for an alb, gloves and embroidered sandals to be given to the bishop of Reiz and for three mitres, one for the archbishop of Embrun, one for the bishop of Reiz and one for 'an abbot who came with the Countess of Provence'. In the same year he supplied copes and embroidered chasubles, orphreys, tunics and dalmatics, all to be offered at Westminster by the King.[21]

William of Gloucester, another man listed by craft historians as an embroiderer, was, in fact, a goldsmith. He acted as artist, supplier and royal clerk to the King. In 1257 he was responsible for the commission of an embroidered altarcloth to adorn the shrine of Edward the Confessor at Westminster. Four embroiderers worked on the project for four years.

Twentieth-century historians have largely accepted the Victorian assumption that professional embroiderers were 'mostly men' because mostly male names do appear in connection with embroidery commissions. This was due to woman's place in the structure of mediaeval craft production. Within the towns the growing number of embroiderers, like other craftworkers, formed a guild as a form of self-government in the face of an increasingly competitive economy.[22] Unfortunately early records relating to the Embroiderers' Guild were burnt in the Great Fire of London. But the situation of women within the guild was no doubt much the same as in other craft guilds: women entered them from a position of legal and financial subordination. The household was the unit of production and the husband was its legal representative. *His* name would therefore figure in transactions.

Mediaeval crafts were certainly open to women, who were, for example, chandlers, painters, ironmongers, netmakers, shoemakers, smiths or goldsmiths.[23] No frontier existed between professional and private life, between the domestic and public sphere. The household was the centre of both domestic and mercantile activity; the workshop was in the dwelling place and members of the household worked together at their trade. Workers could include father, mother, unmarried sister or brother, possibly grandparents, children, servants and apprentices.[24] Women embroiderers were however paid less than men. By the fifteenth century, male embroiderers received 7¼ to 10¼ pennies a day while women were paid 4¼ to 6¼ pennies a day. There were eight divisions in scale of payments, with each embroiderer paid according to qualifications.[25] Then, as now, women assumed responsibility for babies and young children. But the span of childhood was short. Children were expected to play their part in household labour from an early age, and both men and women supervised the older children. Both boys and girls would be apprenticed. A court case of 1369 records that embroidery apprentice Alice Catour's father brought a bill against her master for ill-treating her.[26] That women also took in apprentices is evident from another court case of 1385. A woman was accused of 'taking in a certain serving woman and others as apprentices in the craft of embroidery, whereas her real intent was to set up a house of infamy'.[27]

Not only did women work in guild workshops as masters' wives or daughters, they also laboured independently, judging from the number of laws directed at 'femmes soles'. Moreover, after a husband's death, women were able to carry on the family business and guilds made special provisions for widows. The Tailors of Exeter permitted a widow to have as many workers as she wanted provided that she paid them, and had taken part in the work for at least seven years before she became her husband's successor. Women were even named by their occupation. During the fourteenth century a prayer was offered at Old St Paul's for Alice Aurifraigeria, or Alice Gold Embroiderer.[28] Her name proves that, contrary to Hartshorne's theory, women did embroider gold and metal threads.

Clearly, then, it is misleading to assert that women dropped out of professional production at the time of Opus Anglicanum. Moreover, although they rarely held sufficient economic or civic power to act as suppliers to the King, royal records do name women in relation to embroidery commissions. In May 1317 the Exchequer Issue Roll records that Rose, wife of John of Burford and merchant of London, received payment for a cope ornamented with coral, purchased from her by Queen Isabella to present to the Pope. This is believed to have been the Pienza Cope.[29]

The presence of women's names in royal household accounts is explained by both nineteenth- and twentieth-century historians of embroidery entirely in the light of prevailing ideologies of femininity. The concept of a woman merchant trading independently is so far from twentiety-century assumptions about mediaeval women that it is thought that Rose de Burford was an embroiderer. For example A.F. Kendrick in *English Needlework*, 1967, and Mary Eirwen Jones in *A History of Western Embroidery*, 1969, and Harriet Bridgeman and Elizabeth Drury in *Needlework*, 1978, name her as one of the few women amongst the 'mostly male' professionals. She was in fact a wool merchant from a powerful London family. After her husband's death she carried on his business as a wool merchant, but even before that she was trading on her own account.[30]

Another widow named in relation to an embroidery commission in Henry III's Liberate Roll was 'Joan late the wife of John de Wuburn' who was paid for a cope of 'samite embroidered with the Jesse Tree which the King offered in St Peter's church at Westminster at St Hillary's'.

There was, however, one embroiderer of the thirteenth century whom few historians have overlooked. The name of Mabel of Bury St Edmunds appears twenty-four times between 1239 and 1245 in the Liberate Rolls of Henry III. For a mediaeval artist Mabel is well documented. She was an independent worker rather than an employee of the King's merchant suppliers. In 1239 the King ordered that she be paid £10 for embroidering a chasuble and an offertory veil. The order was an important one, so the King must already have known and respected her work. Two years later pearls were purchased for Mabel to use on the chasuble, and she was given 40 shillings to buy gold.[31] The King then commanded that the value of the chasuble be appraised by 'the sight of discreet men and women with a knowledge of embroidery' to establish Mabel's fee. The appraisal does not appear to have been carried out. Another order was soon issued. This time the appraisal was requested from the 'better workers of the city of London . . . such as will speak and know how to speak of such work', and the King emphasised that he needed embroiderers to advise him on the value of the finished work, the cost of materials and Mabel's fee because 'he did not want to offend in this matter nor incur to some extent condemnation of himself'.[32] That Henry invited embroiderers to establish the worth of work he commissioned indicates the esteem in which the art and its workers were held.

After Mabel had completed the chasuble she was paid for an offertory cloth, apparels, a stole, a fanon, an amice, collar and cuffs. Her last commission for the King was an embroidered banner or standard to be hung near the altar in Westminster

Abbey. Henry supplied the subject – The Virgin and St John – but left the composition and design up to Mabel as she 'would best know how to see to them'. That Henry allowed Mabel control over the design of the banner casts doubt on the widely accepted view that mediaeval embroiderers were the humble executants of ideas supplied by painters, monarchs and churchmen. In 1244 Mabel was given money to finish the banner 'that it may not remain unmade for want of money', and a year later a payment was made for silk used in the banner 'which Mabel de Sancto Edmundo made for the King'.[33]

Mabel then disappears from royal records until 1256, when the King made a pilgrimage to Bury St Edmunds. There he issued the following order: 'Because Mabel of St Edmunds served the King and Queen for a long time in the making of ecclesiastical ornaments . . . that the same Mabel be given six measures of cloth agreeable to her and the fur of a rabbit for a robe.'[34] The gift of a fur robe was a traditional mark of considerable respect.

Mabel of Bury St Edmunds was the last woman to achieve such prominence as an embroiderer in royal service during the middle ages. Susan Mosher Stuard, introducing *Women in Mediaeval Society*, 1976, a collection of feminist essays on the position of women at the time, writes, 'The tendency as the middle ages progressed was toward a lessening of the public activity of women, a lower place in ecclesiastical opinion, fewer roles in guild organisations.'[35] R.W. Southern's *Western Society and the Church in the Middle Ages*, 1970, declares that this constituted progress: 'These ladies of the dark ages have some remarkable religious and literary achievements to their credit, but their period of splendid independence did not last long. As society became better organised and ecclesiastically more right-minded, the necessity for male dominance began to assert itself.'[36]

In the mode of production as well as in the form and content of Opus Anglicanum, we can detect a growing contradiction between the increasingly misogynist stance of the mediaeval church and women's importance in mediaeval society. The *Decretum*, the systematisation of church law laid down in the twelfth century, declared that 'Woman's authority is nil; let her in all things be subject to the rule of men . . . And neither can she teach, nor be witness, nor give guarantee, nor sit in judgement.'[37] Yet women as well as men were employed in workshops making art for the church and, as we have seen, Henry III left the design of an ecclesiastical banner up to Mabel of Bury St Edmunds.

Not only was there a disjuncture between women's place in mediaeval art production and the church's repudiation of women codified in the *Decretum,* but also in the actual content of Opus Anglicanum. Although the form and content were controlled by the church, and intended to glorify and ratify ecclesiastical power, the preoccupations of the women and men workers were nevertheless powerfully present. Close examination of the copes reveals a conflict between the interests of the ecclesiastic patrons and the craft workers. However, this divergence was controlled by the very form and content of the embroidery.

To understand this, it is first necessary to look at the form and technique of the embroidery on the copes. The way the narrative content is distributed over the surface displays the hierarchical and church-dominated character of the society in which they were stitched. Scenes are arranged in descending order of importance. The key image – frequently the Coronation of the Virgin rather than the Crucifixion – was placed high on the cope, lying on the upper part of the priest's back when he officiated in church. Below this key image would be scenes from the Bible and apocryphal Gospels[38] and saints from *The Golden Legend*,[39] with the figures arranged in such a way that they would appear upright when the copes were worn. In the last decades of the thirteenth century, narrative scenes and images of saints were usually displayed in shaped panels – circles or quatrefoils – as for example in the Copes of Ascoli Piceno, the Vatican, Madrid, Syon and Steeple Aston. This design framework was identical to that used in contemporary painting and stained glass.

The later copes of Pienza, Bologna and Toledo employ designs of concentric arcades. The East Anglian school of manuscript illumination which flourished when the copes were stitched worked with the same motif. The most elaborate arrangement of arcades is found on the Pienza cope with its three rows of decorative arches supported on twisted columns.

Another popular pattern was the Jesse Tree. A vine springs from the Old Testament figure of Jesse at the hem of the cope, and snakes upwards, forming circles containing Christ's ancestors, and terminating at the centre of the cope with a triumphant Virgin and Child. The importance of the Jesse Tree design was that it identified the nobility and royalty with Christ, by providing him with a royal ancestry: 'The Patriarch Jesse belonged to the royal family, that is why the root of Jesse signifies the heritage of Kings', wrote the monk Herreus in the twelfth century.[40]

The technique of Opus Anglicanum similarly reflected ecclesiastical power, because embroiderers had developed a way of working gold threads that allowed maximum movement and play of light over the surface of the cope, enhancing the splendour of the church spectacle. Underside couching, as it is known, involved laying metal thread on the surface and fastening it with a linen thread at the back of the material at regular intervals. The spots where the metal threads were pulled down formed a pattern on the surface. A hinged effect was created, offsetting the stiffness of the metal threads and permitting the garment to flow and glitter when worn in procession.

Solid gold grounds were inspired by Near-Eastern fabrics. The crusaders plundered rich textiles and brought them to Europe, where embroiderers adopted not only the use of gold but also certain motifs. Paired symmetrical animals and the Tree of Life entered the embroiderer's repertoire. The Tree of Life is a stylised tree descended from the sacred trees of goddess-worshipping cultures, represented in murals of Crete and Egypt, and referred to in the Old Testament as asherah or asherim that stood alongside the altar at shrines of the Goddess.[41] Both the Tree and paired creatures remained a feature of embroidery, becoming popular sampler motifs in the eighteenth century.

The designs, with their shaped panels distributing the holy scenes in order of importance, the technique with its underside couching and appliquéed jewels, all emphatically celebrated the hierarchy and announced the power of the male-dominated church over the people. It is at the level of the content of embroidery that a tension appears.

Early mediaeval art had been the exclusive possession of a clerical élite, and was intended to convey the solemnity and transcendental character of the Christian religion. The art of the Gothic period, which encompasses Opus Anglicanum, displayed a concern with nature and the everyday life of the craftworkers.[42] For example, a dog barks at the angel who appears to the shepherds during the Nativity, and the Cope of the Passion at St Bertrand de Comminges includes thirty-two different varieties of birds and sixty animals.

Although the development of relatively independent household craft workshops in towns, and the prevailing religious ideology, created conditions of production which allowed for the introduction of details of earthly life to sacred scenes, the church nonetheless attempted to ensure that the representation of women in no way contradicted church dogma.

As we have seen, the majority of the copes were dominated by the Coronation of the Virgin – an image which at once acknowledged and contained the power of women. Mary as Queen can be read in a number of ways. As Queen she ratifies feudal hierarchy, as Virgin she denies the sexuality of earthly women, she is enthroned as Queen of Heaven yet she bows her head to her son who confers power upon her.[43] Marina Warner in *Alone of All Her Sex*, 1978, points out that 'by projecting the hierarchy of the world on to heaven, that hierarchy – be it ecclesiastical or lay – appears to be ratified by divinely reflected approval . . . the cult of Mary as Queen served for centuries to uphold the status quo to the advantage of the highest echelons of power.'[44] She describes how at times of upheaval and change, like that of the period of the great copes of Opus Anglicanum, the Virgin as Queen is utilised to consolidate worldly hierarchy.

She also relates the image of Mary seated beside Christ to an ancient tradition of nuptial imagery, rooted in goddess-worshipping cultures of the Middle East, for example, the annual marriage of the Canaanite god Baal to his sister Anat, the Syrian goddess Ishtar to her lover Tamuz, and Cybele and Attis, Isis and Osiris in Egypt. The nuptials of these divinities mirrored the greater nuptials of the sky and the earth, from which comes forth plenty: the rites of regeneration each year imitated the original union of sky and earth at the beginning of the world. So while the Virgin Mary symbolised asceticism and virginity, because she blossomed spontaneously she also functioned as a powerful fertility symbol: 'The quickening and obstetric functions of the classical goddesses like Hera and Demeter have been taken over by the Virgin.'[45]

It is precisely in the way that images of fertility, pregnancy and childbirth repeat across the ecclesiastical garments that the contradiction between the place of women in mediaeval society and the misogynist stance of the church becomes visible. An emphasis on reproduction was a feature of the apocryphal Gospels, and representations from these Gospels, particularly from the *Life of Mary*,[46] play a large part in the imagery of Opus Anglicanum. A preoccupation with childbirth was shared by

22,23 *The Syon Cope*, Victoria and Albert Museum, London. 1300–1320.
292.2 × 134.6 cm.
During the reign of Elizabeth I, nuns from Bridgetine Convent of Syon fled to
Lisbon, taking the cope with them. About 1810, nuns from the order returned to
England and brought back the cope. The arrangement of linked quatrefoils was
developed slightly later than the Jesse Tree pattern. Detail below.

24 *The Butler-Bowden Cope*, Victoria and Albert Museum, London. The cope was included in the exhibition of mediaeval Opus Anglicanum in London, 1908. Images of the Coronation of the Virgin, the Homage of the Magi and the Annunciation are surrounded by saints.

25 *The Pienza Cope*, Museo Civico, Pienza. Second quarter of the fourteenth century. Gold, silver, silk and pearls on linen, 350.6 × 163.9 cm. Photo: Lombardi–Siena.

26 *The Cope of St Bertrand de Comminges,*
France. c 1300. 144.8 × 22.9 cm; diameter of
roundels 25.4 cm. Photo: Archives de la Haute
Garrone.
The pattern worked in gold upon the ground
resembles the gilt gesso ground of The
Coronation Chair at Westminster Abbey by
Walter of Durham – a reminder of how nearly
related were different media during the middle
ages, before the establishment of a hierarchy of
art forms.

27 *The Butler-Bowden Cope*, Victoria and Albert
Museum, London.
The detail is the Coronation of the Virgin, which
dominated so many of the Opus Anglicanum
copes. Mary seated beside Christ has been related
to an ancient tradition of nuptial imagery, rooted
in goddess-worshipping cultures of the Middle
East. The image both acknowledges and contains
the power of women in mediaeval society. As
Virgin, Mary denies the sexuality of earthly
women. And although she is enthroned as a
goddess, she bows her head in worship of her son,
who confers power upon her.

28 *Embroiderers*, Italian, British Library, London. Fourteenth century.
Both women and men worked as professional embroiderers throughout the middle ages.

29 *The Luttrell Psalter*, depicting Sir Geoffrey and Lady Luttrell, British Museum, London. c 1340.
Lady Luttrell's clothing is embroidered with her coat of arms impaled with that of her husband. (See B. Snook *English Embroidery*, Mills and Boon, London 1974).

30 *The Wilton Diptych*, detail, National Gallery, London. c 1400.
The detail above shows Richard II presented to the Virgin and Child by his patron saints. The king's personal badge of the white hart is embroidered on his clothing, providing some indication of the extent and magnificence of embroidered clothing among royalty and nobility of the period.

33 *The Steeple Aston Cope*, Church of Steeple Aston, Oxfordshire. Photo: Oxford
University Press.
A detail from the cope shows St Margaret erupting from the devil disguised as a
dragon. St Margaret was patron saint of childbirth, and her frequent presence in
embroidery and wall painting was part of the general concern with fertility and
reproduction evident in Opus Anglicanum.

31 (top left) *The Cope of St Maximin*, church of St Maximin, Provence. Late thirteenth
century. Diameter of roundel 35.9 cm. Photo: Oxford University Press. Said to
have been bequeathed to the Preaching Friars of St Maximin by St Louis, son of
Charles II, the embroidery could be either French or English. The detail shows
Mary working cloth in the temple with other virgins – a scene from the apocryphal
Life of Mary.

32 (bottom left) *The Pienza Cope*, detail. Photo: Lombardi–Siena.
The detail shows one of the apocryphal midwives assisting at the Nativity.
Although the church had condemned the images of the midwives, they continued
to appear in embroidery throughout the period of Opus Anglicanum. The
inclusion of details consistent with the everyday life of the people was a feature of
Opus Anglicanum and other arts of the Gothic period.

34, 35 *Apparels of Albs*, Victoria and Albert Museum, London. 1320–1340.
Velvet embroidered with coloured silks, silver-gilt and silver thread, 165.2 ×
26.8 cm.
The Life of Mary allowed for repeated representations of conception and childbirth.
The celebrations of fertility were nevertheless distanced from women's sexuality
and procreative power by the insistence on immaculate conception and virgin
birth. Here we see the Annunciation to Anna, Mary's mother; the Meeting of
Joachim and Anna; the Birth of the Virgin; the Annunciation to Mary; and the
Visitation, when Mary went to see her cousin Elizabeth, pregnant with John the
Baptist.

both the embroiderers and their ecclesiastical patrons. But their interests diverged significantly. The circumstances of mediaeval life – a labour-intensive economy with the household as major productive unit – gave a central importance to fertility and child-birth. Because of the high rate of infant and maternal mortality, childbirth was regarded with considerable fear and apprehension by all craftworkers. To the church, however, childbirth was a sign of women's sinfulness and the manifestation of the curse of Eve: 'As long as woman is for birth and children, she is different from men as body is from soul. But when she wishes to serve Christ more than the world, then she will cease to be a woman and be called a man.'[47]

Despite the church's condemnation, childbirth was celebrated in ecclesiastical embroidery through apocryphal imagery. The stories are an amalgam of Old Testament material and aspects of goddess-worshipping cultures in the areas where the legends originated. The Cope of the Church of St Maximin in Provence, for example, depicts Mary weaving in the temple with a group of young women. After Mary's engagement to Joseph, she continued to spin for the temple and the High Priest allowed her companions in her work. The story manifests elements of Judaism and the religious cults of Syria where the Book of James was written: Mary as weaver relates to Moses who wove purple and scarlet for the Tabernacle. However, because women were not allowed beyond the outer court of the temple at Jerusalem, Marina Warner suggests that the weaving virgins are drawn from the virgin priestesses of Syrian culture.[48] The story appears only once in the embroidery of Opus Anglicanum which survives today. More common are the images of birth and conception from the apocryphal *Life of Mary*. Anna, the Virgin's mother, conceives miraculously after she and her husband are resigned to childlessness. In embroidery – and in painting – the two are shown embracing, signifying the miraculous conception. Anna is then shown in bed attended by a midwife after delivering the child.

The Annunciation by the Angel Gabriel to Mary heralds Jesus' immaculate conception. The Visitation – Mary's visit to her Cousin Elizabeth – is invariably stitched adjacent to the Annun-ciation, although it was soon to sink to relative insignificance in Christian iconography. In St Luke's Gospel the Angel Gabriel told Mary that her cousin 'hath also conceived a son in her old age'. Therefore Mary visited her cousin whose baby, John the Baptist, leapt in her womb at the sound of Mary's greeting. Elizabeth then spoke the words, 'Blessed art thou amongst women, and blessed is the fruit of thy womb. And whence is this to me, that the Mother of my Lord should come to me.' The apocryphal gospels add a human dimension to the story: Mary and Elizabeth embrace so that the words coming from Christ's mouth in Mary's womb might enter Elizabeth's ear and descend to John, annointing him prophet. In Opus Anglicanum the two women are shown in each other's arms – the greeting of two women relatives, one of whom had come to help the other in childbirth. And indeed some versions of the story show Mary officiating as a midwife at the birth of John the Baptist. In mediaeval mystery plays too Mary appeared as a midwife. During the middle ages female relatives and friends automatically attended a birth to provide support at what was possibly a dangerous ordeal.

The final birth scene in the narrative sequence on the copes is the Nativity of Christ. Unlike later representations of the Nativity the emphasis is placed on the mother, not the child. Mary is depicted resting in bed with Joseph seated nearby and a midwife in attendance. The homage of the three kings to the child occupies a separate frame.

The presence of two midwives is described in the apocryphal *Gospel According to the Pseudo Matthew*: Joseph leaves Mary in a cave while he goes to find a midwife. He returns with two, Zelemie and Salomie, only to discover that Mary has already given birth. When Zelemie examines Mary and finds she is still a virgin, she exclaims 'No defilement was at birth and travail bringing forth, virgin she conceived, virgin she gave birth and virgin she remained.' The other midwife asks in disbelief if she too can examine Mary. As soon as she touches the Virgin her hand painfully withers and she cries out, 'Lord, thou knowest that I have ever held thee in awe . . . and behold by reason of my incredulity I am become wretched because I dared to doubt thy Virgin.' A beautiful young man then appears and informs the midwife that the child can heal her. As she touches the child's swaddling clothes her hand is made whole.

The Fathers of the Church had repudiated the apocryphal midwives. St Jerome singled them out for attack, insisting that Mary gave birth alone, delivering the child herself, independent of other women.[49] However, Zelemie and Salomie survived the attack and at the period of Opus Anglicanum constituted part of the imagery of the Nativity, for they were still useful to the church. Salomie's withered hand is healed not by Mary the Virgin but by the Lord. Mary's virginity, which was considered a source of considerable power in the societies where the apocryphal Gospels originated, is shown to be secondary to the might of the male protagonists.

And, of course, the midwives testified to Mary's virginity. The continual emphasis on Mary's virginity successfully undermined the iconography of fertility seen in the Coronation of the Virgin, with its echoes of goddess worship, and in the repeated scenes of childbirth and conception.

The Church did, however, become increasingly antagonistic towards the midwives because their presence allied the Virgin too closely with earthly women. A woman was eligible for worship only once she was set apart from her sex; and reproduction could be celebrated only once it was divorced from female sexuality. Moreover the presence of the midwives at the Nativity evoked the particular circumstances of childbirth during the middles ages which the male-dominated church regarded with deep suspicion. Women conceived repeatedly and birth was accompanied by elaborate ritual, sometimes involving sympathetic magic. No man was allowed in the birth chamber. Midwives attending the birth rubbed oils on the woman's belly and tossed her in a blanket to speed delivery. Herbal aids like ergot to dilate the cervix were employed by midwives. All pins would be removed from the room, all doors, cupboards and drawers in the house opened and all knots untied.[50]

The midwives thus represented an autonomous female event. Adrienne Rich has argued that taboos surrounding childbirth spring partly from male fear of reproductive power, but equally from the fact that all-female groupings are threatening in themselves: 'The deliberate withdrawal of women from men has almost always been seen as a potentially dangerous or hostile act, a conspiracy, a subversion, a needless and grotesque thing . . .'[51]

The intimate link between the content of embroidery and changes in society is illustrated by the way that, as part of a sustained attack on midwives, the church evicted the apocryphal midwives from ecclesiastical art. Banished from embroidery by the fifteenth century, midwives did not of course disappear from society, but they ceased to receive vital ideological ratification from sacred art. Ecclesiastical authorities did all they could to discredit midwives and control their practice. The rationale was that they alleviated women's suffering which had been ordained by God, and that they practised magic. Sprenger and Institoris in the *Malleus Maleficarum*, c.1486, claimed that no one did more harm to the Catholic faith than midwives who 'surpass all other witches in their crimes'. The infamous treatise on witches urged that midwives should take an oath to eliminate witchcraft. In England, under an Act of 1512, a system of licences for midwives was instituted with the threat of severe punishment for any woman who practised without a licence. Midwives had to take a lengthy oath at the Bishop's Court. The actions besides witchcraft that they were forced to forswear indicate the fears that lay behind their persecution. They swore not to make false attributions of paternity, not to substitute children or destroy foetuses.

The male-dominated church faced a formidable task in its determination to control reproduction, its management in society and its representation in art. In Opus Anglicanum, the overwhelming importance of fertility and reproduction is apparent not only in images of the Virgin but also in the fact that St Margaret, patron saint of childbirth, was such a popular figure.

Patron saints were an important aspect of mediaeval culture and each craft guild had its own. Emile Mâle in *The Gothic Image*, 1913, observes that the cult of the patron saint had its roots deep in the life of the people, who felt closer to their patron saints than to an omnipotent, distant God.[52] St Catherine and St Margaret were the most frequently embroidered female saints. Just as the church had attempted to suppress the apocryphal midwives, so there had been moves against St Margaret. The Pope had repudiated her in 494, but she appears in *The Golden Legend*, c. 1260, and was represented not only in embroidery but in illuminated manuscripts, sculpture and murals, for example, at Hayles Church in Gloucester, Wiston Church in Suffolk and Cliffe-at-Hoe in Kent. Echoing pre-Christian ceremonies when fine textiles and embroideries would be offered at the shrines of the goddesses, clothes would be dedicated to St Margaret. Sir William Stokes of Loughborough left to the image of St Margaret his wife's second best kerchief.

In the image of St Margaret we can see represented the

importance of fertility and reproduction to mediaeval society, and the church's determination to control reproduction, using the tactic of divide and rule in relation to women.

St Margaret was the patron saint of childbirth because, as described in Chapter Two, after God, 'delivered' her from the body of the dragon, she prayed that she might be permitted to become intercessor for women in labour. Her story is one of great physical courage. She not only survived repeated torture and escaped from the dragon but she also wrestled with the devil in the form of a man: 'She caught him by the head and threw him to the ground, and set her right foot on his neck saying: "Lie still, thou fiend, under the foot of a woman".'[53]

The particular power of St Margaret – her extraordinary physical endurance – is explicable in terms of the original context of the legends of the holy women of Christianity. They emerged in the third century when Christians, not yet politically powerful, were persecuted by the Roman Government. The majority of the women came into conflict with society over the issue of chastity. St Margaret fought for her Christian faith, not for her chastity, but relinquishing Christianity would ultimately have meant the loss of her chastity to the governor. In an analysis of the legends, *Structural Patterns in The Legends of the Holy Women of Christianity*, 1978, Birte Carle suggests that 'one possible explanation of the sexual conflicts in the legends is that chastity, by the women, was considered to be a female potential. The abstention from a sexual life was not a dissociation from the female sex as such, but a way of keeping it mighty.'[54] She links the holy women to the particular place of virginity in the goddess cults that preceded Christianity, specifically the cult of Vesta: 'The virgin priestesses of Vesta represented the people in their relationship to the power of the universe. The service by chastity was the contribution of the female part of the population to guarantee the public wellbeing.'[55]

In the Opus Anglicanum image of St Margaret, we can see overtones both of a culture which considered female chastity to be a source of power, and a mediaeval representation of the power of women's fertility. The mediaeval church, however, undercut the militant St Margaret. The legends of the saints whose stories turned on the might of virginity in conflict with the evil power of the world were rewritten at the time of the production of Opus Anglicanum. *The Golden Legend* characterises St Margaret as 'white by virginity, little by humility and virtuous by operation of miracles'. The *Hali Meidenhad Treatise,* a guide for female holiness penned by men, quotes the saints Margaret, Juliana, Cecilia and Catherine as maidens of irreproachable meekness.[56] Meekness was considered even more important than virginity: 'A maid as regards the grace of maidenhood surpasses the widowed and wedded, but a mild wife or meek widow is better than a proud maiden.'[57]

The gap between the militant Margaret depicted by embroiderers and the church's official description of the saint as the representative of the virtues of meekness and mildness is, perhaps, explicable in terms of audience. Written descriptions were aimed at the nun or anchorite – women who committed themselves to living out their lives enclosed in cells attached to castles, churches, monasteries and convents. Both nuns and anchorites were predominantly from the nobility. The characteristics ascribed to the virgin martyrs – slenderness, grace and fairness – corresponded to the developing contemporary ideal of aristocratic femininity. The embroidered image of St Margaret, patron saint of childbirth, addressed the needs of other women, amongst them the embroiderers themselves, for she provided a powerful intercessor for women in labour.

Women were thus divided into those who inhabited women's realm of fertility, and those allowed a place in the masculine spiritual hierarchy on condition that, like Mary Queen of Heaven, they were chaste, solitary, maidenly and meek.

To a certain extent the representations of St Margaret, humble in writing and militant in thread, were a compromise between the church's attitude to women and the domestic and economic facts of mediaeval life. St Thomas Aquinas voiced the thirteenth-century church's necessary compromise towards the 'devil's gateway':

As regards the individual nature, woman is defective and mis-begotten, for the active forces in the male seed tend to the production of a perfect likeness in the masculine sex; while the production of women comes from a defect in the active force or some material indisposition or even some external influence. . . On the other hand, as regards human nature in general woman is not misbegotten, but is included in nature's intention as directed to the work of generation.[58]

To the church, women and childbirth were a necessary evil, to the embroiderers of Opus Anglicanum, men and women who worked at the same craft within the household, childbirth was a time of anticipation and celebration. Thus the church countenanced St Margaret as dragon slayer, but curtailed and controlled her influence by emphasising her virginity and providing a written commentary in praise of her compliance and obedience. In her we see a contest between fertility as women's strength, and chastity as male control of that realm. Similarly the repeated apocryphal scenes of birth – midwives and all – were prevented from endowing earthly women with power and importance because Mary remained above all, the Virgin.

The same dynamic that informed the content of mediaeval art can be seen in lived rituals around childbirth. The ceremony known as Churching allowed a measure of independent ritual to develop around childbirth but imposed a stricture which returned ultimate control to the church. A month after giving birth a woman, accompanied by a female relative, entered a church holding a candle. The priest then recited the following lines, 'Enter the temple of God, adore the Son of the Holy Virgin Mary who has given you the blessing of motherhood.' Before Churching a woman was forbidden to make bread, serve food or have any contact with Holy Water. She was considered polluted and dangerous. The Christian rationale for dubbing the postpartum woman a danger to society was that God had cursed women to bring forth their children in pain.

The practices which isolated women after childbirth, although they are often accompanied by apparent control of childbirth by women, are closely linked to male domination. Conception and birth, as I have stated, are central to the content of Opus Anglicanum. Yet they are presented in such a way as to circumscribe the power and significance of women. The ritual from which men were excluded was made public on the garments worn by the priests, taken out of the hands of women and placed on the backs of priests.

4: The Domestication of Embroidery

'In the practice of embroidery the needlewoman has an advantage not now shared by workers in any other craft, in that technical processes are almost a matter of inherited skill,' wrote W.R. Lethaby in *Embroidery and Tapestry Weaving*, 1906.[1] The notion that women are selected by nature for needlework – genetically programmed to embroider – conceals the fact that up to the eighteenth century the majority of embroiderers to the Kings were men. However, the social and economic forces that were to categorise embroidery as a feminine, *domestic* art (and finally as almost a secondary female sexual characteristic) were set in motion in the sixteenth century, a transitional time for the art.

During the Renaissance a new and powerful link was forged between women and embroidery, ideologically within discourses on sexual difference, and materially by changes in the economic and social structure of European society. Feminist historians have argued convincingly that women did not *enjoy* a Renaissance, that the period had remarkably little effect on loosening the restrictions circumscribing women's lives.[2] Indeed, within craft production the tighter regulations and increasingly hierarchical organisations worked to exclude women from positions of responsibility and prestige; while among the upper classes an extraordinary preoccupation with the differences between men and women actually limited women's sphere of action when their family's financial position meant they no longer worked in the family craft or trade.

The essential differences between the sexes had become a central subject of theology and medicine, and of the ethical, political and artistic writings of the day.[3] For example, Baldassare Castiglione in his highly influential *Book of the Courtier*, 1528, a fictionalised discussion on the characteristics of the perfect courtier at the Palace of Urbino, devotes space to a debate on the role of women in social and political life. One protagonist offers the mediaeval understanding of sex difference: '. . . very learned men have written that since Nature always plans and aims at absolute perfection she would if possible, constantly bring forth men; and when a woman is born this is a mistake or defect, contrary to Nature's wishes.'[4] His opponent offers the Renaissance humanist view that, 'male and female always go naturally together, and one cannot exist without the other, so by very definition, we cannot call anything male unless it has its female counterpart, or anything female if it has no male counterpart.'[5]

The humanist view is an advance on the mediaeval view that women were the outcome of a 'mistake', but an ideology of sexual difference – in which notions of masculine and feminine have meaning only in relation to each other – leads to an endless assertion of women's feminity to provide an opposite against which men sustain their dominance. An anxious insistence on absolute sex difference is evident in Castiglione's text:

I hold that a woman should in no way resemble a man as regards her ways, manners, words, gestures and bearing. Thus just as it is very fitting that a man should display a certain robust and sturdy manliness, so it's well for a woman to have a certain soft and delicate tenderness with an air of feminine sweetness in her every movement, which, in her going and staying and whatsoever she does, always makes her appear a woman without any resemblance to a man.[6]

Lying behind this dogmatic assertion of how men and women

should differ from one another was contemporary medical opinion, which had undermined the mediaeval certainty that women were innately defective. Instead, it was argued that women were as perfect in their sex as men in theirs. Numerous texts on gynaecology and gynaecological diseases countered earlier notions that women were dangerous and unclean during menstruation, but provided new justification for women's subordination. Women were inferior to men because of the psychological effects of their cold and moist humour,[7] which made them unable to control their emotions. This, together with their less robust physique, predisposed them, it was argued, to a more protected, less prominent role in the household and society.[8]

The medical justification for women's restriction to the home, and exclusion from public office, was accompanied by a body of prescriptive writings on marriage, which closely defined the particular roles of husband and wife. Embroidery was extolled as the quintessential occupation for women. Thus Frederigo Luigini, in *Il Libro dell bella Donna*, 1554, asks 'What about the needle, the distaff and wheel, do they belong only to low, mechanic and plebeian females?' After citing examples of high-ranking ladies who sewed, he concludes that the needle belonged to 'all women both high and low, but where the poor find only utility in these arts, the rich, the noble and beautiful lady wins honour also'.[9] Luigini's words would have had their greatest impact not on high- or low-ranking women but on the increasing number of women below the level of the court, yet above that of the artisan, who no longer laboured in the family business.

Leon Battista Alberti in his work *On The Family*, 1437, depicted the ideal merchant's wife:

> She said her mother had taught her only how to spin and sew, and how to be virtuous and obedient. Now she would gladly learn from me how to rule the family and whatever I might teach her. I did not imagine for a moment that I could hope to win obedience from one to whom I had confessed myself a slave. Always therefore I showed myself virile and a real man.[10]

The fears aroused by the Renaissance recognition that the attributes of masculinity and femininity existed only in opposition to one another appear most markedly in Alberti's insistence that he is 'a real man'. Interestingly, the 'real woman' was a curiously cross-class image. The model merchant's wife was to be entirely subservient to her husband and to practise domestic crafts. Ruth Kelso has pointed out in *Doctrine for The Lady of The Renaissance*, 1956, that the model generally proposed for the lady was not a woman of leisure at all. It was the woman in the home who was held up as the ideal – cooking, cleaning, sewing, waiting on her husband and looking after the children. While the Renaissance gentleman was distinguished by his activities from the men of the lower social classes, the lady was not.[11]

Although her sex was considered a stronger characteristic than her class in determining a woman's behaviour, femininity – that 'certain soft and delicate tenderness with sweetness in every movement' – was derived from the nobility's ideal of womanhood. The merchant class wanted wives who combined the appearance of nobility with the activities of the labouring class. Needlework, particularly embroidery, as Luigini realised, evoked the femininity of the nobility and yet suggested the service and subservience required of the merchant's wife. By her femininity a wife provided evidence of the status of her husband and family in society. Sewing may have suggested a pleasing modesty, but embroidery conferred noble distinction. It was, traditionally, a badge of status.

The lady was encouraged to abandon previously sanctioned activities associated with masculinity: '. . . it is not becoming for women to handle weapons, ride, play the game of tennis, wrestle or take part in other sports that are suitable for men.' Instead she was to practise those suited to women 'very circumspectly and with the gentle delicacy we have said is appropriate to her'.[12] Music and embroidery were singled out as the ideal occupations for the lady. Pattern books for the art began to appear, invariably dedicated to a great lady to confirm the art's association with social standing and to attract those who aspired to aristocratic distinction. Among the first was a volume published by Peter Quentel in Cologne and translated into English in 1530 as 'A neawe treatys as concerning the excellency of the nedle works spanisshe stitches and weaving in the frame'. The Venetian Frederico Vinciolo published a pattern book in 1587 dedicated to Catherine de Medici with a sonnet 'Aux Dames et Demoisilles':

. . . ladies, please accept (I pray you will so do)

These patterns and designs dedicated to you,
To while away your time and occupy your mind.

In this new enterprise there's much that you can learn.
And finally this craft you'll master in your turn.
The work agreeable, the profit great you'll find.

G. Ciotti also included a poem in his book dedicated to the Lady Isabell Dowager of Rutland for 'the singular vertue, wherewith God hath graced you, and therewithal the excellent knowledge you have in Needleworkes'. The verses explained why embroidery was a pre-eminently female occupation:

Women's strength is unequal to the strenuous toil by which men show their wit, but with the needle, in silk and gold their white hands may reveal their own sharp and pregnant wit. Great knowledge, pains and skill are required to win the prize in needlework, which is suitable employment for all women, queens and noble ladies as well as maids of low degree, who by their skill and fame often come to be companions of noble ladies and even teachers of the daughter of a king, and thus raise their own rank. [13]

The role of embroidery in creating an appearance of femininity and nobility could not be more clearly exhibited. No other activity so successfully promoted the qualities that Renaissance man, anxious to define sex difference, wanted in a wife. Embroidery combined the humility of needlework with rich stitchery. It connoted opulence and obedience. It ensured that women spent long hours at home, retired in private, yet it made a public statement about the household's position and economic standing.

The new significance of the home for the merchant class was concurrent with the development of an ideology of domestic femininity. This was articulated not only in books on marriage but also in religious imagery. Embroidered images of the Virgin and female saints in the fifteenth century began to assume a new humility. Mediaeval iconography had endowed Mary and the virgin martyrs with admired aristocratic feminine attributes. But in the fifteenth century, the willowy figures acquired a new domesticity and intimacy, representing the emerging ideals of the burgher class. Typical is the hood of a cope embroidered between 1460 and 1490. Although the Virgin is still enthroned, she is a young woman smiling as she breastfeeds her baby. Her gentle nurturing qualities are placed above her queenly characteristics. Childcare, not childbirth, was becoming a central cultural concern.

Marina Warner attributes the new intimate 'democratic' virgin to the Franciscans who 'remoulded her to their revolutionary ideal'.[14] But as important is the prescription of the ideal family: 'For just as their frailty makes women less courageous, so it makes them more cautious; and thus the mother nourishes her children, whereas the father instructs them and with his strength wins outside the home what his wife, no less commendably, conserves with diligence and care.'[15]

St Monica, who dedicated her life to her son St Augustine, was held up as a model for women. Texts on the family and marriage advocated that the mother should have exclusive care and education of her sons until they were seven years old and of her daughters until they left home.

The new emphasis on meekness and motherhood affected the patron saint of childbirth, and on a Flemish cope hood, for instance, St Margaret is depicted as a young, helpless girl at the moment of her execution, rather than as a dragon slayer, so familiar from mediaeval embroidery.

Counterbalancing the 'down to earth' image of the madonna, representations of the Assumption of the Virgin were increasingly embroidered on ecclesiastical vestments. The Assumption – the image of Mary borne to heaven bodily after her death – emphasises Mary's power and status, complementing the image of Mary as breastfeeding mother and making of her a more impressive manifestation of humility, and a more compelling role model for women. Yet the Assumption acted as a reminder that Mary's achievements were beyond the power of earthly women.

The story of Mary transported to heaven had been popular since the twelfth century when a German nun, Elisabeth of Schonau, d.1164, had a vision of the Virgin rising to heaven. The *Pseudo Melito*, a Greek document attributed to Melito, a second-century bishop of Sardis, described how Mary rose from the dead and was transported to Paradise by angels because she was uncorrupted by original sin. Plate 39 is a typical example of a fifteenth-century embroidered Assumption: an image of Mary is appliquéed on brocade and surrounded by lilies and angels.

Not only did the ideological conception of the Virgin change during the fifteenth century, but technically and stylistically the embroideries of the period exhibit a move away from Opus Anglicanum. English embroidery, like other arts, absorbed European stylistic developments, emphasising a deep spatial setting and modelled, weighty forms. The embroiderers concentrated on a single homogeneous image rather than the dramatic narrative sequences which had characterised Opus Anglicanum. And instead of working images directly on to couched gold backgrounds (see Chapter Three), embroidered motifs like that of the Assumption were appliquéed on to imported textiles: brocades, satins, damasks and velvets were all used for ecclesiastical garments.[16] The economic conditions which had favoured the slow and costly embroidery of Opus Anglicanum had been swept away by repeated plagues, famines and the Hundred Years War with France.

The ecclesiastical houses in Britain were decimated by the Black Death of 1348: at least half the nuns died. Centres of ecclesiastical embroidery were thus drastically reduced. But it was not until the Reformation that ecclesiastical work was all but extinguished. However this did coincide with a remarkable expansion of embroidery for private houses.

In the secular sphere embroidered images of renowned women of the past parallelled the Assumption of the Virgin in popularity. During the middle ages theologians had eulogised women who had transcended the supposed limitations of their sex. Because women were considered innately evil and defective, their virtuous acts were hailed as truly remarkable. Renaissance writers, convinced of the frailty of the sex, extolled the paradox of strength in weakness, contrasting the grace of saintly women with the failings of womankind. Thus the heroic woman who transcended in virtue all women and all humans became a favourite theme not only of those who demanded respect for women, but also of those who advocated limiting women's sphere of action. Ovid's *Metamorphoses* and Boccaccio's *Famous Women of Antiquity* (*De Claris Mulieribus*) provided a source of heroines. Zenobia, Lucretia, Dido, Penelope, Portia and Caesar's wife were all cited for heroic defence of their chastity. Plate 40 is an embroidered image of Lucretia's banquet. At Hardwick Hall in Derbyshire

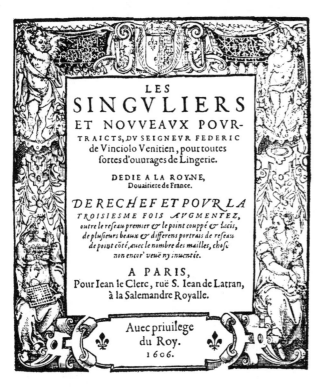

38 *Hood of a cope*, Victoria and Albert Museum, London. c 1460–1490. Linen
embroidered with coloured silks and silver-gilt.

39 *Cope*, Victoria and Albert Museum, London. 1510–1558. Silk damask, the
hood and orphrey of velvet, embroidered with gilt thread and coloured silks.
Two complementary representations of the Virgin were popular during the
fifteenth century: the Assumption – the image of Mary borne bodily to heaven
after her death – emphasises her power and status; and the mother and child
presents her domestic nurturing qualities. Taken together, the two images
discourage the worship of Mary from raising the status of earthly women, while
nonetheless glorifying domesticity.

40 *Penelope*, from a set of embroideries *Heroines Accompanied by Virtues*, National Trust, Hardwick Hall. c 1575.

41 *The Story of Myrrah*, embroidered bed valance, Victoria and Albert Museum, London. Sixteenth century. Linen embroidered with wool and silk. The story of Myrrah is taken from Ovid's *Metamorphoses*. Myrrah is about to hang herself because she is in love with her father. Her nurse suggests that they drug the father and contrive to have him make love to his daughter. Myrrah becomes pregnant, and her father is about to strike her with his sword when Venus turns her into a tree. Supposedly sexually rapacious women, and women whose virtue transcended the virtue of all women, became favourite themes in the art of the sixteenth century. Chaste heroines like Penelope were invoked by those who demanded respect for women, but also by those who advocated limiting women's sphere of action.

there is a set of five sixteenth-century patchwork appliqué wall hangings depicting heroines accompanied by Virtues – Lucretia, for example, is accompanied by Chastity and Liberality.

Twentieth-century historians of embroidery suggest that these embroideries were the work of professionals. However, historians have displayed a tendency to attribute any work of considerable size and skill to professionals, projecting the conditions of later embroidery production on to the sixteenth century when the division between amateur and professional work had not yet become firmly established. Differences between male and female, amateur and professional workers were nevertheless developing. Women's place within professional embroidery had changed since the thirteenth century. At that time, although London workshops which produced Opus Anglicanum were largely controlled by men, there was nothing in the structure of craft production that directly prevented women from working as professional embroiderers.

However during the reign of Edward III the guilds were reconstituted and in 1394–5 the first livery companies were formed. The master craftsmen had risen in the social scale, eventually becoming rich traders who employed journeymen. The leading crafts formed themselves into twelve great livery companies wielding considerable civic power. During the fifteenth century women were not debarred from participation in most craft guild workshops, but increasingly rigid regulations did circumscribe their access. To preserve the status of the master craftsmen from aspiring journeymen the number of people entering a craft was restricted, by limiting apprentices to three for one of the craft's governing body, two for a guild member eligible to wear the craft's livery, and one for an ordinary member. Apprentices had to be under twenty-one years of age and could be bound to householders only in corporate or market towns. Those who wanted to enter a trade were required to produce some elaborate and costly evidence of skill which the majority of women and men could afford neither in time nor money.[17]

Ordinances governing the art of embroidery have been traced to the early years of the fifteenth century, when in 1402 wardens were empowered to search out inferior work. That both women and men were active as professional embroiderers is evident from a commission issued by Henry IV to his embroiderer John Mounshill. He ordered that embroiderer to take 'needleworkers and broiderers, both men and women, necessary for the King's works and to superintend the said works for certain charges to the King's wages; also to take silk thread, silver and gold of copper and solder, and to imprison all men and women who resist.'[18] However, when the guild was finally incorporated in 1552 all the officials were men.[19]

The crown used by the Broderers' Company in the ceremonial crowning of a new warden – a band of crimson velvet embroidered in metal thread and silk with pomegranates, straw- berries and roses – is still in possession of the company.

The livery companies with their formal ceremonies and pageantry created a new demand for embroidery.[20] The dis- tinguishing feature of their livery was stitched on to badges, banners, streamers and palls.

As well as city companies, individual merchants commissioned ceremonial embroidery. A member of the Fayrey family com- missioned a pall for the Fraternity of St John the Baptist, set up at Dunstable in 1442 and surviving until 1547. Scenes from the life of John the Baptist preaching are appliquéed to cloth of gold and violet velvet grounds. On the panel at the end and sides are stitched portraits of John and Mary Fayrey, Henry and Agnes Fayrey.[21]

The Fayrey women are dressed in fine embroidered clothes, providing visible evidence of their families' fortunes. Throughout Europe such women frequently came under attack for their embroidered finery. The Perugian chronicler Francesco Maturanzi wrote that the wives of artisans and other men of mean birth who 'emulated with their jewels and dress the ladies of noble birth were much hated by the latter'.[22] And Sebastian Brant in the *Ship of Fools*, 1497, ridiculed the tradesmen's wives who 'wear more gauds of various kinds, skirts, rings, cloaks, broid'ries scant and rare. It's ruined many a good man's life. He must go begging for his wife.'[23] However, Christine de Pisan blamed the men 'who encourage their wives in their folly and are angry if they don't keep up'. She described the same 'senseless struggle' at every level: the labourer's wife wants to dress like an artisan's wife, the artisan's wife like her 'better' and the merchant's wife like those above as far as his wealth will carry her.[24] She noted the embroidery which adorned a merchant's wife's lying-in chamber – embroidery of a richness once confined to the nobility. The room was curtained with hangings made to her own design and worked in gold thread. The bed was hung in beautiful embroidered fabric, its coverlet was of gold embroidery, and embroidered rugs lay on the floor. By the reign of Elizabeth I, lying-in had become a social occasion – excitement was considered beneficial to the mother. The wealthy vied in the magnificence of their beds. The Countess of Salisbury had a bed with white satin-embroidered hangings decorated with silver and pearls at a cost of fourteen thousand pounds.[25]

Below the level of the great landlord class, the class of 'gentlemen' was expanding – the merchants, lawyers and others who had accumulated property as a seal of respectability. Their houses displayed an increasing level of comfort and luxury with panelled walls and glass windows – attributes of status. Although the vast majority of the population still lived in flimsy two-roomed dwellings, Edmund Harrison, a contemporary chronicler, observed that 'In the houses of knights and gentlemen, merchantmen and some other wealthy citizens it is not so geson [rare] to behold generally their great provisions of tapestry and fine silk hangings and their tables with carpets and napery . . . whereby the wealth of the country . . . doth infinitely appear.'[26]

The distribution of wealth was increasingly polarised between those whose only resources lay in what their hands could provide and the propertied classes. By the 1520s the effects of the low population levels of the fifteenth century were disappearing and conditions developed which favoured embroidery production. Population growth created a cheap pool of labour for the embroidery workshops, and this coincided with a demand for embroidered fabrics from the newly affluent.

The changed social and economic conditions not only promoted professional embroidery, evidenced by the incorporation of the Broderers' Guild, but, most significantly for the future of the craft, created the amateur embroiderer. Women, newly detached from paid production, whose households' still uncertain status demanded embroidered furnishings, were largely responsible for the extraordinary spread of domestic embroidery. Every conceivable surface became a site for embroidery: sheets, valances and coverlets, table carpets, cupboard carpets, cushions for benches and chairs, coifs, stomachers, sleeves, handkerchiefs, bags, hawking gear, needlecases, book covers, book marks, book cushions, shoes, gloves and aprons. Functional articles of clothing heavily embroidered indicated a life 'unsullied' by manual labour. Embroidered gloves were particularly significant. Heavily embroidered with slender elongated fingers, they set their owner apart from manual labourers, who in the days before antiseptic treatment against infection had to protect their hands with more functional gloves. Gloves encrusted with raised embroidery and scented with, for example, civet, musk or jasmine were exchanged by the wealthy at New Year. Queen Elizabeth I employed a woman specifically to care for her collection of fine gloves in their scented boxes.

A sewing casket with the embroidery carefully itemised appears amongst the inventories of women's possessions. Dame Agnes Hungerford, arraigned for murder in 1523, owned, for example, a casket containing 'twenty-four quarterons of Venyse golde, three pypes of damaske golde and sawing silk'.[27] Wealthy women both practised embroidery themselves and employed professionals. In an angry exchange of letters between Bess of Hardwick and her third husband George Talbot, the latter claims that he paid the professional embroiderers who made some rich hangings and that they therefore belonged to him. He wrote,

> First, rich hangings made by Thomas Lane, Ambrose, and William Barlow, and Henry Mr Cavandish's man, and had copes of tissue, cloth of gold, and other things towards the making thereof; meat, drink and wages paid to the embroiderers by the Earl during the working of them; and of hangings of green velvet, birds and fowls and needlework set upon the velvet.

The Countess in response denied that she employed so many professionals and insisted that her husband's men were not involved in embroidering the hangings:

> The copes brought by Sir William St Loe at Chatsworth at the time of the Deed of Gift. Most of the hangings made at Chatsworth, and some of the Countess's grooms, women and some boys she kept, wrought the most part of them. Never had but one imbroiderer at one time that wrought on them. His Lordship never gave the worth of five pounds towards the making of them.[28]

The letters confirm that at that time both men and women still embroidered, but unfortunately the sex of the 'one imbroiderer' is not specified. Ann Sutherland Harris has suggested that by the fifteenth century the existence of itinerant professional embroiderers created 'a situation incompatible with extensive female participation'.[29] However, household accounts do name women in connection with embroidery purchases. For example, expenses incurred by the marriage of Lord D'Arcy to Mary Kytson of Hengrave Hall in 1583 include payments to two women for embroidered clothing: 'Payde to Mrs Crockston for three wrought smocks and 2 coyffes £6.10. Payde more to her 2 smockes wrought all over the sleeves and bodys £6. Payde to Mrs Barbor of Bushe for 2 cawls of silver and golde and one smocke wrought with greene, redd and silver £6.10.'[30]

From the mid-sixteenth century professional embroidery practice changed within the guilds towards a more rigid, hierarchical organisation, and during the same period amateur embroidery dramatically expanded. But the place of embroidery within Elizabethan culture in relation to other arts changed slowly. It was still one art among many – it had not yet been designated and categorised as women's domestic art or working-class craft. Embroiderers continued to share the same stylistic and iconographic concerns as painters, sculptors and metal workers.

Embroiderers inherited and developed the concern with both naturalism and symbolism which had been manifest in Opus Anglicanum. Plate 44 is a typical example of embroidery for domestic furnishings. The coiling stems are the descendants of Celtic ornament and the later Jesse Tree pattern of Opus Anglicanum. The stem provides a formal framework for the 'slips' – animals, birds, or flowers usually applied to the background material.

Each flower and creature could carry a number of symbolic meanings for the Elizabethan embroiderer. Its physical qualities, its medicinal properties and heraldic associations all determined a plant's symbolism. The Elizabethans believed that the qualities of flowers were influenced by neighbouring plants, except for the strawberry whose purity protected it. The repeatedly embroidered rose was a flower of considerable symbolic importance. It was believed that inhaling the scent of dried roses comforted the heart and quickened the spirit. In heraldic terms the rose signified the unification of the Houses of Lancaster and York under Henry VII. Some embroidery would actually be perfumed with flowers. In the *Newe Herball* William Turner recommended spikes of lavender: 'quilted in a cap and dayle worne they are good for all diseases of the head that do come of a cold cause and they comfort the brain very well.'[31]

Today flower embroidery is so closely associated with women that it is easy to overlook that in the sixteenth century flowers were not considered primarily the province of women. John Gerard in his herbal wrote that they 'Admonish and stir up a man to that which is comely and honest: for flowers through their beautie, variety of colour, and exquisite form, doe bring to a liberall and gentlemanly minde the rememberance of honestie, comeliness and all kinds of vertues.'[32]

A fascination with plants was part of a developing interest in botany and gardening. In *Embroidered Gardens*, 1979, Thomasina Beck traces the association of gardening with embroidery. During the Elizabethan era she sees this as a relationship between equals. The language of the early gardening books employed the terminology of embroidery, and embroiderers depicted the new species that were being planted in the gardens laid out around the new, spacious private houses.

In 1586 when Jacques Lemoine de Morgue published *La Clef des Champs* (ninety-eight woodcuts of animals, birds, flowers and plants coloured by hand) he intended it for the use of craft-workers and their patrons, especially goldsmiths, embroiderers and tapestry makers, 'tant chez les Nobles, que parmi les Artizans, et mesme pour toute d'ouvrage a lequille' (as much for the nobility as for the artisans and for all workers with the needle).

The dedication is significant. The author's insistence that the book is intended for all craft workers in all media across class boundaries suggests that artistic divisions along the lines of media, sex and class were beginning to be drawn up. Nevertheless, the fact that the woodcuts could be offered to amateurs and professionals, nobility and artisans indicates that the categories had not yet become rigid.

If we look at the place of the art of embroidery in the education of young girls of the privileged classes, we can see the effects of the fruitful interaction between embroidery and other media, as well as the setting of a pattern for the future. Richard Mulcaster's curriculum for girls, written in 1561, lists reading, writing, sight singing, music and skill in needlework as necessary subjects. However, he distinguishes the education of girls in 'high position' from that of others, and embroidery is the mark of difference:

> If a young maiden is to be brought up with a view to marriage, obedience to authority and similar qualities must form the best kind of training; if from necessity she has to learn how to earn her own living some technical training must prepare her for a definite calling; if she is to adorn some high position she must acquire suitable accomplishments . . . [including drawing] . . . to beautify [her] needlework.[33]

The place of needlework in a woman's education was to become primary by the seventeenth century. In the sixteenth century it served two functions: endowing an education with elevated class associations, and making an education, which might otherwise have been deemed dangerously masculine, safely feminine.

Plate 44 is a book cover embroidered by Elizabeth I when she was eleven. She stitched the cover for her own translation of *The Miroir or Glasse of The Synnefull Soul* which she gave to Katherine Parr as a New Year's gift. Interlacing strap-work of chain stitch in metal thread traces the initials K.P. and pansies are embroidered on each corner of the book. The gift, with its combination of scholarship and skilled embroidery, represented the Renaissance education received by the most privileged women at the time. The interest in education amongst the upper classes has been ascribed in part to the upward mobility within European society during the 1530s and 1540s. C.S.L. Davies in *Peace, Print, and Protestantism*, 1977, suggests it was 'stimulated by the apparent success of clever humanist-trained graduates in royal service'. He adds that 'To some extent the new upper-class interest in education may have been a defensive reaction against this sort of social threat by the educated outsider.'[34] Within some families a humanist education was provided for girls who shared their brothers' tutors. The court gave a lead when Katherine of

Aragon imported Continental ideas on girls' education in the person of Luis Vives, author of *A Plan of Studies for Young Girls*. Although Vives advocated education for women, it was not to be at the cost of those female virtues, silence and obedience, for opponents of women's education argued that it would endanger their chastity by making them talkative and thus less careful of honour which is best preserved by silence. The underlying fear that educating women would disrupt sex distinctions and under-mine male dominance was expressed in *The Book of The Courtier*. Baldassare Castiglione has one of the protagonists in the debate on women exclaim, 'I am quite surprised that since you endow women with letters, continence, magnanimity and temperance, you do not want them to govern cities as well, and to make laws and lead armies, while the men stay at home to cook and spin.' He concluded that the whole idea was 'something one can neither tolerate nor bear listening to'.[35]

Women's education became tolerated only when it was suffici-ently differentiated from men's by the addition of music, dancing and *embroidery*. Praise for a woman's learning was invariably accompanied by words of admiration for her skill with a needle. Contemporary commentators remarked that the ladies at Queen Elizabeth's court were renowned for their knowledge of Latin, Greek, modern languages, spinning, needlework and music.[36]

Needlework was designated a frontline position in the defence of women's chastity. Even Christine de Pisan, proto-feminist as she was, advocated embroidery for ladies as a means of avoiding the temptations that lay in idleness. Prescribing the behaviour of a court lady she writes that 'On a week day, when the lady at court retires to her chamber, if she has not great occupation she will take up some handwork to avoid idleness. Around her will be assembled to work her women and girls.' Yet she recognised that women's restriction to the home and domestic work was a major impediment in their education: 'If they understand less, it is because they do not go and see so many different places and things but stay at home and mind their own work.'[37] Christine de Pisan, like other Renaissance writers, wanted women to maintain their difference from men. She urged them not to compete with men, suggesting a separate but equal policy. Thus she advocated embroidery *and* education, even though she recognised that con-finement to the home and domestic tasks limited women's intellectual possibilities. Other supporters of women's education feared that embroidery and other domestic arts were becoming too all-encompassing. Erasmus wrote, 'The distaff and spindle are in truth the tools of all women and suitable for avoiding idleness. Even people of wealth and birth train their daughters to weave tapestries or silken cloths . . . it would be better if they taught them to study, for study busies the whole soul . . .'[38]

Sixteenth-century feminist poet Louise Labé of Lyons had no doubt that the demand for women to practise domestic arts prevented them from doing anything else: 'All I can do is to beg our virtuous ladies to raise their minds above their distaff and spindles and try to prove to the world that if we were not made to command, still we should not be disdained as companions in domestic and public matters by those who govern and command obedience.'[39]

The key word here is *virtuous*. Domestic arts were equated with virtue because they ensured that women remain at home and refrain from book learning. Ignorance was equated with innocence; domesticity was a defence against promiscuity. By the nineteenth century embroidery was to become synonymous with chastity. The root of this later development lay in the Renaissance, when embroidery was considered as both defence and evidence of chaste femininity. The following epitaph for Elizabeth Lucar, wife of a London merchant, who died in 1537, demonstrates how embroidery permitted a woman to acquire a humanist education without threatening the boundaries between masculinity and femininity. Elizabeth Lucar's considerable academic abilities are carefully prefaced by praise for achievements with the needle.

ELIZABETH LUCAR'S TOMB

Every Christian heart seeketh to extoll
The glory of the Lord, our onely Redeemer:
Wherefore Dame Fame must needs enroll
Paul Withypoll his child, by loue and nature,
Elizabeth, the wife of Emanuel Lucar,
In whom was declared the goodnesse of the Lord,
With many high vertues, which truely I will record.

She wrote all Needle-workes that women exercise,
With Pen, Frame, or Stoole, all Pictures artificiall.

Curious Knots, or Trailes, what fancie could devise,
Beasts, Birds, or Flowers, even as things natural:
Three manner Hands could she write them faire all.
To speak of Algorisme, or accounts in every fashion,
Of women, few like (I thinke) in all this Nation.

Dame Cunning her gave a gift right excellent,
The goodly practice of her Science Musicall,
In diuers Tongues to sing, and play with Instrument,
Both Viall and Lute, and also Virginall;
Not onely one, but excellent in all.
For all other vertues belonging to Nature
God her appointed a very perfect creature.

Latine and Spanish, and also Italian,
She spake, writ, and read, with perfect utterance;
And for the English, she the Garland wan,
in Dame Prudence Schoole, by Graces purveyance,
Which cloathed her with Vertues, from naked Ignorance;
Reading the Scriptures, to judge Light from Darke,
Directing her faith to Christ, the onely Marke.

In the hands of such women, embroidery became infused with an often complex symbolic content, in line with the intellectual preoccupations of the time. Plate 45 is an example of emblematic embroidery by Mary Queen of Scots. Emblems and their use in art, literature and conversation were central to the culture of the Elizabethan upper classes. They remained popular until the mid-seventeenth century. An emblem consisted of an image and a saying or motto. The two lacked any apparent relationship; the challenge was to establish an intellectually convincing link. Colour, gesture and action all had a double meaning. As Rosemary Freeman has pointed out, in *English Emblem Books*, 1948, emblem art depended upon a close interrelation between the art of poetry and the plastic arts. Poetry was regarded as a 'speaking picture' and painting as 'dumb poetry'.[40]

The nobility adopted emblems as personal badges. Mary Stuart represented herself with the motto 'sa vertu m'attire' – a play on her name, Marie Stuart. This personal emblem was included as a 'signature' on much of her embroidery. Her education in needle-work began when she was at the court of France. Accounts

42 Gloves, English,
Museum of London.
Sixteenth century.
Encrusted with embroidery
and scented, they were exchanged
by the wealthy at New Year.

43 Coif, English,
Victoria and Albert Museum, London.
Sixteenth century.

44 Book cover for *The Miroir or Glasse of the Synneful Soul*, Elizabeth I
(1533–1603), Bodleian Library, Oxford. Filigree of gold and silver wire on blue
corded silk.

Elizabeth embroidered the book cover when she was eleven years old for her own
translation of the Latin text, and gave it to Katherine Parr as a New Year's gift.
The combination of scholarship and skilled needlework well represents the
education received by the most privileged of Renaissance women.

45 Embroidered Panel, Mary, Queen of Scots (1542–1587), Victoria and Albert Museum, London.

In the hands of women who had received a Renaissance lady's education, embroidery shared the preoccupation with emblems common to other Elizabethan arts. Mary Stuart stitched this panel in 1569, while she was under the surveillance of George Talbot, husband of Bess of Hardwick, and sent it to the Duke of Norfolk, whom she hoped to marry. The Latin motto reads 'Virtue flourishes by wounding'. The knife cutting dead branches from a vine carries the concealed message that the unfruitful branch of the royal family (Elizabeth I) was to be cut off, while the fruitful branch (Mary) would live and bear fruit. (See M. Swain, *The Needlework of Mary Queen of Scots*, VNR, 1973.)

46 *The Birth of John the Baptist*, designed by Antonio Pollaiuolo, Florence. Fifteenth century. Photo: Mansell-Alinari.

Embroiderers were able to achieve the same perspectival effects as painters during the Renaissance, by employing the technique known as *or nué*. Gold threads laid horizontally were shaded by coloured silk in couching stitches.

relating to the Queen of Scots in 1551 when Mary was nine years old list the purchase of worsteds (twisted woollen yarn) for Mary to 'learn to make works'. She continued to embroider throughout both her reign in Scotland and captivity in England. A visiting English envoy to the Scottish court described how in council meetings the Queen 'ordinarily sitteth the most part of the time, sewing at some work or another'.[41] Once in capitivity embroidery became her major occupation.

Early in 1569 she was placed under the surveillance of George Talbot, Earl of Shrewsbury and third husband to Bess of Hardwick. When Mary first entered their charge, Shrewsbury reported that 'The Queen continueth daily to resort to my wife's chamber where with the Lady Lewiston and Mrs Seton she useth to sit working with the needle in which she much delighteth and in divising works.'[42]

While working together the two women stitched emblematic embroideries. Bess made a memorial to her late husband depicting tears falling on quicklime and the Latin motto 'Tears witness that the quenched flame lives' which had been Catherine de Medici's emblem, so Mary may have suggested that her mother-in-law Catherine's emblem would make an appropriate feature for a memorial. In the border are symbols of grief: a fan with falling feathers (a play on the words *pleurer, plume* and *peine*), a glove, the symbol of fidelity cut in two, broken and interlaced cords, a cracked jewelled mirror and a snapped chain. Mary's panel shows a hand with a pruning knife cutting dead branches from a vine with a Latin motto that reads, 'Virtue flourishes by wounding'. Mary's cipher is impaled in the Greek letters standing for her first husband Francis of France, and it is surrounded by a trellis of flowers and fruit. The apparently innocuous panel was sent to the Duke of Norfolk whom she hoped to marry. The hidden message was that the unfruitful branch of the royal house (Elizabeth I) was to be cut down while the fruitful branch (Mary) would be left to flourish and bear fruit.

Another emblematic embroidery referring to her relationship with Elizabeth depicts a marmalade cat wearing a golden crown watching a mouse. It represents the red-headed queen playing with Mary, the mouse. *The Catte* was one of a series of emblematic devices and mottos stitched on to a rich green velvet ground and known today as the Oxburgh Hanging. The gallery of strange and wonderful creatures with enigmatic mottos 'would exercise the wit of courtiers well-versed in the contemporary language of emblematic writings'.[43]

The contemporary interest in emblematic embroideries is voiced in a letter to Ben Jonson written from Edinburgh in 1619. William Drummond describes an embroidered bed which he believed to have been the work of Mary Stuart: 'The workmanship is curiously done, and above all value, and truely it may be of this Piece said Materiam superbat opus.' But what really concerns him are the embroidered emblems. He describes roughly forty images and mottos, some of which he recognised as emblems of members of her family. He speculated on the meanings of others: 'This is for her self and her Son, a Big Lyon and a young whelp beside her, the word, unum quidem, sed Leonem [one only, but a lion]. An emblem of a Lyon taken in a Net, and Hares wantonly passing over him, the word, et lepores devicto insultant Leone' [and hares insult the defeated lion].[44] The embroidered bed has disappeared, but examples of Elizabethan emblematic embroidery still exist.[45]

Historians' views on the meanings of emblematic embroidery have swung from one extreme to the other. Nineteenth-century historians claimed that it indicated a generally high level of education amongst *all* Elizabethan women. Clearly such claims can be discounted, but twentieth-century embroidery historians have tended to go to the other extreme. J.L. Nevinson, for example, writes that, 'Often one may presume, the deficiencies of women's education and lack of feminine scholarship caused decorative value to be preferred to recondite allusion.'[46]

While not denying that education was limited to the privileged few, Nevinson's opinion overlooks the relationship between embroidery and other cultural pursuits. 'Recondite allusion' was a feature of the Elizabethan arts. Embroidery had not yet definitively separated from the other arts. Nevertheless comparisons were beginning to be made between the different art forms – to the detriment of embroidery. For example, Nicholas White, envoy of Elizabeth I, reported the following exchange with the Queen of Scots:

I asked her Grace, since the weather had cut off all exercise abroad, how she passed the time within. She said that all day long she wrought with the needle and that the diversity of the colours made the work seem less tedious, and continued till very pain did make her give over and with that she laid her hand upon her left side and complained of an old grief newly increased there. Upon this occasion she entered into a pretty disputable comparison between carving, painting and work with the needle, affirming painting in her own opinion for the most considerable quality.[47]

Mary was not alone in her opinion. The emerging artistic values of the Renaissance finally favoured painting above embroidery. At first, professional embroiderers participated in contemporary artistic developments. Like painters they experimented with perspective effects, discovering a technique known as *or nué*. Initially they laid gold threads on material directionally to follow architectural lines, but the perspective effect, so successful from one angle, fragmented when the light fell on a different angle. *Or nué* overcame distortion: gold threads laid horizontally were literally shaded by the irregular spacing of coloured silk couching stitches.[48]

It is usually assumed that technical limitations prevented embroidery from attaining the *trompe l'oeil* effect achieved in oil painting, so that as illusionism became the aim of art, embroidery fell behind painting. However, technical problems could have been overcome and indeed with *or nué* they were. Far more important for the future of embroidery was the changing role of the artist and accompanying developments within art production, coinciding with the rise of the female amateur embroiderer.

It was in Italy that the ideals of the Renaissance artist first emerged and spread across Europe. The new emphasis was on the intellectual claims of the artist as opposed to manual skill. Artists wanted to be distinguished from those who were mere manual executors of other people's ideas and designs. But as long as the mediaeval guild system persisted for painters and embroiderers, the modern notion of the artist as a special kind of person with a whole set of distinctive characteristics, rather than a kind of worker, did not gain general currency. Painters themselves did not distinguish between the designs produced for tapestries, banners, flags, chests, armorial bearings or shop signs. It was not divine talent that entitled them to practise as professionals, but instructions according to guild rules. The painters Neri De Bicci, Antonio Botticelli and Squarcione are examples of painters who produced designs for professional embroiderers. Antonio

Pollaiuolo designed a set of embroidered vestments for the Church of San Giovanni in Florence. Embroiderer Paolo da Verona took twenty-six years to complete them.

The very fact that Pollaiuolo and da Verona were jointly responsible for the vestments indicates one of the reasons why embroidery was devalued as an art form. More often than not it was a collective art form with a division of labour between designer and executant, whose particular skill lay in the disposition of colour, texture, and stitches rather than drawing. However, the emerging rhetoric about the artist meant that evidence of a divine, inspired *individual* was the measure of greatness in a work of art. Alberti, 1404–1472, considered painting the highest among the arts because it contained 'divine force'. This Renaissance notion was partly derived from classical ideas of divine madness in the arts, as well as from the mediaeval concept of God the Father, the architect of the universe.

The handwriting – the recognisable, individual touch – of the artist became important as the direct trace of the inspired individual. Drawings and sketches were for the first time valued as evidence of the creative process. Speed, and an appearance of ease, were qualities admired in an artist: 'In painting, a single brush stroke made with ease, in such a way that it seems the hand is completing the line by itself without any effort or guidance, clearly reveals the excellence of the artist.'[49]

Embroidery, on the other hand, had always been admired for the hard labour it demanded, the patience and persistence it required.

Two examples serve to illustrate the changing professional relationship between embroiderer and artist – and their place in society. In the fifteenth century Cenino Cenini, in his treatise on artistic techniques (1437), instructed artists on how to draw on linen for embroidery. By the sixteenth century, however, artists were no longer working closely with embroiderers. The latter were using existing sketches rather than designs specially prepared for them, and transferring the sketches to material by the technique of pricking and pouncing. The artist was *above* collaborating with embroiderers.

This attitude is exemplified by Nicholas Hilliard in his *A Treatise Concerning the Art of Limning*, c. 1600. He insists that painting has no connection at all with other arts such as embroidery or tapestry: 'It tendeth not to common men's use, either for furnishing houses or any patterns for tapestries.' Hilliard here expresses the class aspirations of the artist and the determination to emancipate painting from the mundane, the functional, and the domestic. Behind his words lie enormous economic and social changes that both facilitated the aspirations of the artist and increased the demand for domestic embroidery. The wealthy who furnished their houses wanted paintings; fees rose, and artists were able, to some extent, to free themselves from direct commission. The demand for embroidered works of art was largely supplied by the women of the household.

In the hierarchy of the art forms which then developed, a very particular division occurred in embroidery because of the increase in amateur domestic workers. Within the professional sphere, painting was valued as the expression of the individuality of the painter, while professional embroidery was placed lower in the artistic hierarchy because it was a collective effort associated with workers lower on the social scale than aspiring painters. It was the amateur embroiderers who expressed in embroidery the new individualism of the age. Women amateur workers were in a significantly different position to professionals. They came from the class to which the male painters aspired; the class associated with intellectual as distinct from manual skills, the class which was to express the developing individualism. For women this meant that their creative work was to exhibit not a powerful artistic personality but a feminine presence. Texts on women's behaviour and embroidery patterns all advocated needlework to promote the virtues of femininity – primarily chastity, humility and obedience. The process had begun which not only divided embroidery from painting, but sub-divided embroidery into a public craft and a domestic art – an art so inextricably bound up with notions of femininity that the nineteenth-century craft historian Ernst Lefebure confidently and chivalrously exclaimed of womankind: 'She is the sovereign in the domain of art needlework; few men would care to dispute with her the right of using those delicate instruments so intimately associated with the dexterity of her nimble and slender fingers.'[50]

Few men would risk jeopardising their sexual identity by claiming a right to the needle. Behind Lefebure's words lies an ideology of sexual difference in which notions of masculine and feminine are meaningful only in relation to each other – and a society which uses embroidery as a signifier of sexual difference.

5: The Inculcation of Femininity

'. . . Females are made women of when they are mere children, and brought back to childhood when they ought to leave the go-cart for ever,' wrote Mary Wollstonecraft in *The Vindication of The Rights of Women*, 1792.[1] She is describing – and criticising – the creation of feminine behaviour in middle-class women: a process which began in the seventeenth century. Girls, she claims, were encouraged to be precocious but sedentary, obedient but seductive, in preparation for a lifetime of subjugation to a husband whose manhood was affirmed by his wife's infantile ways, naïvety and ignorance. Wollstonecraft emphasises that her description of middle-class women was a generalisation, that exceptions existed. But by the late eighteenth century it was the rare woman of the upper classes who escaped an education in femininity, with embroidery taking pride of place in that process.

Philippe Aries has pointed out the new importance of childhood in the seventeenth century.[2] However, for girls childhood was significantly less separated from adulthood than it was for boys. Whereas boys passed from childhood, through puberty, to manhood, girls were early instructed to be little women, and embroidery was a continuum in their lives that linked childhood and womanhood. It was taught in such a way as to inculcate obedience and patience during long hours spent sitting still, head bowed over an increasingly technically complex, demanding art.

Girls were taught embroidery in the family, although some, from the gentry and nobility, learned the art at school. Boarding schools for girls, many of which did little more than teach accomplishments, were on the increase.[3] The school in Edinburgh to which Sir Hugh Campbell sent his daughters in 1677 offered music, dancing, embroidery and pastry baking.[4] Susanna Perwich, who attended her mother's school in Hackney, established in 1643, learned music, dancing, calligraphy, accountancy, housewifery, cookery, crafts in silver, straw, glass, wax, gum and fine embroidery for which she was famed:

> Pictures of men, birds, beasts and flowers,
> When Leisure serv'd at idle hours,
> All this rarely to the life,
> As if there were a kind of strife
> Twixt Art and Nature: trees of fruit
> With leaves, boughs, branches, body, root
> She made to grow in Winter time
> Ripe to the eye.[5]

The vast majority of young girls left no record of their feelings about embroidery, but those who raised their voices against it characterise the art as the activity which separated them from childhood and 'masculine' pursuits. Ann Fanshaw wrote:

> Now it is necessary to say something of my mother's education of me, which was with all the advantages that time afforded, both for working all sorts of fine works with my needle, and learning French, singing, lute, the virginals, and dancing; and not withstanding I learned as well as most did, yet I was wild to that degree, that the hours of my beloved recreation took up too much of my time; for I loved riding in the first place, and running and all active pastimes: and in fine I was that which we graver people call a hoyting girl.[6]

A hoyting girl was a tomboy. The existence of the term is revealing. Femininity did not come naturally to little girls, it was difficult to instil, but because it was inculcated at a very early age it appeared to be innate. Girls who chafed at it – those who were characterised as inappropriately masculine 'hoyting girls' – declared their dislike of the instrument of femininity: 'and for my needle I absolutely hated it', wrote Lucy Hutchinson.[7]

Her attitude is in marked contrast to Grace Sherrington's feelings for her needle in the previous century. She learned to embroider during the sixteenth century, when the art signified that a girl's education was suitably differentiated from a boy's, rather than an instrument for teaching femininity. Married aged fifteen, Grace Sherrington described how she passed her days:

> . . . also every day I spent some time in the Herball or books of phisick, and in ministering to one or another by the directions of the best phisitions of myne aquaintance; and ever God gave blessing thereunto. Also every day I spent some tyme in works of myne owne invention, without sample or patterns before me for carpett or cushion worke, and to drawe flowers and fruitt to their lyfe with my pulmmett upon paper. All which varietie did greatly recreate my mynde; for I thought of nothing else but that I was doing in every particular one of these exercises . . . .[8]

The young seventeenth-century embroiderer appears to have enjoyed no such freedom: not for her the all-absorbing pleasure of creating her own patterns from fruit and flowers. Whereas the Elizabethan embroiderer used a relatively restricted range of stitches to represent the flora and fauna usually culled from herbals and natural histories, the Stuart embroiderer laboured at a range of demanding techniques through an ordained series of embroidery projects. A poem which prefaces a seventeenth-century embroidery pattern book illustrates the techniques that an embroiderer was expected to employ. The vast range was facilitated by the manufacture of finer, more versatile thread.

> For Tent-worke, Rais'd-worke, Laid'worke, Frost-worke, Net-worke,
> Most curious Purles, or rare Italian cutworke,
> Fine Ferne-stitch, Finny-stitch, New-stitch and Chain-stitch,
> Braue Bred-stitch, Fisher-stitch, Irish-stitch and Queene-stitch,

The Spanish-stitch, Rosemary-stitch and Mowse-stitch,
The smarting Whip-stitch, Back-stitch and the Crosse-stitch,
All these are good and we must allow
And these are everywhere in practise now.[9]

Changes in sampler making illustrate the new emphasis on
virtuoso technical perfomance in embroidery. A dictionary published in 1530, compiled by John Palsgrave, defines sampler as an
'exampler of a woman to work by'. Sixteenth-century samplers
had been broad linen rectangles stitched with a collection of
motifs often drawn from herbals or bestiaries. Shakespeare
evokes two girls embroidering a flower on a sampler:

O is all forgot?
All schooldays' friendship, childhood innocence?
We, Hermia, like two artificial gods,
Have with our needle created both one flower,
Both on one sampler, sitting on one cushion,
Both warbling one song, both in one key,
As if our hands, our sides, voices and minds,
Had been incorporate.[10]

By the seventeenth century samplers were becoming educational
exercises in stitchery – individual tests of skill rather than store-
houses of motifs. They provided evidence of a child's 'progress'
on the ladder to womanhood. Measured bands or rows of symmetrical patterns on strips of linen up to three feet replaced the
random motifs of Elizabethan samplers. Of course the change
occurred gradually; spot samplers and band samplers co-existed
for a long time, even sharing the space of the same sampler. The
long band samplers were usually stitched in progressively harder
exercises. The first bands would be devoted to coloured border
patterns – stylised flowers and alphabets in silks. Often the colour
would disappear in bands of whitework embroidery – exquisite
cut work, drawn work and fine needlepoint lace. The latter was in
demand for the lace-edged ruffs and caps of contemporary
costume. The alphabets too had a practical application. The
increasingly affluent households of the seventeenth century
'marked' their newly acquired household linens. In 1619, for
example, the accounts of Lady Shuttleworth's household contain
an entry for 'coventrie blue thred to make letters in needlework
on the bed sheets'.[11]

85

The first indication of the sampler's changing role is that signatures and dates appear on them in the late sixteenth century. A process had begun which can be understood only in the context of both the ideology of individualism and the developing ideas of education and child discipline. Christopher Hill relates the rise of individualism to the Reformation and the ideology of Protestantism: 'Protestantism popularised the idea of the individual balance sheet, the profit-and-loss book-keeping of diaries. This presupposes an atomic society of individuals fighting for their own salvation, no longer a community working out its own salvation as it cultivated its fields in common.'[12]

The slow, hard, concentrated labour of the Stuart long sampler instilled the ethics of Protestantism and charted a girl's growth as a feminine individual. The work demanded was, in part, a response to the changing significance of domestic labour. Calvin had replaced the old injunction 'Sell all thou hast and give to the poor' with the idea that 'God sets more value on the pious management of a household.' The Protestant idea of a 'calling' allowed a secular craft or occupation to be seen as God's work. Numerous books on household management published by men encouraged middle-class women to see domestic labour as a calling. And by the end of the sixteenth century European pattern books, dictating arduous exercises for needlewomen, were translated into English.

John Taylor, 'The Water Poet', wrote a poem 'In Praise of The Needle' to preface a very popular pattern book, *The Needle's Excellency*, that appeared in 1624 and was in its tenth edition by 1631. The poem provides a royal heritage for the craft, naming Katherine of Aragon, Mary I, Elizabeth I, Lady Mary Countess of Pembroke and Lady Elizabeth Dormer as ladies who immortalised themselves in thread. While extolling the needle on account of the powerful women who used it, his real praise is reserved for the fact that it renders women powerless, silent and still:

> And for my countries quiet, I should like,
> That woman-kinde should use no other Pike,
> It will increase their peace, enlarge their store,
> To use their tonges less, and their needles more.
> The Needles sharpness, profit yields, and pleasure
> But sharpness of the tongue, bites out of measure.

Taylor's jocular lines are important. They suggest that embroidering was deeply implicated in the debates about women that rumbled throughout the seventeenth century. Taylor was himself involved in the pamphlet war over the right behaviour for women. In 1639 he published 'A Juniper Lecture with the description of all sorts of women, good, and bad: From the modest to the maddest, from the most Civil to the scold Rampant, their praise and dispraise compendiously related.' He called this misogynist tract a Juniper Lecture because juniper wood burns a long time like revengeful women harbouring malice. He followed it by the equally provocative 'Crab-tree Lectures' in which 'Mary Makepeace addresses her sister women and advises them never to act in such a way as to deserve the names Tabitha Turbulant, Franks Forward, Bettriss Bould Face, Ellen Ever-heard and so on.' He was soon challenged by Mary Tattlewell and Joan Hit-him-home with 'The Woman's Sharpe Revenge'. Derisively they wrote, 'Now concerning your very passionate, but most pittiful Poetry, a question may be made whether you be a Land Laureate or a Marine Muse; a Land Poet, or a Water Poet; A Scholler or a Sculler; of Parnassus or Puddle Dock . . .'[13]

The ideological position represented by Taylor in his poem in praise of the needle as an instrument of suppression, and his 'lectures' full of fear of women as disorderly and desiring to dominate men, took a material form in the series of needlework projects imposed on small girls. They marked a gradual initiation into full femininity. Martha Edlin, born in 1660, made a sampler in 1668 covered with coloured bands. Then she undertook a lace and whitework sampler, and finally applied her wide knowledge of stitchery to pictorial embroidery on a casket or cabinet. A similar cabinet was completed by Hannah Smith when she was nearly twelve years old. She wrote a note which she placed inside one of the drawers, revealing how important the needlework projects were to the children who carried them out, how closely bound in with the project was the child's sense of herself:

The yere of our Lord being 1657 if ever I have any thoughts about the time; when I went to Oxford; as It may be I may when I have forgotten the time to sarifi myself; I may Loock in this paper and find it. I went to Oxford in the yere of 1654 and my being there; near 2 yere; for I went in 1654 and I stayed there 1655 and I cam away in 1656: and I was allmost 12 yers of

age; when I went and mad an end of my cabbinete; at Oxford
. . . my cabinet was mad up in yere of 1656 at London. I have
ritten this; to sartifi my self; and those that shall enquire about
it Hannah Smith.[14]

The exactitude of the progression of sampler and casket
making, and its obsession with time, was part of the general
ideology of discipline and structured day that developed during
the seventeenth century. The problem of labour discipline – how
to establish a regular rhythm of labour (abolition of saints' days,
emphasis on the Sabbath rest, establishment of regular meal-
times) – greatly concerned social thinkers. The importance of this
regularity, and of saving time, seems to have been accepted by the
middle class during the seventeenth century.[15] The sampler
system was a manifestation of the same ideology, applied to
women's lives. Sampler making also related to the changing
circumstances of seventeenth-century family life. Sheila
Rowbotham in *Hidden from History*, 1973, writes that 'There
was a need for a substitute for the shaken rule of priest and king.
The father assumed a new importance in the hierarchy of authority. The puritans saw children as naturally sinful, and believed
they had to be beaten into holiness.'[16]

The importance of parental discipline increased with the advent
of Protestantism, when the celebration of the mass gave way to
the reading of scriptures as the central act of worship. The church
was tending to lose ground to the domestic hearth, and the
household was becoming the agency for moral and religious
control. The advent of samplers with embroidered pledges of
obedience to mother or father, and moralising verses, signifies the
changes:

> My Father Hitherto Hath done his Best to make
> Me a Workewoman Above the Rest. Margaret
> Lucas 1681 Being ten year Old come July The First

> I am a maid but young my skill
> Is yet but small but god
> I hope will bless me so I may live
> To mend this all Rachel Loader
> Wrought this sampler being
> Twelve Years old the Tenth

Day September 1666

Martha Salter
The Fear of God is an excell
Lent Gift

Occasionally a sampler inscription deviates from the submissive obedience the work was intended to inculcate. The following verse is taken from an unsigned, undated sampler of the late seventeenth century:

> When I was young I little thought
> That wit must be so dearly bought
> But now experience tells me how
> If I would thrive than I must bow
> And bend unto another's will
> That I might learn both art and skill
> To get my living with my hands
> That I might be free from band
> And my owne dame that I may be
> And free from all such slavery.
> Avoid vaine pastime fle youthful pleasure
> Let moderation allways be they measure
> And so prosed unto the heavenly treasure.

This curious mixture of resentment and acquiescence, piety and rebellion illustrates the strength of the ideology of sampler making. The proud assertion of independence ends with an entirely conventional sampler sentiment, heavy with renunciation of personal pleasure.

The topmost section of a sampler sometimes contained figurative work. The biblical scenes selected for pictorial embroidery depict parental power at its most absolute and violent. Jephta's daughter and the sacrifice of Isaac were commonly depicted. Jephta swore to God that if he was granted victory in battle he would sacrifice the first person he met on coming home. It was his daughter who was duly sacrificed. The story of Abraham preparing to follow God's commands and sacrifice his son Isaac was well established as a subject for embroidery by the seventeenth century. But the constant repetition of the theme suggests it had a powerful resonance within the family where the parents, particularly the father, were assuming a new authority. Nevertheless, biblical embroidery became the butt of male wit:

> Sir, she's a Puritan at her needle too . . .
> . . . she works religious petticoats, for flowers
> She'll make church histories. Her needle doth
> So sanctify my cushionets, besides
> My smock sleeves have such holy embroideries,
> And are so learned, that I fear in time
> All my apparel will be quoted by
> Some pure instructor
> > Jasper Mayne, *City Match*, Act II Sc 2, 1639[17]

Despite the reference to 'she's a Puritan', embroidery as an education in femininity crossed religious and political boundaries. It continued to be an important aspect of aristocratic life. Thus, for many puritans pious subject matter could not erase the art's association with vanity and decadence. So, paradoxically, while they promoted it as a defence against idleness it was also castigated as evidence of idleness:

> Fear God and learn woman's housewifery,
> Not idle samplery or silken folly
> > Thomas Milles, *Treasure of Ancient and Moderne Times*, 1613[18]

As Roberta Hamilton points out in *The Liberation of Women*, 1978, whatever differences Puritans and Anglicans maintained over Church matters, they were surprisingly in agreement where conduct in the family was concerned.[19] Embroidery was to prepare upper- and middle-class girls for their place as wives occupied with 'housewifery'.

The content of the samplers and embroidered pictures that girls were set to stitch presented marriage as their natural destiny. The ideal was that all women would marry. *The Lawes Resolution of Women's Rights*, published in 1632, states that 'All of them (women) are understood either married or to be married . . . The Common Law here Shaketh Hands with the Divine.' In among the stylised flowers and geometric shapes which characterise the pattern books prefaced by John Taylor's poem *The Needle's Excellency*, is a pattern for a man and a woman – a couple who become part of the vocabulary of samplers. The earliest surviving of these 'family figures', as they are known, is dated 1630. The representations of marriage and parental authority became more common as the century continued. The Protestant idea of the family was produced from two sources; the family partnership which prevailed in the homes of the yeomen and craftsmen, and the patriarchal families of the Old Testament. The appeal of the Patriarchs of the Jewish people was that they had not only controlled the economic fortunes of their families, but also guided their large households through spiritual crises, holding themselves responsible only to God.[20]

In the iconography of samplers and embroidered pictures, the image of man and woman, Adam and Eve, Abraham and Sarah, standing hands clasped, celebrated the new ideology of the conjugal bond as productive partnership and effective tie – made in heaven. Sarah and Abraham were particularly popular. Sarah represented obedience, wifely fortitude and submissiveness. St Paul had invoked Abraham and Sarah to ratify women's absolute subjugation in marriage: 'Let women be subject to their husbands as Sarah obeyed Abraham calling him Lord.' Adam and Eve were almost as frequently stitched. However, embroiderers stressed not Eve's wickedness but her role as Adam's companion and helpmate. Thus a sampler verse reads:

> Adam alone in Paradise did grieve
> And thought Eden a desert without Eve
> Until God pitying his lonesome state
> Crowns all his wishes with a lovely mate
> Then why should men think mean, or slight
>   her
> That could not live in Paradise without her.

The verse conveys the contradictory place of women in the ideology of marriage which developed under Protestantism and pre-industrial capitalism. The Protestant reformers of the sixteenth century, arguing for the right of clergy to marry, asserted the superiority of marriage to celibacy, a belief based on a mélange of the Bible and biology. Luther wrote, 'Men have broad shoulders and narrow hips, and accordingly possess intelligence. Women have narrow shoulders and broad hips. Women ought to stay at home, the way they were created indicates this, for they have broad hips and a wide fundament to sit upon, keep house and raise children.'[21] But he also emphasised that marriage should be a productive partnership: 'The greatest blessing is to have a wife to whom you may entrust your affairs, and by whom you may have children.'[22] Family life, of course, differed from class to class, but where the family functioned as a self-contained productive unit it furnished the basis of a new ideology of the family, linked with the new emerging ideas of private property and individualism.

There were uneasy contradictions for women within the Holy State of Matrimony: the partnership may have been productive, but it certainly was not equal. Religious, legal and political changes enhanced the powers of the head of the household. A woman's legal rights rested in her husband who had complete control over her property and children. And while Protestantism sanctified matrimony, it simultaneously asserted the power of the individual consciousness which implied the right to choose one's own marriage partner – a potentially disruptive notion when a major function of marriage in the middle and upper classes was still to cement alliances between families and transmit property. The educationist Hannah Wooley wrote, 'But of all the acts of disobedience, that of marrying against the consent of parents is the highest. Children are so much Goods and Chattels of a Parent, that they cannot without a kind of theft give themselves away.'[23]

The concentration of the conjugal couple in samplers was part of the proliferating contradictory discourses on marriage. On the one hand, the couple were represented as secure and symmetrical, stitched in the centre of the sampler; on the other hand, they were embroidered in the context of the constant emphasis on the virtue of obedience – the major message of so many sampler verses and, indeed, taught to girls by the act of embroidery itself.

The image of the married couple, a flower clasped between them signifying fertility, was transferred from samplers to embroidered pictures. Within the framework of a biblical narrative they are the most common motif in stump work – the pictorial embroidery practised by young girls of the middle and upper classes, that gained popularity during the middle decades of the century. The name comes from the small blocks of wood or stuffing that embroiderers used to give their embroidered figures the new plasticity of post-Renaissance art. Wire was also employed, allowing butterflies to fly from the satin background, petals to stand out, and canopies to overhang the people beneath them. Victorian embroidery historians strongly disapproved of stump work. Marion Alford considered that it revealed 'how high art can in a century slip back into no art at all'. She deplored 'the utter want of beauty or taste in the whole effect'.[24] Later historians with a twentieth-century appreciation of the 'primitive', and patronising enthusiasm for the 'naïve', disinterred stump work.

Pictorial embroidery for its own sake, rather than as part of furnishing, developed during the 1630s. The construction of the seventeenth-century tent stitch and stump-work pictures, with key scenes from a biblical narrative co-existing in the same frame, clearly owes a debt to the Elizabethan tent-stitch valances where consecutive scenes from a story form a frieze around the top of a fourposter bed, and to the embroidered carpets where disparate scenes occupy the same piece of material.

In stump-work pictures the same motifs appear again and again. In the background a spacious house or castle stands against a sky where the sun breaks through the clouds. The narrative unfolds in a garden with the pool or fountain popular in Stuart gardens. Spangles and seed pearls adorn costumes, and tiny pieces of mica glint in castle windows. The new metal threads and fine silks provided a variety of textures, enhanced by the range of techniques the needleworker had acquired in sampler making. Different textures are used with ingenuity and care. Lacework, couched thick metal thread, and delicate silk are juxtaposed and contrasted, sometimes primarily for compositional purposes, at other times to signify the character of the personage portrayed. Royalty is garbed in smooth, gleaming silk embroidery in split stitch, lesser personages are stitched in opaque thread with rougher techniques. Their dress is always contemporary rather than biblical. In a picture illustrating the story of David and Bathsheba, the women's clothes are virtuoso technical performances. The outer garments are slightly raised and detached, embroidered with flowers and edged with needlepoint lace. The underskirts are stitched in silver-gilt thread. The towel clasped about Bathsheba is carefully edged with chenille and the folds conveyed not only by shaded colour but by padding and directional stitches.

Despite such plentiful evidence of the thought and care that went into the construction of these pictures, with their skilled handling of texture and colour that echoes across the satin, commentators have dismissed stump work as simply 'quaint' because of the embroiderers' disregard for correct scale. Flowers tower above people; birds are the size of trees, snails the size of a man's head float beside him. This lack of scale has been attributed to the embroiderers' inability to draw and the slavish adherence to patterns. Sheets of flower engravings were being produced by the mid-seventeenth century and an embroiderer could have copied them straight on to the satin. This could explain the lack of perspective and the discrepancy of scale that characterises stump work. There is no doubt that prints were used in this way. But if stump-work pictures are considered within the history of embroidery, rather than measured against the norms of oil painting, the lack of perspective appears no accident and by no means the aberration of a child faced with a printed sheet of flower engravings. Stuart embroidery was the direct descendant of Elizabethan appliqué work, with its individual pictures of flowers and animals. Had the Stuart embroiderer worked to scale, the flora and fauna in her pictures would have been so small that their species and special characteristics would have been lost to sight.

The prominence given to the flora and fauna in the biblical narratives was a manifestation of contemporary interest in the properties of the natural world, in gardening, and the rural occupations of the class whose children stitched the pictures. A huntsman with his hounds pursues hares around the lids of countless embroidered caskets; representations of the seasons repeatedly appear – a reminder of the extent to which the lives of the embroiderers and their families were dominated by harvests and the weather. The gardens can be linked to developments in contemporary horticulture. They often represent what was known as a nosegay garden: pansies, roses, violets, carnations and marigolds. Thomasina Beck, in *Embroidered Gardens*, relates curious objects to be found in the embroidered pictures – birds with men's heads, distinctly odd plants and trees – to the then current interest in grafting, dwarfing and topiary which Alexander Pope derisively described: 'Adam and Eve in Yew, Adam a little shattered by the Tree of Knowledge in the great storm: Eve and the serpent very flourishing . . .'[25]

There was nothing new about the inclusion of details from contemporary gardens in embroidery; during the sixteenth century a reciprocal relationship existed between gardening and embroidery, with gardening borrowing terms from embroidery and embroiderers depicting the new imported plants grown in the country. What changed with the seventeenth century was that both flower gardening and embroidery were increasingly becoming the particular province of women, though professional embroidery was still controlled by men. When John Evelyn visited Lady Clarendon's house at Swallowfield in Berkshire in 1685, he admired the garden: 'My lady being so extraordinarily skilled in the flower, and my lord in diligence of planting . . .'[26]

Another explanation for some of the flowers and animals embroidered is that they may be royalist symbols. Thus the ubiquitous presence of lion, stag and leopard can be attributed to the fact that they were the supporters of the royal arms. The caterpillar is said to have symbolised Charles I, while the butterfly stands for the Restoration. Given that royalist women declared their allegiance to the Stuarts by embroidering portraits of the royal family – particularly Charles I – it seems highly likely that royalist meanings played an important part in the choice of motifs for stump-work pictures.

There is however, another possible reason for the prominence of certain floral motifs in Stuart embroidery. The content of mediaeval embroidery had revolved around reproduction and childbirth. By the seventeenth century, much of the apocryphal imagery of reproduction and fertility had been repudiated by the church, in conjunction with changing attitudes towards childbirth and motherhood. Male control over childbirth was increasing; persecution of midwives as witches reached new and appalling proportions, the male midwife was coming into his own and, significantly, the worship of the mother of God was, under Protestantism, the object of ridicule. Writing on religion in France in 1673, Peter Heylin mocked Catholicism for honouring a mother: 'If they will worship her as a Nurse with her Child in her arms, or at breast, let them array her in such apparel as might beseem a Carpenter's Wife, such as she might be supposed to have worn before the world had taken notice that she was the Mother of her Saviour. If they must needs have her in her state of glory as at Amiens; or of honour (being now publicly acknowledged to be the blessedness among Women) as at Paris: let them disburden her of her Child. To clap them thus both together, is a folly equally worthy of scorn and laughter.'[27]

The 'commanding mother' was banished. Childbirth was no longer the subject of art in England. But the symbols of the Virgin's fertility lived on in women's work. All the flowers associated with the Virgin were included in sampler and stump work; a spray or branch with one full flower and a bud symbolised the mother and child, fruit piled in a basket and a lily in a pot were traditionally associated with the Annunciation. The 'flower pot of the Annunciation' was worked on the crown of a baby's cap.[28] How consciously these symbols were used is impossible to tell. Possibly they had become incorporated as part of the basic floral vocabulary of embroidery since the middle ages, but the stitching of the symbol of the Annunciation on babies' clothes suggests that embroiderers knew what they were doing.

The landscapes and flora and fauna of stump work indicate the particular place women were beginning to occupy within culture. Their work was inextricably part of the general culture of their time, yet it was beginning to be concentrated upon particular themes. What was appropriate for women was being defined for them, according to ideas of sexual difference and an ideal of femininity. Women themselves employed subjects to declare their conformity to the feminine identity they were designated. Yet in the embroidered pictures of biblical scenes we can also see how women gave their own interpretations and particular emphasis to the feminine ideal. Certain subjects were repeated again and again.

The most popular Old Testament subjects were the stories of Esther and Ahasuerus, David and Bathsheba, Rebecca and Eleazar, Jael and Sisera, Ruth and Naomi, Judith and Holofernes, David and Abigail, Miriam and Moses, Solomon and Sheba, Susanna and the Elders, Jephta's Daughter, Abraham and Hagar and the Sacrifice of Isaac. With the exception of the latter, all represent heroic acts by women, whether locked in combat with men, triumphing over evil in partnership with men or suffering at men's hands. It is tempting to attribute the embroiderer's choice of subjects to a feminist consciousness – an assertion of women as active beings in the very medium intended to teach obedience and passivity. However, a number of different factors determined the stitching of biblical heroines.

First, there was the availability of patterns. London print sellers marketed sheets of flower prints, animals, birds and biblical narratives. Peter Stent, active from 1643 to 1647 at the sign of the White Horse in Giltspur Street, London, sold books and individual sheets of prints. Embroidery historians have identified the most popular sources of engravings used by embroiderers: biblical illustrations by Bernard Salamon (1508–1561), Jost Amman (1539–1591) and Gerard de Jode (1531–1591). Nancy Graves Cabot has traced thirteen existing embroideries of 'Abraham banishing Hagar' by de Jode.[29] However, embroiderers were selective in the prints they chose to copy. Among those available from Peter Stent, 'Susannah and the Elders' and 'The Sacrifice of Isaac' were often embroidered, but no embroidery survives of 'Moses Lifting the Serpent'. While historians have diligently traced the printed sources of embroidered pictures, they have not asked why certain subjects were preferred above others.

The common theme in the chosen subjects – the female heroine – was not limited to needlewomen or to embroidery. Famous women of the Bible were popular subjects for artists – men and women – in all media. The theme of the female heroine had traditionally been employed in arguments about the characteristics and potential of women since the middle ages. Heroines were used to exemplify both women's power and their perfidy. In the seventeenth century their depiction gained a new popularity. Thomas Heywood's publications, *Nine Books of Various History Concerninge Women*, 1624, and *The Exemplary Lives and Memorable Acts of Nine of the Most Famous Women of the World*, had countless imitators.

Sixteenth-century embroidered hangings, carpets and cushions had been stitched with allegorical female figures and scenes from Ovid's *Metamorphoses*. As discussed in Chapter Four, the stories selected turned on a woman's heroic defence of her chastity, or those which depicted women's capacity to rule. Possibly the representations of Queen Elizabeth I in paintings and woodcuts as goddess or biblical heroine – Deborah, Astrea, Judith, Cynthia or Ceres – encouraged their use in embroidery.

However, the seventeenth-century embroiderer largely eschewed profane subjects in favour of Old Testament stories. Biblical heroines became particularly popular with the widespread vernacular translations of the Bible, some in pocket editions. Indeed, Bible covers, book marks, Bible cushions and bags became increasingly important sites for embroidery. The same Bible stories appear in embroidery and in the tapestries produced by the Mortlake workshops which were started in 1619. It has been suggested that the tapestries inspired the embroiderers, but in fact workers in both media drew on the same pattern sources: European prints. Painters, sculptors, metal engravers and embroiderers all produced interpretations of the same engravings, for the different media had not yet entirely divided.

The particular characteristic of the favourite seventeenth-century biblical heroines was their participation in planned acts of violence. When the embroidered pictures were produced, the representation of women as potentially violent and sexually in-satiable still held sway. So in choosing to portray violent women, embroiderers were not deviating from accepted representations of women. Where amateur women embroiderers differed from male workers, both within professional embroidery and other media, was in the particular biblical figures they depicted. Whereas Delilah, Salome and Jezebel frequently figured in male art and literature, amateur embroiderers ignored the women who tempted and destroyed men in favour of Judith or Esther, whose acts of courage saved their people.

Stories about women's power within marriage were popular with embroiderers: Sarah who forced her husband to evict Hagar from their household, Esther who successfully interceded with her husband Ahasuerus on behalf of her people the Jews. The Story of Esther illustrates how the same image can have different specific meanings for men and women. Esther was often invoked to symbolise a persecuted minority: the Royalists under the Commonwealth, the Puritans under James II and the Jacobites under William and Mary and the Hanoverians. But her particular significance can be gauged by the pseudonym and title chosen by a woman who replied to one of the first of the century's misogynist tracts written by Joseph Swetnam in 1615. Offering an opening salvo in the pamphlet war over women's place, he attacked women as idle, forward and inconstant. 'Ester Sowerman' immediately replied with a pamphlet titled 'Ester hath hang'd Haman or An Answere to a lew'd Pamphlet'. Haman was executed after Esther revealed his plot against the Jews.

The stitched stories of Queen Esther, too, gave prominence to the hanging of Haman. Indeed they are recognisable largely by the inclusion of the gallows in the background.

47 Sampler, Victoria and Albert Museum, London. 1603–25. Silver thread and silk on linen, 50.8 × 30.5 cm.
The random embroidering of individual motifs characterised sixteenth-century samplers. During the seventeenth century the samplers changed, becoming long bands of progressively more testing stitchery, in accordance with the new emphasis on child discipline and parental control.

48 Samplers, embroidered casket and contents, Martha Edlin, Victoria and Albert Museum, London. 1668–71.
A girl's childhood was structured by a series of projects from sampler to embroidered casket, intended as much to inculcate an ideal of feminine behaviour as to teach stitching skills.

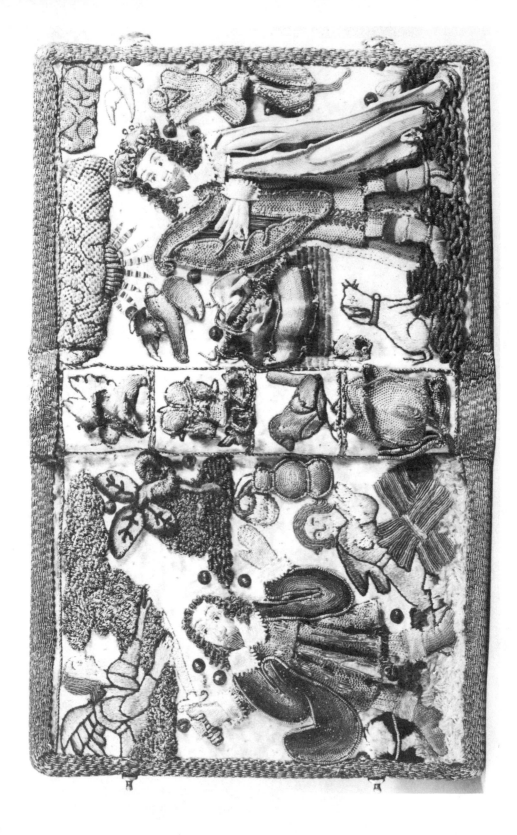

49 *The Sacrifice of Isaac.* Bible cover, Bodleian Library, Oxford.
Second half of the seventeenth century. Stumpwork.
Biblical scenes popular in pictorial embroidery depict patriarchal power at its most
violent and absolute. The story of Abraham preparing to follow the command of
God the Father to sacrifice his son Isaac was an established subject for embroidery
by the seventeenth century, but the frequent repetition of the theme suggests that
it had powerful resonance within the family, where the parents, particularly the
father, were assuming a new authority.

50 *The Judgement of Solomon,* stumpwork panel, Victoria and Albert Museum,
London. 1686.

52 Sampler, detail of *Adam and Eve,* Fitzwilliam Museum, Cambridge.
Seventeenth century.

51 Sampler, Susanna Wilkinson, Fitzwilliam Museum, Cambridge. 1699.
The sampler couple are taken from a popular pattern book, Richard Shorleyker's
The Scholehouse of the Needle, in print by 1624.

53 *The Story of Abraham and Hagar,* panel, Victoria and Albert Museum, London.
Second half of the seventeenth century. Stumpwork, 35.6 × 25.4 cm. The
relationship between husband and wife first became a dominant theme of
embroidery during the seventeenth century. Adam and Eve, Abraham and Sarah,
or simply the image of man and woman standing side by side were often stitched.
Sarah, seen in the tent, here represents wifely fortitude.

54 (top right) *Esther and Abasuerus,* panel, Victoria and Albert Museum, London.
Second half of the seventeenth century. Stumpwork.

55 (bottom right) Print sold by Peter Stent, British Library, London. c 1643–47.
Embroiderers copied motifs from sheets of engravings. The tulip, lion and parrot
which can be seen in Plate 55 appear in numbers of embroidered pictures. The
flora and fauna, stitched large to be instantly recognisable, were a manifestation of
a growing interest in properties of the natural world as well as carrying of symbolic
meanings. It has been suggested that the ubiquitous lion, stag and leopard –
supporters of the royal arms – declared the Royalist allegiance of the embroiderer.

57 *Jael and Sisera: Deborah and Barak,* casket doors, Hannah Smith, Whiteworth Gallery, Manchester. 1654–56. Silk.

56 Sampler, detail of *Judith with the Head of Holofernes,* Fitzwilliam Museum, Cambridge. Seventeenth century.

Biblical heroines who engaged in acts of violence were popular subjects in all the arts throughout Europe in the seventeenth century – evidence of the era's embroilment in issues of sex roles and power. Whereas male painters depicted Delilah, Salome and Jezebel as well as Esther, Judith and Jael, women and girl embroiderers, from the surviving evidence, seem to have eschewed those women who destroyed men in favour of those whose acts of courage saved their people. They celebrated 'masculine' behaviour in women through the very medium intended to inculcate femininity.

58 *The Betrothal of the Virgin,* Edmund Harrison, Fitzwilliam Museum, Cambridge. 1637. Silk and silver-gilt thread on linen.
Edmund Harrison was embroiderer to James I, Charles I and Charles II. One of a set of images from *The Life of Mary* made for William Howard, Lord Stafford, *The Betrothal of the Virgin* offers a considerable contrast to the work of amateur women. Technically it resembles European embroidery, with its use of *or nué*.

Esther and the Hanging of Haman, Judith decapitating Holofernes, Jael driving a tent peg through Sisera's temple, were popular subjects with needlewomen because they proved women's potential for heroic action. Some idea of the meanings their chosen biblical heroines had for seventeenth-century women can be gleaned from their pamphlets and poems. Educationalists such as Bathsua Makin and Anna Maria von Schurman often referred to the feats of famous women of the past. Makin offers these women as inspiration for contemporary women and employs biblical heroines such as Deborah, 'deliverer of Israel', and Miriam, 'a great poet and philosopher', to provide scriptural justification for women's education.[30] The poet Ann Finch, Countess of Winchilsea (1661–1720), quotes Deborah as proof that women's subjugation is imposed by man and not part of the natural order:

> Good breeding, fassion, dancing, dressing, play
> Are the accomplishments we shou'd desire;
> To write, or read, or think, or to enquire
> wou'd cloud our beauty, and exaust our time,
> And interrupt the Conquests of our prime;
> Whilst the dull manage, of a servile house
> Is held by some, our outmost art, and use,
> Sure 'twas not ever thus, nor are we told
> Fables, of Women that excell'd of old;
> To whom, by the diffusive hand of Heaven
> Some share of witt, and poetry was given . . .
> A Woman here, leads fainting Israel on,
> She fights, she wins, she tryumphs with a song,
> Devout, Majestick, for the subject fitt,
> And far about her arms, exalts her witt,
> Then, to the peacefull, shady Palm withdraws,
> And rules the rescu'd Nation, with her Laws,
> How are we fal'n, by the mistaken rules?
> And Education's more than Nature's fools,
> Debarr'd from all improve-ments of the mind
> And to be dull, expected and dessigned . . .
>
> *The Introduction*[31]

Finch, von Schurman and Makin quote the exploits of women who exercised power, comparing their achievements with the limited lives of seventeenth-century women. But the comparison carried meanings only because the horizons of middle-class women were expanding. It was the contradictions that such women experienced in their lives that led them to question women's position in society, and gave the biblical heroines such resonance. In England the Cromwellian Revolution of 1640 brought new opportunities and fresh responsibilities to women of all political, and religious persuasions. 'A book might be wholly filled with a story of the part taken by women in the political and religious struggles of this period,' wrote Alice Clark in 1919.[32] She also cited the women who perpetually besieged the court for grants of wardships, monopolies and patents. Royalist women were often forced to take on the running of the family affairs and defence of their property after 1640. Puritan women became famed as travelling preachers and faith healers. Sheila Rowbotham in *Women, Resistance and Revolution*, 1972, comments that 'Despite the distrust of female sexuality, despite the narrow scope offered them, heresy proved consistently popular with a section of women. These were the women in the growing towns freed from constant labour but not admitted to the privilege of court or convent.'[33]

Puritanism allowed women certain restricted dignity and provided for a more humane concept of relationships between the sexes. Objections were raised to wife beating, and women were no longer churched after childbirth. Yet most women's legal and financial position was deteriorating. The changing organisation of industry and agriculture slowly forced women into an increasingly subordinate relation to their husbands – or into extreme poverty. Many avenues of work gradually closed to married women. And the associations which were formed at this time for public purposes – educational, scientific or political – did not include women in their membership.[34]

It was these contradictions in women's position, the manner in which their lives both expanded and contracted, that determined the delicate needlework renderings of the violent biblical heroines. The co-existence in stump work of content celebrating 'masculine' behaviour in women with a form intended to confer 'femininity' indicates the extent to which the seventeenth century was a time of upheaval and transition in the development of what was considered acceptable behaviour in women. There were two schools of thought; one insisted that women should be submissive, devout, obedient wives; the other claimed men and women were equal before God. The stump-work caskets are part of the era's embroilment with issues of sex roles and power. Judith, Jael and Esther assert women's potential.

For women they were affirming, for men they were pre-occupying but fearful. Men repeatedly attacked 'masculine' behaviour in women. A publication appeared in the 1620s titled *Hic Mulier: Or The Man-Woman* in which the author accused women of changing 'needles for swords'.[35] In 1620 John Chamberlein described how the Bishop of London called together the clergy and announced that King James had given an express commandment to them 'to inveigh vehemently against the insolencie of our women, and they're wearing of brode brimmed hats, pointed dublets, theyre hayre cut short and shorne, and some of the stilettoes and poniards, and other such trinkets of like moments; adding withal that if pulpit admonitions will not reform he wold proceed by another course.'[36] Similar anxious preoccupation with gender identity were manifested in William Prynne's *Another Blast against Manly Women and Effeminate Men*, and in *Muld Sacke* which charged all men with effeminacy who allowed wives or daughters any authority, and accused any woman of being a 'Man-Woman' who claimed independence from her parents or challenged the supremacy of her husband.[37]

It was in this climate of acute consciousness and anxiety in relation to sex roles amongst the middle and upper classes that women embroidered the 'masculine' women of the Bible. In addition to the active heroines, another group of subjects displayed male aggression and power over women. The Judgment of Solomon, for example, was hugely popular with embroiderers. Two women both claim ownership of a baby, and to ascertain who is telling the truth Solomon threatens to cut the baby in half. Jephta's rash vow mentioned above, which led to his sacrifice of his own daughter, was another favourite. David and Bathsheba, another constantly repeated subject, tells the story of how David arranges to have Bathsheba's husband killed after she has become pregnant by David. Initially David spied Bathsheba bathing and asked that she be sent to him. It was usually with this salacious scene that artists chose to represent the story, but embroiderers included the entire narrative in a sequence of images around the central bathing scene. Less popular but nevertheless frequently stitched was the story of David and Abigail. Abigail's husband, Nabal, refused hospitality to David and his troops. Realising what a dangerous error her husband had committed, Abigail rode out to the troops with provisions. Ten days later God 'Smote Nabal; and he died' and David sent for Abigail to marry her. We can thus identify three basic categories of embroidered Bible stories: those which revolve around masculine power and violence, those of women's heroic resistance, and those images which suggest that reconciliation and partnership between the sexes was possible.

Embroiderers employed the needle, not the pen – they left no records of their attitudes towards their subject matter. We cannot claim them as proto-feminists who stitched their heroines in conscious opposition to their ordained role, in rebellion against the inactivity, immobility and obedience enforced by embroidery itself. But their work was undoubtedly a declaration in favour of their sex. From all the heroines who abounded in seventeenth-century art of every kind, they embroidered those who reflected well on their sex, the same women whom writers evoked to support their arguments in favour of wider opportunities for women. Embroiderers throughout history were rarely in the vanguard of the fight for women's rights – but it is in their work that we can see reflected the constraints and contradictions that drove some women to speak out.

By the end of the seventeenth century embroiderers had abandoned the three-dimensional, minute, skilled silk stitchery demanded by stump work, and women themselves had repudiated the biblical heroines. Judith, Jael and Esther were no longer invoked to justify women's rights: 'The justification for women's rights was no longer that of being God's handmaidens or daughters of Jael but the demand to make women reasonable beings.'[38] Scriptural role models came in for ridicule from women themselves. In 1699 a woman calling herself Eugenia mocked Sarah and Abraham, the subject of so many stump-work pictures. In a reply to a sermon delivered at a wedding, she wrote a pamphlet titled 'The Female Advocate; or a plea for the just liberty of the Tender Sex, and particularly of married women, Being Reflections on a late Rude and Disengeneous Discourse delivered by a Mr John Sprint in a Sermon at A Wedding May 11th at Sherburn Dorsetshire'. Sprint, in his sermon, had praised Sarah for calling Abraham 'Lord'. Eugenia remarked caustically that 'it would look a little odd for a Man of low degree to be greeted, My Lord, Your Lordships most obedient Servant etc by his Lady in a blew apron.'[39]

Women were recognising that the biblical role models – indeed the entire famous women genre – far from proving women's potential, implied that by comparison the vast majority of the sex were wanting and incapacitated. An anonymous essay of 1696 attacked the male writer 'who levels scandal at the whole sex, and thinks us sufficiently fortified, if out of the story of 2,000 years he has been able to pick up a few examples of women illustrious for their Wit, Learning or Vertue. . .' 'Pedants and schoolboys' is how she describes those who 'rake and tumble the Rubbish of Antiquity, and muster all the heroes and heroines they can find to furnish Matters for some wretched Harangue, or Stuff a Miserable Declamation with instead of Sense or Argument'.[40]

Throughout the century embroidery had become ever more closely associated with femininity, until it was almost axiomatic that a woman wanting to enter a supposedly 'masculine' sphere of activity repudiated femininity in the form of embroidery. In 1659 *The Learned Maid, or Whether a Maid may be a Scholar* by Dutch feminist Anna Maria von Schurman was translated into English. She argued that embroidery – 'pretty ornaments and recreations' – should be replaced in girls' curriculum by maths, music and painting: 'Some object that the needle and distaff supply women with all the scope they need. And I own that not a few are of this mind. . . But I decline to accept this Lesbian rule, naturally prefering to listen to reason rather than custom.'[41]

Anna Maria von Schurman represents an attitude towards embroidery that was to appear more and more frequently amongst critics of the state of women's education. Embroidery became *the* object to attack for the women who spoke out against the constraints of femininity. This was regrettable. Embroidery was no more innately feminine than are women; it had simply become part of the construction of femininity. By pouring scorn on embroidery, critics of femininity found themselves in the same camp as men who belittled women's activities and sneered at sewing. Two British followers of von Schurman were more circumspect in their criticism of embroidery.

Both Hannah Wooley and Bathsua Makin were middle-class women who earned their living by teaching and writing. Hannah Wooley set herself midway between the women who were distrustful of their own capacities and the convinced feminists. Her best known book *The Gentlewoman's Companion*, 1675, lays forth her views on education: 'Man is apt to think we were merely intended for the World's propagation and to keep its human inhabitants sweet and clean; but, by their leaves, had we the same Literature he would find our brains as fruitful as our bodies.'[42] Nevertheless her ideal curriculum includes all the 'pretty ornaments and recreations' dismissed by von Schurman, '. . . works wrought with the needle, all Transparent works, Shellwork, Mosswork . . . Frames for Looking glasses, Pictures or the like. Feathers of Crewel.' Frames for mirrors were used as sites for pictures in raised three-dimensional embroidery; feathers of crewel refer to the worsted embroidery which was becoming increasingly popular during the latter half of the seventeenth century. Wooley's inclusion of considerable amounts of embroidery in her curriculum was pragmatic; both a tactic to make education for girls acceptable, and a tool for producing the characteristics she deemed necessary for women within marriage. 'Think not though grown to women's estate that you are freed from obedience,' she wrote, because 'all such as are entered into the honourable State of Matrimony [are] to be loyal and loving subjects.'[43]

Bathsua Makin's views are more radical than Wooley's. She included embroidery in her curriculum to convince her critics that her desire was to educate, not to unsex: 'I do not deny that women ought to be brought up to a comely and decent carriage, to their needle, to neatness, to understand all those things that do particularly belong to their sex. But when these things are competently cared for, then higher things ought to be endeavoured.'[44] Accordingly, half the day at her school was given over to 'all things taught in other schools, works of all sorts, music, singing, writing, keeping accounts,'[45] while the rest of the girls' time was devoted to Latin, French, Greek, Hebrew, Italian and Spanish.

Bathsua Makin is tacitly acknowledging that femininity is inculcated not innate, as well as the extent to which embroidery is enmeshed with women's sexual identity. They were 'brought up to their needle', it was particular to their sex.

Like Wooley, Makin makes a great point of the fact that education will not interfere with the marriage relationship. Indeed she claims that an educated woman would be more likely to accept her husband's superiority and be satisfied 'if her husband would consult and advise with her'. Similarly Mary Astell, author of *A Serious Proposal to the Ladies for the Advancement of their True and Greatest Interest*, 1697, while suggesting that an education which would 'furnish our minds with a stock of useful knowledge, that the Souls of Women may no longer be the only unadorn'd and neglected things', nevertheless claims that the 'making of good wives' would be an important outcome of her ideal seminary.

The extraordinary care that campaigners for women's education took to include embroidery in their curriculum, and to emphasise that their project would not undermine marriage, relates to the dominant view of education post 1660. It was considered politically dangerous to spread learning beyond a chosen élite. 'Nineteen out of twenty of the species were designed by nature for trade and manufacture', wrote a correspondent of *The Grub Street Journal*. 'To take them off to read books was the way to do them harm, to make them not wiser or better, but impertinent, troublesome and facticious.'[46] A similar fear of insubordination, and an insistence on the present hierarchical relationship between men and women, lay behind the resistance to women's education. As Makin herself said, 'A learned woman is thought to be a comet which bodes mischief whenever it appears.'[47] Makin, Wooley and Astell all basically accepted the conventional definition of women's nature, including the identification of women with embroidery. They were demanding that women's capacity to use their minds be recognised and allowed. The Restoration did extend that possibility to some women. It was a relatively advantageous time for women writers.

Cora Kaplan in *Salt and Bitter and Good*, writes that 'slightly less repressive attitudes toward the female role in court society meant that a few courageous women dared to write and show their efforts to others'.[48] These women, such as Anne Bradstreet, the Puritan poet, and Ann Finch, Countess of Winchilsea, employed embroidery as a metaphor for the constraints of femininity:

> I am obnoxious to each carping tongue
> Who says my hand a needle better fits, . . .'[49]

> My hand delights to trace unusual things,
> And deviates from the known and common way;
> Nor will in fading silks compose
> Faintly the inimitable rose . . .'[50]

Numbers of women were, however, dedicated to composing the inimitable rose not in silk but in wool. The latter half of the seventeenth century saw an upsurge in the embroidery known as crewel work. Embroiderers covered large hangings with a mass of coiling vegetation rising up from small rolling hills, alive with exotic birds and animals. The designs owe a debt to Eastern textiles. During the seventeenth century, trade with India and China expanded, giving access to Chinese embroideries and Indian printed or painted cotton. Whereas stump-work cabinets were related to European art, by the end of the century embroiderers were drawing on textiles for inspiration. This is welcomed by historians of embroidery, who deplore what they consider to be the seventeenth-century needlewoman's subservience to the pictorial effects of oil painting, inhibiting her from developing the art's own specific qualities and potential. However, the embroiderer's alignment with other textile arts also signifies the divisions that developed between different media, and the increasingly rigid categorisation of Art versus Craft.

In accordance with the new rational spirit of the age, the crewel hangings could withstand constant and prolonged use and were produced at comparatively little cost: the traditional embroidering of backgrounds was abandoned, so the labour involved was considerably lessened.

Worsted wools, usually in shades of blue and green, were stitched on a light background of cotton strengthened with linen. Worsted embroidery was not a new phenomenon, but it increased and evolved during the latter half of the seventeenth century. A change in sheep's diet made worsted more easily available. Christopher Hill writes that, 'Sir Thomas More's bitter joke about sheep eating men turned out to be truer than he knew. For in the sixteenth century, whilst the living standards of men and women of the lower classes fell catastrophically, the living standards of sheep improved equally remarkably. Enclosure and the floating of water meadows led to better grass; this produced sheep with coarser and longer wool, though more of it. This in turn contributed to the decline of English broadcloth . . . and to the rise of worsted.'[51]

At the same time housebuilding increased from the late sixteenth century, with styles which gave an important place to embroidered hangings. The houses of people who were neither very rich nor very poor grew bigger, and were subdivided so that yeoman farmers, for example, began to have bedrooms, an important move towards the notion of individuality and sexual privacy.[52] It was the women of the household who embroidered the superb crewel embroidered curtains which festooned the beds. Low Elizabethan rooms had beds perhaps seven feet high, but the lofty ceilings of post-Restoration England allowed for monstrous tent beds. A letter of 4 August 1683 from the correspondence of the East India Company provides some indication of the work involved in bed hangings: 'You know that only the poorest people in England lye without any curtains or vallances .... The vallances to be 1 foot deep and 6½ yards compass. Curtains to be 3½ yards wide and 2 yards long. Each bed to have 2 small carpetts, 1½ yards wide and 2 yards long, each bed to have 12 cushions for chairs of the same work.'[53] A bed required between three and five curtains, sometimes supplemented with narrow draft excluders, three valances, three bases, a coverlet and cushions, all of which could be embroidered.

I have concentrated on amateur embroidery in the seventeenth century because it is there that we can see the advent of children's education in femininity through sampler making and, in embroidered pictures, perceive a reflection of women's resistance and resignation to the imposition of rigid sex-role differentiation. But, of course, the religious, political, economic and social forces that led to the vast increase of amateur embroiderers and the insistence on femininity for women also gave rise to changing conditions among professional embroiderers.

Charity schools spread, and the education of working-class girls, like that of upper- and middle-class girls, included the stitching of samplers. In 1713 the curriculum of a girls' school in Lambeth, London, comprised reading, writing, spinning, knitting, plain sewing and marking (lettering samplers). But frequently such schools were merely a means of exploiting the girls' labour. The Red Maids school of Bristol, for example, was founded by John Whitson in 1627 so that daughters of 'dead and decayed freemen of the City' could be taught reading and plain needlework, since the latter was 'laudable work towards their maintenance'. The initial excuse for exploiting the children's labour was that their industry provided a salary for their instructor. But by the end of the century the Red Maids were simply apprentices carding wool.[54]

There was no rapid or sudden break with the conditions that had prevailed in embroidery production during the sixteenth century. Men continued to dominate and control the Broderers' Company. Edmund Harrison, whose work is illustrated in Plate 57, was embroiderer to James I, Charles I and Charles II. Records exist of commissions he received to embroider coats for yeomen of the chamber and other servants, as well as for costumes used in masques and pageants. But the only works surviving by his hand are New Testament scenes in a style that resembles the European rather than the pictorial techniques of amateur work, since he employed the *or nué* technique developed in fifteenth-century Florence to provide perspectival effects.

Women are listed as receiving payments for embroidery, but their domain as professionals seems increasingly to have been restricted to embroidered clothing. In 1630 a woman named Alice Beardon received one hundred pounds for 'certain cutworks furnished to the Queen for her own wearing'.[55]

The future pattern of professional work began to be established. Working-class women were employed as sweated labour in trades associated with embroidery, and middle-class women became embroiderers because the craft's aristocratic and feminine associations made it an acceptable occupation. John Milton's daughters, for example, were apprenticed as gold and silver embroiderers and makers of tinsel laces.[56] And when Jane Martindale left her yeoman family in the North of England for London, she was confident that her skill with a needle would enable her to find employment with a wealthy household.[57] At the other end of the social spectrum, signs of the future appeared in the conditions of women workers associated with the crafts stimulated by embroidery. Gold and silver thread were important ingredients of seventeenth-century embroidery. The production of metal thread had been in the hands of women, but a proclamation of 1622 forbade the exercise of the craft by all except members of the Company of Gold Wire Drawers. Few, if any, women became members. 'Hampered by want of specialised training, [women] were beaten down into sweated industries.'[58] Within metal thread production, women were employed as spinners for starvation wages, working in crowded sheds. In the parish of St Giles, Cripplegate, there were eighty-five spinning sheds that employed paupers. Despite the increased use of metal thread, the demand for it was limited and capable of little expansion. The labour available in the pauper class was therefore sufficient to satisfy it.[59]

In the more privileged area of embroidery production, the fortunes of professionals fluctuated throughout the seventeenth century. The Broderers' Company presented Charles I with a petition stating that the trade had decayed and members were forced to work as porters, waterbearers and the like – all revealingly masculine occupations.[60] There are a number of possible explanations for the troubles facing the Broderers; amongst them were the increase of work by amateur women, and the fact that glossy materials were replacing embroidered clothing, which was becoming limited to small, richly decorated articles like stomachers, the triangles of material worn point downwards in front of a dress to create an impression of a tapering waist.

After the Restoration, the Broderers' Company appear to have tried to enforce their control over embroidery production. Amendments to the Company's by-laws, 1609, provided that no woman should be taken on as an apprentice, and thus permitted the Company to fine women embroiderers as 'unlawful workers'.[61] Hence, for example, Margaret Wadding and Elizabeth Coleman were fined during 1681. In each case the Company ordered that their work be destroyed, but relented on the payment of a fine.

A judgment against the Company in 1710, ruling that their legislative powers did not extend beyond their members, marked the end of their privileges in relation to the work. Economic and ideological factors together increasingly militated against embroidery practice by male professionals. In 1630 the Sumptuary Laws – regulations limiting the wearing of embroidery and costly materials to people of rank – had been revoked. Embroidery increasingly became the signifier of private circumstances rather than public position, and ever more closely intertwined with notions of femininity, as the division between public and private spheres deepened, and masculine and feminine areas became more rigidly distinguished.

6: From Milkmaids to Mothers

'My wife finished the sewed work in the drawing room, it having been three and a half years in the doing,' Sir Walter Calverley wrote in his diary for 1716, adding with admiration and satisfaction that 'The greatest part has been done with her own hands. It consists of ten panels.'[1]

The panels were originally worked for the drawing room at Esholt Hall, but Lady Calverley's son removed them to Wallington in Northumberland where they can be seen today. Contemporary account books record the move: 'Item 4, a large trunk with Lady Calverley's work in the best drawing room.' Item 17 in the inventory was another large embroidery packed carefully in a case, 'a six leaft skreen, Lady Calverley's work'. The screen is of particular interest because it demonstrates the role of women's domestic furnishing embroidery in representing her family's social position, while also revealing the extent to which the constraints of femininity were limiting what women could depict.

Each of the six leaves is five feet nine inches high, and twenty and a half inches wide. The whole is signed and dated 1727 and stitched with scenes from Virgil's *Eclogues* and *Georgics* in fine tent stitch on canvas in wools with some silk. The size of the undertaking, the care with which Lady Calverley's husband recorded her work and her son transported it, testify to the importance of the work to the family. Its value lay not only in sentimental attachment to the work of wife and mother, but because it offered a representation or rural life which the family wanted – and needed.

Comparing the screen with late seventeenth-century pastorals, we see what a change in content had come over embroidered pastoral pictures. The stump-work and silk pictures of the Restoration, though nominally of biblical subjects, are celebrations of rural, aristocratic life. Couples garbed in contemporary courtly dress stand before stately homes in luxuriant gardens while huntsmen pursue hares forever round the rims of embroidered caskets. Here there is no hint that the land on which the mansions stand is cultivated by the labourers who take an important place on Lady Calverley's screen. The seventeenth-century pictures can be read as one symptom of a reaction to the Commonwealth and Puritanism, of the 'almost deliberate paganism, hunting and open-air virtues contrasted with book keeping sordidness.'[2]

Plate 60 is a transitional piece. It contains elements of the stump-work pictures – a couple stand in a garden before their house – but all biblical references are gone and the embroiderer displays a concern with perspective and proportion that was quite foreign to the young women who made the stump-work pictures. The scene represents the new order – the great pastoral estates and houses which replaced castles and fortified mansions and provided 'the visible centre of the new social system'.[3]

The Calverley screen reinstates narrative subject matter, but it is now Virgilian rather than biblical. Religion was no longer such a determining factor in the lives of embroiderers nor of such symbolic importance in the decoration of their houses. Virgilian associations in paintings, tapestry and embroideries 'identified their owners as the Augustan patricians they aspired to be'.[4] Scenes from Virgil were stitched on countless chair backs and sofas, pole screens and wall panels. Diligent historians have traced the pictures' origins to Francis Cleyn's illustrations of Ogilby's translations first published in 1654.[5]

Julia Calverley employed Cleyn's illustrations, juxtaposing scenes from the *Eclogues* on the misery of civil war to passages from the *Georgics* on the peace and plenty of rural life. Possibly the screen refers to the Calverley family history, their misfortunes during the Civil war, their recent clearing of debts and restoration of the family fortune. However, the content marks a change in the representation of rural life which was not confined to her screen.

In *The Dark Side of the Landscape, the Rural Poor in English Painting 1730–1840*, 1980, John Barrell usefully analyses the change from Arcadian pastorals to the emergence of a 'more actualised though no more real' representation of rural life. The Calverley screen contains both modes, with the piping shepherds of Arcadia inhabiting the same world as the British ploughman; classically garbed figures stroll over rolling hills while below a basketmaker bends over his work, and a nobleman gallops in pursuit of a stag. The combination of elements suggested English rural life was timelessly harmonious and free of class conflict. The nobility are displayed as both confidently leisured and the benevolent overlords of a well-run, well-worked estate. Only in embroidery, a medium free from the rules and proprieties which governed oil painting, could disparate modes be so successfully combined to make an ideological point. Julia Calverley utilised the design of Chinese lacquer screens to convey 'the double image of the aristocracy as the leisured consumer of Britain's wealth, and as the interested patrons of her agricultural and mercantile expansion'.[6]

John Barrell argues that the inclusion in paintings of a cultivated landscape was necessitated by a changing social and political climate: 'natural property in land was being challenged by the more mobile power of money, the hierarchical coherence of "paternalist" society by what is perceived as a new economic individualism. The disappearance of Arcadian Pastoral, and the emergence of a more actualised poetry and painting of rural life, makes it clear that an account of the ideal life which entirely ignored this awareness could no longer be plausible, and to cease to ignore it meant, inevitably, to admit some degree of concern for work.'[7]

Lady Calverley's screen no doubt provided a pleasing and reassuring image of security and plenty, ease and social control for her family. Moreover, with the ideal image of her class, Lady Calverley designated absolute differences between the sexes. The representation of women on the screen contrasts markedly with the biblical heroines of Stuart embroidery. The latter were shown either in conflict with men or closely cooperating with them, sharing power as queen to king. The women on the Calverley screen are quite separate from the other sex, even to the point of occupying their own leaf. In the sixth leaf, pride of place is given to the lady and her pet squirrel, the attendant who carries the lady's basket of flowers and a milkmaid who balances a pail on her head. Compared with the marked differences between men of leisure and labourers on the other leaves, little distinguishes the women beyond variations in dress. All are static and slender in contrast to the vigorous men on the adjacent leaf of the screen. They are associated with nature and nurture rather than direct labour.

However, the lady represents a feminine ideal which has acquired explicit class connotations, defined not in terms of economics but by a style of living and mode of behaviour associated with the aristocratic lady, and characterised by an absolute absence of visible work. To be feminine was to be seen to be leisured. Lady Julia's own epitaph engraved on her memorial expressed the ideal. It conveys what she was, not what she did:

Endowed with that equal disposition of mind which always creates its own happiness, with that open and flowing benevolence which always promotes the happiness of others; her person was amiable and engaging, her manners soft and gentle, her behaviour delicate and graceful; her conversation lively and instructing.

There is no hint of the determination, application, ambition and education demanded by her monumental embroideries.

The aristocratic feminine ideal dictated the way Lady Julia depicted women – but did not yet entirely dictate what was considered quite proper for women to embroider. The twentieth-century historian of embroidery, Wingfield Digby, described the screen as 'so charming and yet in such robust good taste'.[*] By the middle of the eighteenth century Lady Calverley's depiction of men would have been considered rather too robust. Wingfield Digby's decription of the screen illustrates this shift – typically, he employs notions of charm and taste, terms usually applied to women, when describing this work of art. Women's work from the early eighteenth century onwards was increasingly viewed in terms of what it displayed of the embroiderers' femininity. Julia Calverley, though constrained to embroider women in accordance with the developing feminine ideal, was still relatively free of the imperative to conform to notions of feminine propriety in the composition as a whole.

Lady Julia's permission to be 'robust' in her work was, perhaps, a feature of her class position. Lower down the scale, where a family's class position was more uncertain, maintaining and demonstrating the feminine ideal associated with an aristocratic lifestyle became increasingly important. Correct feminine behaviour was a central subject in the emerging magazines and periodicals for women. *The Ladies Library* of 1714, published by Richard Steele and 'written by a lady', contained essays 'compiled from the Writings of Eminent Divines for a Guide to her conduct to be of some Service to Others of her Sex, who have not the same opportunities of searching into Various Authors themselves'. Volume I contained essays on Chastity, Modesty, Meekness, Wit and Delicacy. Volume II provided directions for femininity in action as The Daughter, The Wife, The Mother, The Widow and The Mistress.

The extent to which embroidery was becoming *the* activity which connoted a feminine, leisured lifestyle is evident in a series of letters to *The Spectator* in 1716. Addison wrote a mocking essay on the art:

> What a delightful entertainment it must be to the fair sex, whom their native modesty, and the tenderness of men towards them, exempts from publick business, to pass their hours in imitating fruits and flowers, and transplanting all the beauties of nature into their own dress or raising a new creation in their closets and apartments. How pleasing is the amusement of walking among the shades and groves planted by themselves, in surveying heroes slain by their needle, or little cupids which they have brought into the World without Pain. This is methinks, the most proper way wherein a Lady can show a fine Genius, and I cannot forbear wishing, that several writers of that sex had chosen to apply themselves rather to tapestry than rhyme. Your pastoral poetesses may vent their fancy in rural landskips, and place despairing shepherds under silken willows or drown them in a stream of mohair.⁹

Addison's satirical praise of the needle had been prompted by a letter to the magazine deploring the lack of needleworking by young girls. The author writes in the guise of an outraged aunt whose nieces' lives are devoted to 'gadding abroad' instead of to embroidery. She begs Mr Spectator to recommend the long neglected Art of Needlework:

> Those hours which in this age are thrown away in Dress, Play, Visits and the like, were employed in my time, in writing out Receipts, working Beds, Chairs and Hangings for the Family. For my part, I have ply'd my Needle these fifty Years, and my good Will would never have it out of my Hand. It grieves my Heart to see a couple of idle flirts sipping their Tea, for a whole Afternoon, in a Room hung round with the Industry of their great Grandmother.[10]

The outraged aunt contrasts the feminine ideal of the industrious wife which had held sway in the seventeenth century with the developing eighteenth-century aristocratic ideal.

Addison's reply included a set of rules and regulations for the practice of embroidery. First he itemised the reasons why embroidery was an excellent occupation for ladies. It distracted from gossip and politics, 'Whig and Tory will be but seldom mentioned where the great Dispute is, whether Blue or Red is the more proper Colour.' Then there was 'the Profit that is brought to the Family where these pretty Arts are encouraged . . . How memorable would that Matron be, who should have it inscribed upon her Monument, that she Wrought out the whole Bible in Tapestry, and died in a good old Age having covered three hundred Yards of Wall in the Mansion House.' He then proposed:

> 1. That no young Virgin whatsoever be allowed to receive the Addresses of her first Lover, but in a Suit of her own Embroidering. 2. That before every fresh Servant, she be obliged to appear with a new Stomacher at the least. 3. That no one be actually Married, till she hath the Child bed, pillows etc. ready Stitched, as likewise the Mantle for the boy quite finished. These laws, if I mistake not, would effectually restore the decayed Art of Needlework, and make the Virgins of Great Britain exceedingly Nimble-fingered in their Business.[11]

The next issue of the magazine carried a reply from a young woman named Cleora.

> Mr Spectator, the Virgins of Great Britain are very much obliged to you for putting them upon such tedious Drudgeries in Needlework . . . I would have you to know that I hope to kill a hundred Lovers before the best Housewife in England can stitch out a Battel, and do not fear but to provide Boys and Girls much faster than your disciples can embroider them. I love Birds and Beasts as well as you, but I am content to fancy them when they are really made. What do you think of Gilt Leather for Furniture? . . . and what is more, our own Country is the only Place in Europe where Work of that kind is tolerably done . . . I am resolved to encourage the Manufacture of my country.[12]

The sexist ridicule that marks this correspondence suggests it to be a male invention. However, male ridicule, like all good satire, was based on accurate observation. Addison was right that women considered their embroidery 'profit that is brought to the family', and his rules on the practice of embroidery directly related to the way in which embroidery structured a young girl's life, and prepared her for marriage. His satirical description of embroiderers 'transplanting all the beauties of nature into their own dress or raising a new creation in their closet' was, moreover, prophetic. Pastoral pictures and floral embroidery became increasingly popular as the century continued.

The manner in which embroiderers changed the modes of pastoral embroidery reveals the extent to which the identification of embroidery and femininity determined what a woman portrayed in her work. By the mid-century, painters of pastoral scenes had discarded Arcadian imagery and adopted what John Barrell terms the 'jolly imagery of Merry England'. Happy peasants labour in a lush countryside suggesting a rich, happy, harmonious land, in which everyone works together and all consume the fruits of that common industry. In fact, the repressive actuality, that the good life is reserved for the rich, and hard labour for the poor is contained within the pictures; their success is to conceal this contradiction by a careful handling of iconography and structure.[13]

Embroiderers were able to participate in the new direction of

59 Bed hangings, Abigail Pett, Victoria and Albert Museum, London. Last
quarter of the seventeenth century. Wool embroidery on cotton with linen.
During the late seventeenth century house building increased and the homes of
people who were neither very rich nor very poor grew larger, and were subdivided
with separate bedrooms. Hangings by the women of the household became a
prominent feature.

60 Embroidered picture, Hannah Downes,
Victoria and Albert Museum, London. c 1690. A
transitional work, the embroidered picture
contains elements of the stumpwork pictures, but
biblical references have disappeared and the
embroiderer shows a concern for perspective in
her desire to depict the couple, their mansion and land.

61 Needlework screen, Lady Julia Calverley,
National Trust, Wallington Hall,
Northumberland. 1727. Each leaf 176.6 × 52 cm.
The screen is based on Francis Cleyn's
illustrations to Virgil's *Eclogues* and *Georgics*
published in 1654. Julia Calverley juxtaposes
scenes on the misery of civil war with
illustrations of the peace and plenty of rural life.

62 *Farmyard Scene,* British, Metropolitan Museum of Art, New York. First quarter of the eighteenth century. 78.1 × 66.1 cm.

When Arcadian imagery gave way to the 'jolly imagery of Merry England', farmyard scenes became a common subject for the needle, portraying another shift in the feminine ideal. A dedication to all that was natural became an important attribute of femininity.

63 Embroidered picture, Sarah Warren, Henry Francis du Pont Winterthur Museum, Winterthur, Delaware. 1748. Silk and wool on linen, 64.5 × 13.7 cm. Fishing Lady or Boston Common Pictures were worked in Boston boarding schools. Like British embroidered shepherdesses they depict women with gentlemen in attendance, and are perhaps related to the preoccupation with changing forms of courtship and marriage.

64 Drawing of Flowers for a Court Dress, Mary Delany. Courtesy of Mrs Ruth Hayden. Mid-eighteenth century.

65 A detail of the petticoat of the court dress, Mary Delany. Courtesy of Mrs Ruth Hayden.

66 Dress and petticoat, Victoria and Albert Museum, London. c 1775–1800. A
move towards naturalism in costume embroidery meant that by 1740 to embroider
and to 'flower' were interchangeable terms. Mary Delany's sketches for her court
dress indicate that drawing as well as embroidery was seen increasingly as a
feminine accomplishment. The division between art and craft was becoming
elaborated by a division between those media and subjects considered the sphere of
ladies and those which were the proper concern of gentlemen.

67 Embroidered picture, Victoria and Albert Museum, London. c 1780. Silk and watercolour on silk.
From about 1780 and during the early decades of the nineteenth century, a new genre of silk picture developed and flourished, depicting ladies in gardens among the flowers which they were said to resemble.

68 Embroidered picture, Christies, London. First quarter of the nineteenth century. Chenille and collaged contents of a workbasket, including needles. 30 × 33 cm.

pastoral art even though farmyard life seems an inappropriate subject for the polite 'feminine' needle, however carefully constructed the image might have been in support of the class aspirations of the family. Throughout the eighteenth century embroiderers reflected every shift in pastoral imagery, using the genre to make meanings specific to their experience as women. A repertoire of motifs developed which each worker adapted to her own purposes. A windmill on a hill, a peasant carrying corn or rake, a duckpond, a shepherd and shepherdess appeared in numbers of embroidered pictures. Ornamental farms were also the latest development in gardening: ducks wandered through ornamental shrubs while cattle and sheep grazed the lawns.[14]

Both embroidered farm scenes and farm gardens were part of the developing ideology of the natural – that what was natural was right. Farm scenes, though a far cry from the pastoral embroidery satirised by Addison earlier in the century, were thus entirely suitable subjects for ladies. An enthusiasm for nature and a dedication to all that was natural became an important attribute of the feminine ideal. Women who desired to abandon society were praised as artless, sensitive, and admirably unmaterialistic. Moreover, the milkmaids and shepherdesses that inhabited this world conveyed specific ideas about femininity. On the right of the farmyard in Plate 62 sits a shepherdess attended by a shepherd. Her clothes mark her out as socially above the other protagonists in the pastoral scene, and she is not shown at work among her sheep but sitting prettily beneath a tree. The other familiar female figure is the milkmaid, who is more of a country girl than the 'silken shepherdess' in accordance with the 'Merry England' image of this type of pastoral; nevertheless she is distinctly feminine. In pastorals painted by men, the emphasis was on the shepherdess's and milkmaid's appeal to male fantasies of the demure but sweetly compliant rustic maid. In pastorals embroidered by women, the shepherdesses and milkmaids suggested that femininity – that highly artificial construct drawn from an aristocratic ideal – was in fact simply part of women's nature. The shepherdess who sits upon the ground is as feminine as the lady who embroiders at home.

However, like all embroidered pictures, the pastorals had many layers of meaning. They are also about courtship: the shepherdess was waited upon – courted – by a man. The 'Boston Common' or 'Fishing Lady' Pictures – the American contemporary counterparts to the English pastoral – are even more explicitly about courtship. They were termed Boston Common pictures because they were worked mostly by girls at boarding schools in Boston and sometimes included John Hancock's house – his was the first signature on the Declaration of Independence – built on Boston Common in 1737. A typical example of such a picture shows each female figure attended by a gentleman, in the same way that the British shepherdess was accompanied by a man.

During the seventeenth century arranged marriages were the norm but by the eighteenth century, middle-class women were beginning to take a more active part in the rituals of courtship and marriage. By 1720 magazines addressed to women were even including sketches of desirable husbands and discourses on love grounded upon reason. In 1744 *The Female Spectator* came out against arranged marriages, and later *The Lady's Curiosity or Weekly Apollo* published an essay on 'The Unreasonableness in Confining Courtship to Men'. By 1780 *The Ladies Magazine* felt able to justify ladies proposing to gentlemen during leap year.

Courtship was becoming an area where women had, however briefly, a sense of themselves as possessing potential power and the ability to act. Jane Austen's heroines show how women believed themselves able to operate and manoeuvre within courtship structures, manipulating them to their own ends. Feminist historians have offered various interpretations of the changing patterns of courtship and marriage. Sheila Rowbotham has pointed out that the middle class was critical of the double standard of behaviour expected of women and men in the aristocracy, and rejected their 'kinship pattern in favour of the idea of the individual in charge of her or his own destiny, in love as in business'.[15] Patricia Branca also argues that 'population pressure created a growing property-less group, for whom dowries and detailed marriage agreements were irrelevant'.[16]

Women's other major art form – the novel – represented eighteenth-century women's concern with courtship and marriage more directly, and reading novels, in Lady Mary Wortley Montagu's view, led young women 'to hope for impossible events to draw them out of misery'.[17] Perhaps embroidering the shepherdess and her gentleman in the 'natural' environment afforded some relief too, and drew the emboiderer 'out of her misery', cooped up as she was in a drawing room.

Sampler verses compare the freedom and harmony of nature with the embroiderer's own possibilities:

> Sweet bird thy bower is evergreen
> Thy sky is ever clear
> Thou has no sorrow in thy song
> Nor winter in thy year.

Moreover, although the stitched shepherdess suggests that femininity is natural – a cross-class characteristic – paradoxically she also suggests that in a natural environment, the constraints of aristocratic femininity can be shed and class barriers crossed. That at least is the role of country people in women's magazine romances. It is necessary to exercise caution in looking to women's magazines for evidence of women's feelings – the more so as many were written by men. However, they were intended to appeal to women. Thus *The Female Spectator* in 1747 published a rustic romance in which 'Mary a Squires daughter had clambered over Hedge and Stile, to give a rampant Jump into the Arms of a young jolly Haymaker . . .'

Running parallel to pastoral embroidery was a move towards greater naturalism in costume embroidery. Women did, indeed, 'transplant the beauties of nature into their dress' as Addison satirically put it. By 1740 the terms 'to embroider' and 'to flower' were interchangeable. In Samuel Richardson's *Pamela* the narrator wrote to her parents that 'Mrs Jervis shewed my master the waistcoat I am flowering for him, and he said, "It looks well enough; I think the creature had best stay till she had finished it." '[18] Her master's mother had instructed her in the arts of femininity, 'to flower and to draw too'. They were in part responsible for gaining her her master's attentions, and Pamela declared that the acquisition of the attributes of aristocratic femininity were inappropriate for her and altogether a dubious advantage: 'To be sure, I had better . . . have learned to wash and scour to brew and bake and such like . . .' In other words it would have been better for her had she learnt to *work* rather than to display leisured femininity which signified her availability for men. For embroidery had acquired an additional connotation. Once it was equated with a lifestyle that necessitated female dependence, it quickly became synonymous with feminine seductiveness. Female dependence was flattering but fearful to men. The helpless, leisured lady affirmed a man's social and economic standing, but simultaneously produced the image of woman as self-interested, subtle seductress. The role of embroidery in *Pamela* – Richardson's attitude towards it as both an instrument of seduction and a waste of time – again illustrates how femininity and embroidery were fused in men's minds.

It is significant that drawing was also increasingly seen as a feminine accomplishment. The division between art and craft was further elaborated by a division within art itself between those media and subjects considered the sphere of ladies, and those which were the 'proper' concern of gentlemen. 'To model well in clay is considered as strong minded and anti-feminine but to model badly in wax or bread is quite a feminine occupation.'[19] Behind the increasingly familiar ridicule lie changes in the status of art and artist, instituted by the growth of academies of art dedicated to making art the intellectual activity of a cultured gentlemanly elite.[20]

Women were excluded from the best of art education in the academy schools and largely prevented from studying the nude model and producing prestigious history paintings. One way they reacted was to develop alternative areas of art practice. There was an extraordinary burgeoning of new media. Women worked with shells, feathers and paper collage. However, the artistic value and potential of these new media were not recognised until the twentieth century, when they were adopted by male artists. The effects of the secondary status of all these materials to oil painting can be seen clearly in embroidery. Rather than valuing the intrinsic qualities of the art – the possibilities it offers in terms of textures, stitches and material – mid-eighteenth-century embroiderers wanted, above all, to imitate the slick *trompe l'œil* characteristics of oil painting. This imitation earned them an entry in Walpole's *Anecdotes of Painting*, 1762. He wrote admiringly, 'This art of copying in work by the eye, with no particular rule for the stitches, was invented by Miss Grey, daughter of a clergyman.'[21] Thus, to work directly from nature became the embroiderers' ambition. A much admired eighteenth-century quilt was described as 'worked in flowers, the size of nature, delineated with the finest coloured silks in running stitch, which is made use of in the same way as by a pen etching on paper . . . Each flower is different, and evidently done at the moment from the original.'[22]

Embroidering from nature was prompted not only by the embroiderer's sense of the inferiority of her own art in relation to the much more admired oil painting, but also because sketching from life had become a feminine accomplishment. A pattern book was advertised as a 'Select collection of the most beautiful flowers drawn after nature, disposed in their proper order in baskets. Intended for the improvement of ladies in drawing and needlework.'[23]

The amateur embroiderer developed a wide knowledge of botany, but an 'interest in plants' was also noted as an important advantage in a professional embroiderer recommended by Mary Delany.[24] Mary Delany was herself an amateur embroiderer and botanist. She was the daughter of a landowner, and the diversity of her art practice was typical of the women of her class. She painted, made shell work, feather work, silhouettes, designed furniture, spun wool, wrote and illustrated a novel and invented paper collage. For the latter she was commended by Robert Walpole who professed that 'he could not resist the agreeable occasion of doing justice to one who had founded a new branch.'[25] She began doing paper collage when she was eighty years old. Using scissors, coloured paper and paste she produced roughly one thousand botanically accurate illustrations of flowers and shrubs collected into ten volumes known as *Flora Delanica*. Well before inventing what she called paper mosaic, Mary Delany had been embroidering plants and flowers. She embroidered her own court dress with over two hundred different flowers on the overskirt, including winter jasmine, hawthorn, sweet pea, love-in-the-mist, lily of the valley, forget-me-not, anemone, tulips, convolvulus, blue bell and roses. Like ladies of her class, she not only embroidered costume but was responsible for the embroidered furnishing of her home, and stitched different chair covers for summer and winter use.[26]

Mary Delany's letters provide useful insights into the attitudes that shaped mid-eighteenth-century embroidery. Writing to her sister Ann Dewes she described a costume she particularly admired:

The Duchess of Queensberry's clothes pleased me best. They were white satin embroidered, the bottom of the petticoat brown hills covered with all sorts of weeds, and every breadth had an old stump of a tree that ran up almost to the top of the petticoat, broken and ragged, and worked with brown chenille, round which were twined nasturtiums, ivy, honeysuckles, periwinkles, convolvuluses, and all sorts of twining flowers, which spread and covered the petticoat. Vines with the leaves variegated as you have seen them by the sun, all rather smaller than Nature, which makes it look very light; the robings and facings were little green banks with all sorts of weeds, and the sleeves and the rest of the gown loose twining branches of the same sort as those on the petticoat; many of the leaves were finished with gold, and parts of the stumps of the trees looked like the gilding of the sun.[27]

For a lady to have a 'landscaped' dress was part of the general glorification of the natural. Fanny Burney remarked caustically of a woman she knew that 'Nothing could she talk of but Dear Nature and nothing abuse but Odious Affectation.'[28] However, Mary Delany's admiration of the Duchess of Queensberry's costume reveals that a lady's embroidery was ideally not only natural but specifically feminine. The leaves on the dress were realistic but *smaller* than nature and the robes and facings were *little* green banks. The whole effect was *light*.

The constraints that femininity laid on form as well as content become clearer from Mary Delany's description of a costume that aroused her disapproval. Lady Huntingdon's petticoat was 'black velvet embroidered with chenille, the pattern a large stone vase filled with ramping flowers that spread almost over a breadth of the petticoat from the bottom to the top; between each vase of flowers was a pattern of gold shells and foliage embossed and most heavily gilt . . . it was a most laboured piece of finery, the pattern much properer of a stucco staircase, than the apparel of a lady.'[29] But of course the Duchess of Queensberry's brown hills and old stump were no more innately appropriate for the apparel of a lady than Lady Huntingdon's stucco staircase. Mary Delany's objection to the latter embroidery was moral. The stitchery transgressed the proprieties of femininity; it was showy and artificial rather than small and natural, it boasted of human finery rather than God's creation. For Mary Delany, a lady's love of nature and the manifestation of her love of nature in her 'work' were equated with love of God and *natural* piety. She prefaced the first volume of *Plants Copied after Nature in Paper Mosaic* with the following poem:

Hail to the happy hour when fancy led
My Pensive mind this flo'ry path to tread;
And gave me emulation to presume
With timid art, to trace fair Nature's bloom:
To view with awe the great Creative Power,
That shines confess'd in the minutest flower;
With wonder to pursue the Glorious line
And gratefully adore The Hand Divine!

Even before Mary Delany's death in 1788 a somewhat different relationship was developing between women, nature and embroidery. Love of nature continued to be considered an important aspect of feminine piety and purity, but, in addition, women were coming to be seen as part of nature.

From about 1780 to the early decades of the nineteenth century this was expressed by a new genre of silk picture – ladies in gardens. Often combining watercolour elements with embroidery, these pictures depict the lady as one flower amongst many. Behind the ever increasing identification of women, or rather femininity, with nature lay the influence of Jean Jacques Rousseau. Amongst all the theorists of the Enlightenment, the intellectual movement that dominated Europe and America in the first three quarters of the eighteenth century, Rousseau gave clearest expression to the values associated with bourgeois femininity.

His theories on education were popularised by English writers on education and his book *Emile,* 1762, was serialised in *The Ladies Magazine* during 1780. An ideal girl's upbringing is prescribed for Sophie, who was designated to become Emile's wife. What in an individual is determined by nature and what by nurture and environment is, according to Rousseau, radically different in relation to the two sexes. For boys he acknowledges that their behaviour, abilities and achievements are an expression of the total environment in which they are reared, but he presents a lengthy list of feminine qualities which he considers to be innate in women. Shame and modesty, love of embellishment and finery, the desire to please and be polite to others, and skilful shrewdness tending to duplicity – all these characteristics are presented as inborn and instinctive in the female sex. [10] His ideal was a homely girl, reared in a rural environment, wearing the loose-flowing dress of Grecian women rather than stays, fed on cream and cakes which she naturally preferred to meat, and entirely unable to run: 'women are not made to run'.[31]

A love of embroidery was, in Rousseau's opinion, natural to women:

> Dress making, embroidery, lace making come by themselves. Tapestry making is less to the young women's liking because furniture is too distant from their persons . . . This spontaneous development extends easily to drawing, because the latter art is not difficult – simply a matter of taste; but at no cost would I want them to learn landscape, even less the human figure. Foliage, fruits, flowers and drapery is all they need to know to create their own embroidery pattern, if they can't find one that suits them.[32]

Rousseau argues that a girl has a primary propensity for the art of pleasing. He wrote that:

> The little creature will doubtless be very desirous to know how to dress up her doll, to make its sleeve-knots, its flounces, its head-dress etc. . . And, in fact almost all of them learn with reluctance to read and write; but very readily apply themselves to the use of their needles. They imagine themselves already grown up, and think with pleasure that such qualifications will enable them to decorate themselves.[33]

He goes on to tell the story of a young girl who repeatedly makes 'O's with her pen as she learns to write until she catches sight of herself in the mirror and sees how awkward the effort makes her appear. She is persuaded to resume her lessons only because without knowing her letters she will be unable to stitch her name on her linen and thus prevent other women from using her family's property. And of course needlework shows off her hands to advantage.[34]

Needlewomen depicted Rousseau's tomb, evoked his representation of ideal femininity in a natural family, stitched portraits of his heroines and even of the philosopher himself. Realising how influential his work was – and how pernicious in relation to women – Mary Wollstonecraft devoted a large section of her *Vindication of the Rights of Women* to attacking his views on natural femininity and the subordination of women which he believed naturally followed. She argued that there was nothing natural about a girl's behaviour; rather 'their understanding is neglected, and [they are] forced to sit still, play with dolls and listen to foolish conversation'. Rousseau, she pointed out, was taking as 'undoubted indication of nature' what was in fact 'the effect of habit'.[35]

The development of an aristocratic feminine ideal, asserted as natural to women, and the role of embroidery in conveying a leisured lifestyle had a disastrous effect on the professional branch of embroidery. Because embroidery connoted 'not work' its status as a profession dropped, and yet the feminine ideal of delicacy, purity and naturalness, preached so persuasively by Rousseau, stimulated the demand for whitework floral embroidery.

The invention of Crompton's mule in 1779 enabled British manufacturers to produce very fine muslin as a base for embroidery. Mills in the West of Scotland concentrated on this type of cloth which was then embroidered by women and children. In 1782 an Italian named Luigi Ruffini set up a workroom in Edinburgh with girls of six or seven as apprentices producing flowered muslin. By 1793 parish ministers all over the West of Scotland reported similar workrooms.[36] One minister offered a somewhat surprising criticism of them:

> About 200 young girls are employed at dotting and tambouring etc. Some of them being at eight or nine years of age, and at this early period gain sixpence or eightpence a day. Although this may be profitable to one class, it is attended with much material inconvenience to another. Farmers complain of the high wages of servants and sometimes have difficulty in procuring them at all. Is there no remedy for this growing evil.[37]

Four girls worked together at a tambour or hoop, with the youngest girls employed at 'dotting' in darning or satin stitch, while the older ones embroidered the flowers with a tambour hook which creates a fine, continuous chain stitch. They followed a pattern placed below the fine muslin. In 1786 Ruffini applied to the Board of Trustees in Edinburgh for three of his boy apprentices to be allowed to learn drawing at the Drawing

Academy maintained by the board. He employed one hundred and ten girls and only four boys. Although there were no regulations preventing girls from training as pattern drawers, no girls were admitted to the school in Edinburgh. In 1797 Sir William Forbes suggested that a second school be opened specifically for women to provide a knowledge of drawing 'to such of them as are engaged in flowering muslin, in tambouring, embroidery and other works of fancy.' Although the plan was approved, a school was never established.

Tambour workshops employed children bound by the parish, and the evidence is that they were often severely mistreated. *The Lancaster Gazetter* of 4 July 1801, for instance, reported the prosecution of a London tambour master who was found guilty of ill-treating his apprentice, Sussanah Archer, aged fifteen. He was charged with assaulting and beating her, 'employing her beyond her strength, at unseasonable hours and times; of neglecting to provide for her proper clothing and necessaries, whereby she was stated to be emaciated and her health impaired.' Five out of the man's seventeen apprentices had already died and at the trial it was admitted that the treatment of tambour apprentices was 'disgraceful to any civilised state'.[38]

Embroidery outworkers were in a marginally less miserable state than tambour workers, but the work was overcrowded and low paid. Its aristocratic associations made embroidery one of the few acceptable forms of employment for women whose class background would normally forbid paid employment. Moreover, needlework was the only manual skill they would have acquired – and thus they entered the trade.

Robert Campbell in *The London Tradesman*, 1747, describing the different occupations in the city, lists embroiderers among the employees of the Lace Man, along with lace weavers, spangle, bugle and button makers, bone lace makers, orrice weavers, silver thread drawers and wire drawers. Campbell had nothing good to say of women workers. He describes, for example, women silver and gold button makers as gin drinkers and thieves who 'reduced the trade to small profits, and small reputation; the women are generally Gin-Drinkers, and, consequently bad Wives; this makes them poor, and to get something to keep Soul and body together work for a mere trifle.'[39] In other words, if women are sweated the fault lies in their womanhood, not in the Lace Man. Embroiderers, on the other hand, he describes as not bad women but simply bad at their work:

> Few of the workers at present can draw, they have their patterns from the pattern drawer, who must likewise draw the work itself, which they only fill up, with gold and silver, silks or worsteds, according to use and nature. We are far from excelling in the branch of business in England. The nuns in foreign countries far exceed anything we can perform . . . This I take to be chiefly owing to the want of taste for drawing in the performers. An embroiderer ought to have a taste for designing, and a just notion of the principles of light and shade, to know how to range their colours in a natural order, make them reflect upon one another, and the whole to represent the figure in its natural shade.[40]

Campbell's expectations of the embroiderers and his employment of the word 'taste' suggest he assumed they came from a more privileged class than the button makers. However, his suggestion that the embroiderers simply had a want of taste for drawing is ludicrous. Elsewhere he makes it perfectly clear that pattern drawing was strictly the province of men. 'If a boy is found to have any scrawling Disposition he may be bound as soon as he can write,'[41] commented Campbell on pattern drawers, and proceeded to outline the trade's requirements:

> This requires a fruitful Fancy, to invent new whims to please the changeable foible of the ladies, for whose use their work is chiefly intended. It requires no great taste in painting, nor the principles of drawing, but a wild kind of imagination, to adorn their work with a sort of regular confusion fit to attract the eye but not to please the judgement.[42]

There is a dichotomy between Campbell's demands for judgment and a sense of design from professional embroiderers, and his expectation of mindless, natural confusion from the lady amateurs.

Apart from the sweated outworkers and workroom apprentices, there were embroiderers with businesses of their own. Elizabeth Watson, for example, in the early years of the century advertised: 'At the sign of the Wrought Bed, all sorts of the richest and newest-fashioned Wrought Beds, being much finer than any ever yet made for Sale. All sorts of lower price Wrought Beds and worked Callicoes, for Bed Linings and Window Curtains, Wrought Quilts, Imbroidered Aprons, and loose Flower fit for Gowns, Scarfs and Aprons.' Miss Hare sold patterns professionally: 'All kinds of silks, gauze or muslin, painted or stained in most elegant tastes for ladies negligees, shawls, or aprons, and . . . drawings of all sorts for every kind of needlework on the shortest notice.'[43]

An ideology of femininity was produced right across society, but it was powerfully reproduced in bourgeois families through the mother/daughter relationship.

In the seventeenth century samplers had been employed to inculcate obedience, submission, passivity and piety. Parental authority and the primacy of the marriage bond were dominant issues in all pictorial figurative embroidery. In the eighteenth century samplers continued to inculcate femininity, but parents – particularly mothers – are represented as not simply honoured, but loved. Ties of affection within the family gained a new importance in the latter half of the century. Women were increasingly locked into a place within the family; femininity was to be realised in child bearing and child rearing. The new ideology of motherhood coincided with and sanctified the effects of a rising birth rate and declining death rate, which meant that women had more living children and the family more domestic responsibilities.

Motherhood became an overriding issue for radical and conservative writers. Thus Rousseau exhorted women to fulfil their 'proper purpose' to which they were destined by nature: 'Where mothers resume nursing their children, morals will be reformed; natural feelings will revive in every heart; the state will be repopulated; this first step alone will re-unite everyone.'[44]

Ironically embroidery came under suspicion in the new concern for motherhood. Embroidery prepared women to be pleasing to men, but was it such a good preparation for motherhood? William Buchan thought not. In *Domestic Medicine, or a Treatise on the Prevention and Care of Diseases by Regimen and Simple Medicines*, 1769, he wrote:

Miss is set down to her frame before she can put on her clothes,

69 Embroidered picture of Rousseau's tomb (died 1778), Christies, London. Silk and chenille, 42 × 52 cm.

70 Embroidered picture, Christies, London. c 1810. Silk and chenille, 32.5 × 40.5 cm. Rousseau's theories on innate femininity, and his prescriptions for a girl's education, were popular throughout Europe. During 1780 his book *Emile* was printed in English in *The Ladies' Magazine*. Embroidered pictures reflect his influence and celebrate his ideal of rural family life. The embroiderer in the garden asserts that femininity is part of women's nature and that the ability to embroider is, in Rousseau's words, 'a spontaneous development'.

71 Bedspread, English, private collection. Late eighteenth century.
For embroiderers of the working class, the invention of Cromptom's Mule led to the production of fine muslin as a base for white embroidery. The flowers and dots were created in fine chainstitch with a tambour hook. Tambour workshops originated in Scotland during 1792. In 1801, at the London trial of a tambour workshop master for cruelty, the conditions of tambour embroiderers were condemned as 'disgraceful to any civilised state'.

72 *La Mère Laborieuse*. Jean Baptiste Chardin
(French, 1699–1779), Musée du Louvre, Paris.
Oil on canvas.
Motherhood became a popular subject in art
during the mid-eighteenth century. Chardin
shows a mother and daughter with their
embroidery – the daughter learning the virtues of
feminine industry from her mother.

73 Embroidered picture, Strangers Hall
Museum, Norfolk. Late eighteenth century. Silk
and water colour.
Mothers and daughters in a rustic setting were
repeatedly depicted in the latter half of the
eighteenth century, as the relationship gained a
new social significance.

74 Sampler, Elizabeth Louisa Money, Christies, London. 1844.

Sampler verses on the brevity of youth, and the pain and ennui of life, from which death is viewed as a release, were extremely common well into the nineteenth century. The concept of reward or retribution in the after-life provided a powerful weapon for instilling obedience and docility. The religious revivals at the end of the eighteenth century appear to have stimulated the use of threats of death in disciplining children.

75 Needlework Memorial, Caroline L Newcomb, The Daughters of the American Revolution Museum, Washington. 1817. Watercolour and silk, 64.8 × 80.6 cm. A concern with death and mourning informed all the arts in the latter half of the eighteenth century when embroidered mourning pictures began to be stitched. Traditionally, embroidery had played an important part in mourning rituals. In the United States, mourning pictures became specifically family memorials.

76 *Woodman in a Storm*, after Gainsborough, Mary Linwood, Leicestershire Art Gallery, Leicester. Worsted wools.
Late eighteenth-century embroiderers reproduced rural genre paintings in thread. They selected pictures that represented the poor as pious, hard-working and deserving of the charitable, concerned compassion which women of the privileged classes were expected to manifest naturally in their life and needlework.

77 *Cherry Ripe,* after a painting by Francis Wheatley, gift of Irwin Untermeyer to the Metropolitan Museum of Art, New York. Last quarter of the eighteenth century. Original mezzotint, partly cut out and applied upon painted and embroidered silk. 50.8 × 41.9 cm.

and is taught to believe that to excel at her needle is the only thing that can entitle her to general esteem. It is unnecessary here to insist upon the dangerous consequences of obliging girls to sit too much. They are pretty well known, and are too often felt at a certain time of life. But supposing this critical period to be got over, greater dangers still await them when they come to be mothers. Women who have been accustomed to a sedentary life generally run great hazard in childbed . . . Would mothers, instead of having their daughters instructed in many trifling accomplishments, employ them in plain work and housewifery, and allow them sufficient exercise in the open air, they would both make them more healthy mothers, and more useful members of society.[45]

Buchan voices the new assumption that mothers would have total responsibility for the mental and physical development of daughters, that they would singlehandedly and devotedly form their children. The ideology rationalised the growing limitation on middle-class women's sphere of action – although Buchan allows them a useful role in society – and sanctioned their economic dependence on their husband. Their 'survival' was thus dependent on conforming to the feminine ideal and they inculcated a feminine identity in daughters – for the children's sake. Motherhood was accepted as a personal, moral duty. Tracts appeared with such titles as *An Unfortunate Mother's Advice to her Absent Daughter*, 1761 and *The Polite Lady, or a course of Female Education in a Series of Letters from a Mother to her Daughter*.

Motherhood became a popular subject in all the arts. A new kind of genre painting developed in France representing childhood and domestic bliss. The subject of *La Mère Laboreuse* by Jean Baptiste Chardin, (1699–1779), shows a mother and daughter both embroidering with a tambour hook. But nowhere more than in embroidery itself was the mother/daughter relationship celebrated and idealised.

A new silk picture subject developed: mother and daughter in a rustic setting. The two are usually represented hands clasped, the daughter a tiny replica of the mother, as they walk together in the countryside to underline the naturalness and healthiness of the relationship. And as Chardin's painting indicated, not only was the mother/daughter relationship a major subject of embroidered pictures, but embroidery itself became a major factor within the relationship. Sampler verses set forth a mother's love and moral duty and called for the daughter's absolute love and obedience:

> All youth set right at first, with Ease go on,
> And each new Task is with new Pleasure done,
> But if neglected till they grow in years
> And each fond Mother her dear Darling spares
> Error becomes habitual and you'll find
> 'Tis then hard labour to reform the Mind
>
> *Ann Maria Wiggins aged 7*

It was precisely because sampler-making and embroidery originated within the increasingly emotive mother/daughter relationship that embroidery, and the femininity it was intended to inculcate, became such a 'habit', to use Wollstonecraft's word for the power of the ideology of femininity. In itself sampler making could not have reproduced femininity, however long a child laboured over pious phrases and selfless sentiments. The key to the hold embroidery and femininity established over middle-class women was that it became implicated in an intense relationship, shot through with as much guilt, hatred and ambivalence as love.

The embroidered picture of mothers and daughters, with the daughters appearing as diminutive versions of the mother, illustrate the intense identification between the two. Because women are the same gender as their daughters they tend not to experience the infants as separate from themselves in the same way as they do sons. In both cases a mother is likely to experience a sense of oneness and continuity with her child. But the sense can last longer and be stronger in relation to a daughter, whom she can experience as an extension or double of herself.[46]

For a daughter, learning to embroider and to absorb the message in samplers took place in the context of her deep, unconscious primary bond with her mother.

The very intensity of this relationship, however, (which began to assume its contemporary character in the latter half of the eighteenth century) creates conflicts. Children seek to escape from the mother as well as to return to her.[47] Yet development for a daughter necessitates growing away from her mother *and* becoming more like her. The conflict appeared at the heart of embroidery. On the one hand sampler making symbolised unity with the mother expressed in obedience and gratitude, on the other embroidering could be experienced as an oppressive forced bonding with the mother – a denial of the child's individuation.

Similarly, a mother's feelings towards her daughter could be played out around embroidery. Mothers react to their daughters' ambivalence towards themselves by wanting both to keep their daughters close and to push them into adulthood. Teaching a child to embroider asserts the identification and unity of mother with daughter, yet instils skills intended for the moment when the daughter leaves parents for husband.

Whether selected by child or imposed by mother, sampler verses are imbued with guilt and the desire to make reparation:

> On this Fair Canvas does my needle write
> With love and Duty both this I indite
> And in these lines dear Parent I impart
> The tender feelings of a Grateful Heart.
>
> Behold the labour of my tender age
> And view this work which did my hours engage
> With anxious care I did these colours place
> A smile to gain from my dear Parents face
> Whose care of me I ever will regard,
> And pray that God will give a kind reward.

An entry in Fanny Burney's diary made at sixteen illustrates the mother/daughter conflicts so strenuously denied by sampler verses:

> I make a kind of rule never to indulge myself in my two most favourite pursuits, reading and writing, in the morning – no, like a very good girl I give that up wholly to needlework, by which means reading and writing in the afternoon is a pleasure I cannot be blamed for by my mother, as it does not take up the time I ought to spend otherwise.[48]

Fanny Burney was in fact referring to her stepmother. Her own mother had died in 1762 – a sampler by her exists at Parham Park in Sussex. Fanny began writing a diary in 1768 after her father remarried. Her stepmother, like her mother, was an educated woman, but considered that Fanny was unbecomingly bookish. By insisting that her stepdaughter embroider, rather than giving all her time over to literature, the stepmother was in all probability recapitulating her relationship with her own mother. That Fanny experienced mixed feelings towards her stepmother's demand is evident in her diary entry with the emphasis on moral imperative and the repeated use of hyberbole. Fanny wanted to be 'a very good girl', loved and at one with the woman of the family, and yet she desires the independence, adulthood and autonomy signified by reading and writing.

The very nature of needlework, the stillness, concentration and patience it required simply made it a penance for some children: 'Polly Cook did it and she hated every stitch she did in it' says one sampler. Aware that embroidery could be a double-edged tool for inculcating femininity, an educational tract for parents observed that the ideal mother 'bred up her children in all the plain and flowery arts of the needle; but it was never made a task nor toil to them.'[49]

Ironically the author was Dr Isaac Watts whose *Divine and Moral Songs for Children*, first published in 1720, provided verses for so many of the samplers toiled over by small girls throughout the century. Dr Watts recommended that parents teach his verses to their children 'that they may have something to think upon when alone and sing over to themselves . . . Thus they will not be forced to seek relief for an emptiness of mind out of the loose and dangerous sonnets of the age.'[50] Amongst Watts' songs, 'The Rose' was particularly popular with sampler makers:

> Then I'll not be proud of my youth or my beauty
> Since both of them wither and fade;
> But gain a good name by doing my duty:
> This will scent like a rose when I'm dead.

Similarly, verses from Watts' *Solemn Thoughts on God and Death* were frequently embroidered:

> There is an hour when I must die
> Nor can I tell how soon 'twill come
> A thousand children young as I
> Am called by death to hear their doom.

Death was of course closer to women's and children's lives than it is today. The family died at home, nursed by the women of the household. But as greater numbers of children survived, death in the family became less familiar, and more dreadful. Threat of death and retribution in the after life was a powerful weapon for instilling obedience and docility. The religious revivals at the end of the century increased the use of death threats in children's upbringing: 'Death at last surprised her; and surprised we all must be, if we do not live as if the present day may be our last,' wrote Jonas Hanway in *Domestic Happiness Promoted: in A series of Discourses from a Father to His Daughter*, 1786, adding that 'half who are born, are dead by seventeen years'.

There was no shortage of doom-laden verses for samplers. The works of Phillip Doddrige and John Wesley both emphasised the transitory nature of life and the desperate importance of virtue for avoiding eternal damnation:

> Dear Child delay no time
> But with all speed amend
> The longer thou dost live
> The nearer to thy end.
>
> *Sampler dated 1713*

> And am I born to die
> To lay this body down
> And must my trembling spirit fly
> Into a world unknown.
>
> *Sampler dated 1819 from Rev. C. Wesley*

But all embroidery, however oppressive the chosen or imposed subject may appear, invariably incorporates a source of comfort, satisfaction or pleasure for the embroiderer. Thus the saddest samplers suggest that there will be an end to tediousness, boredom and constraint:

> There is a calm for those who weep,
> A rest for weary Pilgrims found,
> They softly lie and sweetly sleep
> Low in the ground
> Jesus lover of my soul
> Let me to thy bosom fly.

As One Day Goes Another Comes
And Sometimes Shew Us Dismal Dooms
As Time Rools on New Things We See
Which With us Seldom do Agree
Though now and Then a Pleasant Day
Its Long A Coming and Soon Away
Wherefore The Everlasting Truth
Is Good for aged and For Youth
For Them to Set Their Hearts Upon
For What Will Last When Time is Done.

1755

Sometimes a note of vindictive triumph sounds in samplers –
you'll be sorry when I'm dead – as in the following verse which
was popular throughout the eighteenth century:

When this you see, remember me,
And keep me in your mind,
And be not like a weather cock
That turn at every wind.
When I am dead, and laid in grave,
And all my bones are rotten,
By this may I remembered be
When I should be forgotten.

A concern with death was, of course, not limited to
embroidery but informed all of eighteenth-century culture.
Death was a central subject for Neo-classic art with its 'sobering
lessons in the more homely virtues, stoic exemplars of unspoilt
and uncorrupted simplicity, of abstinence and continence, of
noble self-sacrifice, and heroic patriotism. The stark deathbed
and the virtuous widow replace the chaise longue and pampered
cocotte.'[51] Thus Hugh Honour characterises the shift from
Rococo art to Neo-classicism in terms of representations of
women. There was, indeed, an increasing concentration on
women's behaviour throughout the century, couched either in
highly sentimental or deeply moralistic terms. Because the virtues
of bourgeois femininity were inscribed within every aspect of
Neo-classicism it was a decidedly appropriate style for the
embroiderer to adapt to her own uses. By embroidering the
virtuous widow she became a virtuous widow – for an

embroiderer's personality was considered to be displayed by the form, content and act of embroidering.

Moreover, the Neo-classical insistence on the educative mission of art, appealing to morality through sentiment, helped purge embroidery of its association with vanity and frivolity. The 'severe and chastened style'[52], representing a life of simple, uncomplicated passions, yet moral, rational and touched with sentiment, largely banished the silken shepherdess, replacing her with women mourning at tombs beneath willow trees, strewing flowers sadly upon urn or monument. The mourning pictures referred to in Chapter One dominated pictorial embroidery from the latter half of the eighteenth century until at least 1825.

Neo-classical paintings provided a wealth of patterns for such pictures which could be appropriated as the basis for embroidery. In art, as in life, women played a key role in mourning rituals. For painters and sculptors the inclusion of grieving women provided a note of pathos and emotionality, making the male protagonists appear all the more stoic and heroic by contrast. In Jacques Louis David's *Oath of the Horatii*, 1785, the weeping women allow 'masculine courage and resolve [to be] contrasted with feminine tenderness and acquiescence'.[53] But even though the iconography of Neo-classicism depicted the difference between the sexes as one of weakness versus strength, self-control versus self-abandon, women were allocated significantly virtuous roles. That in part explained the appeal of the 'Neo-classical way of death' to needlewomen – forever judged by the work they had in hand, in terms not of its aesthetic value but of what it said about their value as women.

There is, however, a profound difference between embroidery and painting in the representation of mourning women. The dead are offered as noble, heroic and tranquil in painting, while desolation and loss is expressed entirely by the grief of the survivors – the mourning women – or by the heroic struggle for self-control if the survivor is a man. In embroidery, on the other hand, the mourning woman is endowed with power and self-control. She stands beside the tomb, bravely and dutifully strewing flowers. She becomes the heroic survivor, dutiful in that she treasures the memory of the departed, but very active and alive.

Traditionally, embroidery had played an important part in mourning rituals and, to some extent, mourning pictures and memorial samplers were the eighteenth-century equivalent of the black embroidered beds of the middle ages. But as middle-class women become increasingly detached from the family business, domestic rituals tended to expand. Mourning, in particular, grew ever more complex and important. Mary Delany's letters repeatedly itemise the appropriate clothing for different stages of mourning.

In the United States an embroidered mourning picture followed a sampler as the next stage in a girl's education. Both became popular in the 1790s, when the expansion of the middle classes in the North and Middle Atlantic states led to an increase in private schools and embroidery was taught in emulation of European habits. Writing in the *Feminist Art Journal*, Winter 1976–77, Toni Flores Fratto describes the curiously contradictory ideology of American society which prompted the expanding production of samplers and embroidered pictures:

> It was an age that called itself egalitarian but was less opposed to social distinction than it was individualistic and socially mobile. One of the consequences of this thrust was an intensification of the desire to spread the social graces and the arts, formerly the prerogative of the upper class alone, throughout society. What had once been luxuries were coming to be seen as necessities, and were in fact necessary to the maintenance of a new and not altogether stable standard of gentility.[54]

When Martha Jefferson was at school in Paris in 1787, her father Thomas Jefferson wrote to impress upon her the social importance of needlework: 'In dull company, and in dull weather, for instance, it is ill-manners to read, it is ill-manners to leave them; no card-playing there among genteel people – that is abandoned to blackguards. The needle is then a valuable resource. Besides, without knowing how to use it herself, how can the mistress of a family direct the work of her servants?' Martha Jefferson's reply is unenthusiastic but resigned, 'As for needle-work, the only kind that I could learn here would be embroidery, indeed netting also; but I could not do much of those in America, because of the impossibility of having proper silks; however they will not be totally useless.'[55]

Embroidery silks were soon in abundant supply, judging from the number of samplers and embroidered pictures produced. The European Neo-classical model was adapted for the United States with the addition of Christian and domestic symbols, and the eviction of literary references. The American mourning picture is specifically a family memorial: a house symbolised the dead's earthly home, a church was included for faith and hope, a withered oak for the transitoriness of life, the sea for tears and a ship for departure. Stencils of these individual elements were available for the embroiderer to dispose as she wished. Gradually water-colour mourning pictures replaced embroidery, but stitching carried such important associations that short brush strokes were employed on roughened paper to imitate embroidery.

Writing to his daughter at school, a father directed her to embroider the family a mourning picture:

Dear Daughter
We are well and hope this will meet you with the same. I wish you now to work in embroidery a mourning piece in memory of your brother Strabo – who died June 29 1799 aged eight months and 13 days. You must wright by every post and let me know how fast you progress in your education and at all times remember to behave well and conduct in Decency in all your transactions through life.
from your affectionate father
Isaac Clark[56]

The letter is dated 1806, seven years after Strabo's death, which suggests that for the embroiderer mourning pictures were at times little more than exercises in piety and obedience rather than personal expressions of sorrow. Occasionally, however, a memorial sampler strikes a note of specific grief and guilt – as in this early nineteenth-century British sampler:

On The Death of My Affectionate Mother
Lord thous wast pleased to bestow on me a mother truly kind,
Whose constant care was to bestow good precepts on my mind
And plant the seeds of virtue on my young and tender breast
Ere thou didst snatch her from my sight with thee to be at rest

Grant me O Lord they constant aid to do the holy will
That a tender Mother's pious wish may be in me fulfilled
Eliza Richardson, 10 years old, 1837

Sewing a sampler declaring the child's intention of continued goodness and obedience was a means of maintaining a sense of one-ness with the mother whom embroidery and sampler-making signified. At the same time perhaps the protestations of love and appreciation denied the guilt/ambivalence that characterises the mother/daughter relationship, thus stilling the guilt death invariably brings in its wake. Moreover, the time taken to complete a memorial sampler or picture allowed a period of mourning, and possible acceptance of separation and loss, despite the attempt to 'retain' the mother by maintaining the code of behaviour laid down in sampler making.

Although images of death and mourning were the most popular Neo-classical subjects adopted by embroiderers, other subjects revolving around loss, separation and renunciation were taken up enthusiastically, for example, *Cornelia Mother of the Gracchi* and *Hector Taking Leave of Andromeda*. Hector's parting words to Andromeda were 'Go therefore back to our house and take up your own work, the loom and distaff.' The image evoked all the feelings associated with loss and separation which women constantly conjured up in their work. From the moment of weaning, women's lives were a continual pattern of separation – separation from their mothers, their primary family, their own children. But in Hector and Andromeda a new element of separateness enters the iconography of women's needlework, the separation of the private and public spheres. Hector instructs Andromeda to stay at home, to occupy herself with domestic activities. Femininity was to be lived in terms of specific domestic responsibilities. The aristocratic feminine ideal had been defined in terms of not being seen to work. Middle-class women could not fulfil this ideal, simply because they had to work in the home. The new emphasis on mothering makes this quite clear. The work they did was, however, not viewed as labour but rather as the expression of their innate domesticity. A new feminine ideal was constructed – domestic femininity. And for women urged and instructed to 'achieve' a domestic feminine identity, it became increasingly important that embroidery be seen not primarily as a badge of leisure but as a contribution to the happiness and wellbeing of the home. In the debates on the role and right conduct of women, embroidery became a constant reference point – and the content of the art soon reflected the recodification of ideas about women stirred by the often contradictory effects of industrialisation, evangelicalism and political radicalism.

The Revolution in France prompted debate in Britain about the nature and role of women voiced by Mary Wollstonecraft in *The Vindication of the Rights of Women*. Published in 1792, it was both a demand for bourgeois women to be granted legal and political equality with men and a furious attack on the supposed virtues of femininity. Mary Wollstonecraft claimed that gentleness was a meaningless virtue 'when it is the submissive demeanour of dependence',[57] and obedience was a virtue 'ever sought for by tyrants,'[58] while fragility never provoked real respect'. If the female mind were strengthened and enlarged, she argued, there would be an end to 'blind obedience'.[59] She demonstrated how the construction of feminine characteristics sanctioned middle-class women's subjugation and economic dependence and *why* women embraced the constraints of femininity. She claimed that the only semblance of power women could obtain was through femininity: 'While they have been insulated, as it were; and while they have been stripped of the virtues that should clothe humanity, they have been decked with artificial graces, that enable them to exercise a short-lived tyranny.'[60] Identifying needlework as a prime agent in the construction of femininity, Wollstonecraft summarised the attacks levelled at the art since the seventeenth century. 'This employment', she wrote, 'contracts their faculties more than any other by confining their thoughts to their persons.'[61] Previously, embroiderers had been criticised for vanity and frivolity. Wollstonecraft went further and speculated on the destructive effects of an activity intended not for personal creative pleasure but to enhance the femininity of the embroiderer in other people's eyes. Moreover, because embroidery was a sedentary occupation it 'renders the majority of women sickly . . . and false notions of female excellence make them proud of this delicacy'.[62]

Other considerably less radical women and conservative men were equally concerned about the effect on a woman's health of hours spent at embroidery. Mrs Chapone in *Letters on The*

Improvement of The Mind Addressed to a Young Lady, 1774, recommended needlework only with reserve, observing that it was more important to strengthen the mind by reading, and health by exercise. In *Domestic Medicine*, 1769, William Buchan attributed the weakness he saw in young women entirely to excessive embroidery:

> One hardly meets with a girl who can at the same time boast of early performances by the needle, and a good constitution. Close and early confinement generally occasions indigestion, head-aches, pale complexions, pain of the stomach, loss of appetite, coughs, consumptions of the lungs, and deformity of the body. The last of these indeed is not to be wondered at, considering the awkward postures in which girls sit at many kinds of needlework, and the delicate flexible state of their bodies in the early periods of life.[63]

Buchan's book was an exhortation to mothers to improve the health of their daughters, but ironically the effect of such admonitions was that gratitude for good health became another subject for sampler verses:

> Health seems a cherub Most Divinely Bright
> More soft than Air, more gay than Morning Light,
> Hail, blooming Goddess, thou Propitious power,
> Whose Blessings Mortals Next to Life implore
> Such Grace in your Heavenly Eyes Appear
> That Cottages are Courts when you are there
>   *M. Fennah*

Wollstonecraft felt the most unforgivable aspect of the art was that it made women dull: 'The conversation of Frenchwomen, who are not so rigidly nailed to their chair to twist lappets, and knot ribands, is frequently superficial; but, I contend, that it is not half so insipid as that of those Englishwomen whose time is spent making . . . the whole mischief of trimmings.'[64]

There was no place in Wollstonecraft's polemic for any sympathy for or understanding of the support and pleasure women found in embroidery. An earlier critic, calling for education for women, realised that embroidery and other 'feminine crafts' were a source of creative satisfaction for women in default of any other outlets. Eliza Heywood in *The Female Spectator*, 1746, asked 'Why do they call us silly women, and not endeavour to make us otherwise?' She goes on to claim that 'The Ladies themselves begin to seem sensible of the Injustice which has been done to them, and find a Vacuum in their Minds, which to fill up, they of their own accord invented ways of sticking little Pictures on Cabinets . . .'[65]

Less sympathetic but more searching, Wollstonecraft offered a class perspective of the place of embroidery in women's lives. She recognised that 'women of the middle rank' aped the fashions of the nobility, though 'without catching their ease'.[66] Nevertheless one of the major arguments she offered for middle-class women to abandon embroidery and needlework revealed how deeply embedded she was in the ideology of her time. 'The custom of confining girls to their needle' she wrote, 'and by thus narrowing their minds they are rendered unfit to fulfil the peculiar duties which Nature has assigned them.'[67] An almost evangelical moralism sounds in her solution to the time middle-class women put into needlework:

When a woman in the lower rank of life makes her husband's and children's clothes, she does her duty, this is her part of the family business; but when women work only to dress better than they could otherwise afford, it is worse than a sheer loss of time. To render the poor virtuous they must be employed, and women in the middle ranks of life . . . might employ them, whilst they themselves managed their families, instructed their children . . .[68]

The evangelical Anglican writer and educationalist Hannah More also extolled the virtues of industry for the poor and the duty of motherhood for the middle class. Indeed, More and Wollstonecraft were united in their concern over the importance of mothering and disdain for embroidery. But the profound differences between them cannot be overestimated: whereas Wollstonecraft admitted a 'wild wish' that sex distinction be abolished because it created femininity, that 'weakness of character ascribed to women, her understanding neglected, whilst accomplishments are acquired with sedulous care',[69] Hannah More wanted sex distinctions re-codified: she argued for 'good originals instead of bad imitators . . . to be the best thing of one's own kind rather than an inferior thing, even if it were of higher kind'. She wanted women to be 'excellent women rather than indifferent men'.[70]

Embroidery presented something of a problem for reformers like Hannah More and Maria Edgeworth. They wanted to defend femininity but they nevertheless agreed with Wollstonecraft that embroidery was redolent of both aristocratic decadence and the cardinal sin of vanity. Accordingly they attempted to delineate an attitude towards embroidery appropriate for the industrial bourgeoisie – the class that was defining itself not only in opposition to the new proletariat, but also to the landed classes – the gentry and the aristocracy.

Hannah More claimed that the practice of the art had changed significantly since its hey-day in the hands of the nobility:

> It is a matter of triumph that they [young ladies of the industrial bourgeoisie] are at present employed in learning the polite arts, while others wore out their days in adorning the mansion-house with hangings of hideous tapestry and dis-figuring tent stitch. The superiority of the reigning modes is cheerfully allowed; for certainly there is no piety in bad taste. Still, granting all the deformity of the exploded ornaments, one advantage attended them: the walls and floors were not vain of their decorations; and it is to be feared that the little person sometimes is; and while one admires the elegant fingers of a young lady busied working or painting her ball dress, one cannot help suspecting that her alacrity may be a little stimulated by the animating idea, how very well she will look in it.[71]

Hannah More had a solution to the dangers attending embroidery; the young lady should always embroider for others 'habituating [herself] to the service of those to whom she is bound by every tender tie.'[72]

Maria Edgeworth, novelist and educationalist, enlarged upon More's plan. She warned young ladies away from music and dancing because they encouraged competition, and were 'too often used as a means of attracting temporary admiration'. Embroidery on the other hand was an admirable 'domestic occupation' which she happily endorsed because 'every art, however trifling in itself, which tends to enliven and embellish domestic life, must be advantageous not only to the female sex, but to society in general.'¹³

Wollstonecraft was defeated on her own ground. She argued that the middle class should abandon embroidery for it made them sickly and self-absorbed, and thus unfit for motherhood. More and Edgeworth claimed that embroidery practised in the right spirit made women into selfless, domestic beings and thus ideal mothers. The great upsurge of embroidery in the nineteenth century performed in the name of love (of home and husband) reveal whose arguments carried the day.

The debate on femininity and the doubts about embroidery inevitably combined to affect the content of embroidered pictures. Each shift in the ideology of femininity was part of general social change and just as earlier embroiderers had found appropriate patterns in the paintings of Neo-classicism, so embroiderers in the late eighteenth century turned to rural genre pictures. These paintings endowed the poor with the very virtues demanded of bourgeois women – cheerful dutifulness and simple neatness. Unlike the rural genre of the middle years of the century which celebrated the vitality of rural life, these were images of domestic idylls, the peaceful family life of the honest, contented labourer. In the actions they depict, and in the values they seem to endorse, they are strikingly similar to the essays, tracts, sermons and treatises on the poor which became suddenly more numerous in the 1780s, such as Hannah More's *Cheap Repository Tracts*, moral stories which sold in huge numbers. Their theme was right thinking and right living to be attained through hard work, sobriety, piety and absolute acceptance of the present social order. The paintings – the contemporary rural genre pictures – which embroiderers based their work upon, suggest that poverty is inevitable, thus concealing oppressive labour relations. The rustic appears only to be working for his family and the solution to his poverty is honest industry. Describing the work of the painter Gainsborough and the poet Crabbe, John Barrell observes that both

depict the poor as degraded, as indeed they had become by the process of transforming a paternalist into a capitalist economy; but the sympathy of both men presents itself as a sort of moral compensation for the effects of that process. They become more expansively benevolent in proportion as they represent the poor as more repressed, and congratulate the very classes that were responsible for the repression of the poor for the very humane concern they feel at the results of their own actions.[74]

It is easy to see why embroiderers chose to reproduce the work of Thomas Gainsborough, Francis Wheatley and George Morland, bearing in mind that through the century embroidery was increasingly viewed as an extension of the embroiderer. Because the paintings represented humane concern, the ladies who stitched them conveyed preoccupations which entirely exonerated their art from the accusations of vanity and selfishness.

And rural genre, as importantly, celebrated women's now designated sphere of family life and domesticity. Morland's work was particularly popular with needlewomen. They worked from prints of his paintings which were widely available and thoroughly sanitised. Rustic complexions were cleared and thatched cottages subtly repaired, making them entirely acceptable source material for the feminine needle.

But while affirming the primacy of the domestic sphere, these pictures were, nevertheless, designed to have an effect on the outside world. They signify a change in notions of femininity: the women who at an earlier time had stitched ladies in gardens to represent the naturalness and rightness of femininity had been asserting their own virtue; whereas the women who stitched the rural poor were asserting the power of femininity to evoke virtue, morality and spirituality in others. Morland's *The Blind Beggar*, not lazy but disabled and thus deserving of charity, was stitched to provide an example of the deserving poor. Gainsborough's poor children were similarly popular for they demonstrated children learning the habits of pious industry.

It was perhaps women's sense that their work should have some moral and emotional impact on society that led to the development of needle painting – the exact reproduction of oil painting in stitchery. Once embroidery was indistinguishable from oil painting it was granted entry into the public sphere with public exhibition. Mary Linwood is the best known needle painter. She developed a method of imitating oil painting with specially dyed worsteds worked on thick cloth in small, short and long stitches. An exhibition of her work toured the country and became a regular tourist attraction in London. One hundred needle paintings were on display including six after Morland, Reynolds' *Girl and Kitten*, Raphael's *Madonna della Sedia* and Gainsborough's *Woodman in a Storm*. Linwood placed them in a carefully constructed environment: for example a lioness after Stubbs was hung in a cave strewn with bones. The enthusiastic reviews were concerned not with the quality of embroidery but with the quality of femininity on display. *The Ladies Monthly Magazine*, 1798, praised the exhibition as:

> An effort of ingenuity and indefatigable industry, this Exhibition is equal, if not superior to any that has been produced in this country. The taste and judgement, the variety and gradation of tints cannot possibly be exceeded in effort by the pencil. The *Lodona* from Maria Cosway, is a most happy desplay in excellance in drapery . . . There cannot be a more excellant school for the study of all ladies, who are desirous of attaining proficiency in this wonderful art of needlework.

The Morning Post thought that the greatest praise it could offer Miss Linwood was to record that not only ladies but 'Great numbers of Noblemen and Gentlemen go to Miss Linwood's exhibition.' And typically, *The Library of Anecdote* paid attention to Miss Linwood's person rather than her pictures: 'The ladies of Great Britain may boast in the person of Miss Linwood of an example of the force and energy of the female mind, free from any of those ungraceful manners which have in some cases accompanied strength of genius in a woman.' The reviews amply illustrate the way a woman's embroidery was seen as an extension of her sex and judged accordingly. It need hardly be said what a constraint that was on the embroiderer, or to what an extent it devalued the work once that particular brand of femininity ceased to be demanded of women. When Mary Linwood died in 1845 so did interest in her work. The British Museum refused the collection and it was dispersed.

Mary Linwood is also credited with the invention of 'black and whites' – embroidery that emulated prints and drawings with fine black silk and sometimes human hair. Country houses were the usual subjects of 'black and whites'. *The Library of Anecdote*, 1839, described how Mary Linwood discovered the technique: 'by copying such prints as struck her attention, with rovings of black and puce coloured silk on white sarcenet. The needle in her hand became like the spear of Ithurial; she but touched her ground work and her figures assumed form, and started into life.'[75] In other words, it was all a happy accident, a natural spontaneous production involving no mental effort.

7: Femininity as Feeling

'By far the greater portion of young ladies (for they are no longer *women*) of the present day, are distinguished by a morbid listlessness of mind and body,'[1] wrote Sarah Ellis in 1839. Her books were among the most popular of the guides to gentility that proliferated from the late 1830s. She was addressing middle-class women and blamed their listlessness on their apeing of the aristocracy: 'false notions of refinement are rendering them less influential, less useful and less happy.' Sarah Ellis issued the 'ladies' with a rallying cry: 'This state of listless indifference, my sisters, must not be. You have deep responsibilities, you have urgent claims; a nation's moral wealth is in your keeping.'[2]

Sarah Ellis recognised that notions of femininity were in flux. Indeed, her own books were a symptom of bourgeois society's attempt to encode what women should or should not do for the new order. Here she voices the emerging definition of femininity. It was women's vocation – a vocation not in terms of chosen work but rather women's natural destiny. The process of presenting femininity as natural continued, even while the feminine ideal changed. However, Sarah Ellis inadvertently reveals that far from coming naturally, achieving the Victorian feminine ideal was demanding, debilitating and demoralising.

Women's 'morbid restlessness' was observed not only by conservative writers like Sarah Ellis, but by progressives like Florence Nightingale, who rightly identified the family as the locus of women's oppression within bourgeois society: 'If it wants someone to sit in the drawing room, that someone is supplied by the family, though that member may be destined for science, or for education or for active superintendence by God, i.e. by the gifts within. This system dooms some minds to incurable infancy, others to silent misery.'[3]

The contradictions and constraints engendered by the ideal of genteel domestic femininity were a manifestation of the dark side of Victorian optimism. Walter Houghton in *The Victorian Frame of Mind*, 1957, argues that

> Expanding business, scientific development, the growth of democracy, and the decline of Christianity were sources of distress as well as satisfaction. But since the optimism was expressed more often than anxiety (partly because it was more widely felt, and partly because any pessimistic attitude toward the human situation was considered weak or unmanly), we are still unaware of the degree to which the Victorian consciousness – and especially subconscious – was haunted by fear and worry, guilt and frustration and loneliness.'[4]

That unawareness ends in listening to what the women had to say. Expressions of distress and melancholy denied to men were expected from women. Women were to 'learn to suffer' while it was nevertheless their duty to 'cultivate cheerful conversation'.[5]

In among the complex determinants of women's lives and the curious contradictions they faced, one thing remained constant – women of all classes embroidered. Embroidery, therefore, was viewed by some as the major cause of women's unhappiness, while others insisted that it was their sole solace. Mary Lamb was one of the first of the nineteenth-century writers to accuse embroidery, in a bitter attack on the art published in *The British Lady's Magazine*, 1815, – a regular purveyor of embroidery patterns. Her declared aims were to 'lighten the heavy burthen which many ladies impose upon themselves' and to draw

attention to the plight of professional embroiderers, 'the industrious sisterhood to which I once belonged'. The article, 'On
Needlework', is a curious amalgam of extreme sincerity and
dismissive sarcasm, a style which embroidery too often calls forth
in writers. Arguing that needlework was a drawback to every
family's comfort she asks the editor of the magazine:

> Is it too bold an attempt to persuade your readers that it would
> prove an incalculable addition to the general happiness, and the
> domestic comfort of both sexes, if needlework were never
> practised but for a remuneration in money? As nearly, how-
> ever, as this desirable thing can be effected, so much more
> nearly will women be upon an equality with men, as far as
> respects the mere enjoyment of life. Real business and real
> leisure make up the portions of men's time – two sources of
> happiness which we certainly partake of in a very inferior
> degree.[6]

Mary Lamb claims that amateur embroidery created intellectual
starvation in upper-class women, as the art was 'naturally in a
state of warfare with intellectual development', and material
starvation for working-class women, because amateurs were
throwing them out of work, denying them that 'great staple-
commodity which is alone appropriated to the self-supporting
part of our sex'. She summarily dismisses the usual argument that
amateur embroidery contributed to the family economy: 'a
penny saved in that way bears about a true proportion to a
farthing earned . . . At all events, let us not confuse the motives of
economy with those of a simple pastime.'[7]

Charlotte Brontë took up Lamb's theme that embroidery
limited women's intellectual life. In *Shirley*, 1849, twelve-year-
old Rose Yorke complains that a life devoted to domestic tasks is a
waste of a woman's talents and almost a living death because she
feels 'monotony and death to be almost the same'. Her mother
reprimands her saying,

> 'Rose did you bring your sampler with you, as I told you?'
> 'Yes, mother.'
> 'Sit down, and do a line of marking.'
> Rose sat down promptly, and wrought according to orders.
> After a busy pause of ten minutes, her mother asked –

'Do you think yourself oppressed now? A victim?'

'No mother.'

'Yet as far as I understood your tirade, it was a protest against all womanly and domestic employment.'

'You misunderstood it, mother, I should be sorry not to learn to sew; you do right to teach me, and to make me work.'

. . .

'Where is the use of ranting and spouting about it then?'

'Am I to do nothing but that? I will do that, and then I will do more.'[8]

Charlotte Brontë's own memories of sampler stitching speak through the lines she gives to the servant Sarah in *Shirley*. Observing that Caroline Helstone seems sad, she says, 'How low you seem Miss! But it's all because your cousin keeps you so close to your work. It's a shame . . . You're fit to cry just this minute, for nothing else but because you've sat so still the whole day. It would make a kitten dull to be mewed up so.'[9]

Ten years after the publication of *Shirley*, with the increasing popularity of embroidery, critics of the art became brusquer and less sympathetic. The magazine, *The Young Englishwoman*, commented sarcastically, 'If the upper and middle ranks of life fritter away their time on worsted work. . . we are not aware that anyone demands it of them. Rather than crying "I am a-weary, weary in this dreary do-nothingness" they should go into their father's study and select books or if they have not sufficient brains for this, take a saw and plane and hammer and manufacture a chair, a table, or box.'[10] On a more serious note, Millicent Garrett Fawcett observed that embroidery was a means of appearing to fulfil the vocation of femininity: 'At about eighteen, when a boy is just beginning his university career, a girl is supposed to have "completed her education". She is too often practically debarred from further intellectual progress . . . and it being her supposed duty to be what is called domesticated, she devotes her life to fancy needlework . . .'[11]

For every writer who condemned embroidery there was one who considered it a comfort for a nameless sorrow. Dinah M. Craik claimed the needle was 'a wonderful brightener and consoler; our weapon of defence against slothfulness, weariness and sad thoughts.'[12] Carmen Silva, introducing a book on tatting, wrote, 'I have often pitied men – in the first place because they can't know motherhood, in the second, because they are bereft of our greatest comfort – needlework. Our needlework is so much better than their smoking; it is so unobtrusive.' She goes on to praise embroidery as a true friend, a safe companion and a comfort 'as it occupies the hands when we feel restless'.[13]

Detractors and defenders of embroidery were equally correct. It was both a cause of confinement and a comfort. The two faces of embroidery can best be seen in samplers which instructed a girl in docility and accustomed her to long hours sitting still with downcast gaze. Sampler verses themselves were prayers for spiritual support in a battle against restlessness and loneliness:

> Give me a bible in my hand
> A heart to read and understand
> And faith to trust the lord
> And sit alone from day to day
> And urge no company to stay
> Nor wish to roam abroad
>
> *Sarah Marchant 1834*

However, amongst critics and advocates of the art no one quite understood the significance of embroidery in women's lives or why it had gained a new importance in the nineteenth century. It was neither a manifestation of masochism as *The Young English-woman* suggested nor the art therapy which Carmen Silva described. Rather, it occupied a key place in the exploration of what it meant to be a woman in the middle class, when industrial capitalism was increasingly disrupting the established economic and social structure.

Newly wealthy groups meant greater numbers of women were sequestered in the home where the regulation of life became strictly structured.[14] The distinction between the public and private sphere had changed since the mid-eighteenth century. Then, men had escaped from the social, public domain into the privacy of the family. The Victorian gentleman, on the other hand, escaped from the family to the impersonal privacy of club and café, because the family had become a social and emotional centre.[15] Women presided over drawing-room society, but were not permitted the respite of the impersonal public domain. A lady alone in public risked her reputation. She was to be the guardian of the sphere that was now endowed with critical social significance. She was the symbol of it, the cause of it and its prisoner.

The rash of etiquette books that appeared from the 1830s onwards attest to the enormous importance of women's social role at home – and the increasing uncertainty as to how they should behave.

The act of embroidering came to be seen as correct drawing-room behaviour, and the content was expected to convey the special social and psychological attributes required of a lady. On a broad level it was an index of gentility. In *Jane Eyre*, 1847, for example, Charlotte Brontë gently mocks the class connotations of the art. The servant Bessie questions Jane about her accomplishments. On learning that Jane can play the piano, draw and speak French she asks, 'And can you work on muslin and canvas?' When Jane acknowledges she embroiders, Bessie has all the proof she needs and exclaims, 'Oh, you are quite a lady Miss Jane.'[16]

The early nineteenth-century arbiters of feminine behaviour nevertheless had doubts about embroidery. It provided too easy an access to gentility. The writer Maria Edgeworth, noting the spread of ladylike accomplishments, mocks the scramble to acquire the attributes of the aristocracy. Music, drawing and embroidery, she writes, are only practised by 'high life' until they descend to the inferior class of society: 'They are then so common that they cannot be considered as the distinguishing character-istics of even a gentlewoman's education.'[17] A letter in *The Ladies Magazine* of July 1810 supports Maria Edgeworth's view. While appearing to criticise the lightweight nature of girls' education, covertly the writer is protesting about the social mobility implied by the spread of accomplishments:

> Many of your readers, sir, have doubtless noticed the great increase of schools within these last few years . . . and we not infrequently see the pompous inscription 'Ladies Seminary' in a country village; the governess of which is usually as ignorant as those she undertakes to teach. To these places are the children of farmers, mechanics, and traders sent; where, at an enormous annual expense, they are taught dancing, music, and what are called fancy works.[18]

Yet there was a profound contradiction in embroidery as a status-affirming art – one that had already bedevilled embroiderers in the late eighteenth century: embroidery's very association with the aristocracy made it suspect for the middle class. While women were expected to prove their family's gentility they had to display a pleasing modesty: giving oneself airs was a cardinal sin. Writers of domestic manuals grappled successfully with the problem by establishing the *right spirit* in which women should embroider. Sarah Ellis and Elizabeth Sandford made it clear what was the wrong spirit. Both inherited to a large extent the attitudes of the Evangelicals of the 1790s typified by Hannah More whose feminine ideal was a pious, devoted wife and mother. Believers in the Puritan work ethic, Sarah Ellis and Elizabeth Sandford castigated idleness in ladies. Indeed, women's greatest error was 'that of calling themselves *ladies*, when it ought to be their ambition to be *women* – women who fill a place, occupy a post.'[19] Elizabeth Sandford commented scathingly of ladies that 'The only effort they make in the way of duty is, to order dinner, – and, in the way of occupation, to work a flower.'[20] If, however, working a flower was performed as a service for others, rather than in the service of personal social aspirations, it became an admirable activity of *women*. Sarah Ellis solved the uneasy problem of when embroidery embodied desirable bourgeois qualities by suggesting that there was a natural, God-given link between women's hand work and their moral influence over society. She wrote that 'the feminine qualification of being able to use the hand willingly and well, has a great deal to do with the moral influence of women.'[21] And she described how embroidery could create the ideal early Victorian bourgeois feminine characteristics:

Time was when the women of England were accustomed, almost from childhood, to the constant employment of their hands. It might be sometimes in elaborate works of fancy, now ridiculed for want of taste . . . I cannot speak with unqualified praise of all the *objects* on which they bestowed their attention, but, if it were possible, I would write in characters of gold the indisputable fact that *habits* of industry and personal exertion thus acquired, gave them a strength and dignity of character, a power of usefulness and a capability of doing good which the higher theories of modern education fail to impart.[22]

A comparison between the eighteenth-century ideology of embroidery and that of the nineteenth century preached by Sarah Ellis reveals the tragic aspect of attitudes which might otherwise seem simply laughable. The eighteenth century asserted femininity was natural and that embroidery was the natural expression of femininity, but at least allowed that women achieved some satisfaction in embroidery. It was spoken of, even if mockingly, as a source of creative pleasure. In the nineteenth century, unless embroidery was performed as a moral duty, in the spirit of selfless industry, it was regarded as sinful laziness – redolent of aristocratic decadence.

The economic and social climate which produced this punitive moralism is evident in Sarah Ellis' further justification for the practice of embroidery. Having established it as potentially industrious and useful, she provides a further reason for teaching young girls fine stitchery. Far from endowing a girl with the elegance necessary for coming up in the world, it would prepare her for sliding down the social scale. Addressing 'women of the trade and manufacturing class' she reminds them that their place amongst the privileged was insecure to say the least: '. . . it is no uncommon thing to see individuals who lately ranked amongst the aristocracy, suddenly driven by failure of some bank or some mercantile speculation, into the lowest walks of life. . .' Women accustomed to working with their hands would be able to 'sink gracefully and without murmuring against providence.'[23] All women embroider, but only once a woman shifts on the social scale is her 'work' recognised as work. In the hands of middle-class women, embroidery is a 'duty and their resource', as Lydia Segourney put it in *Letters to Young Ladies*, 1837. It was in fact a resource for fulfilling an impossible role – answering the demands of nineteenth-century femininity. How were middle-class women to be industrious and useful in an industrial capitalist society which scorned idleness and glorified work as the supreme virtue? They had their 'work'. And because they did not 'work' for money it could be seen entirely in the light of their primary duty – to *love* their husbands.

Love could not be expressed sexually or passionately, but through the providing of *comfort*. Comfort becomes the *leitmotif* of embroidery. Every stitch was directed towards domestic comfort. In *Treasures of Needlework*, 1855, one of the early embroidery instruction books, the authors Mrs Warren and Mrs Pullan declared that needlework 'brings daily blessings to every home, unnoticed, perhaps, because of its hourly silent application; for in a household each stitch is one for comfort to some person or other and without its ever watchful care home would be a scene of discomfort indeed.'[24]

Behind the anxious insistence on *comfort* lay profound distress and insecurity. Sarah Ellis warned, 'Never yet was the affection of man fully and lastingly engaged by women, without some means being adopted to increase and preserve his happiness.'[25] She reveals one major source of anxiety which embroidery was intended to still. By making a man's home comfortable with her woolwork chairs and carpets, portières and 'whatnots', a woman was in truth embroidering to gain love.

Middle-class women were increasingly dependent on their husband for economic security, for social status and for love. The ideology of Victorian marriage held love to be a main ingredient – so much so that its absence was remarked with consternation. In 1854 G.R. Drysdale wrote,

> A great proportion of the marriages we see around us, did not take place from love at all, but from some interested motive, such as wealth, social position, or some other advantages: in fact it is *rare* to see a marriage in which true love has been the predominating feeling on both sides.[26]

Women expected to be loved by their husbands and were informed that it was their duty to love. Yet at the same time the gap between the sexes was widening, provoked by the increasingly patriarchal nature of the nineteenth-century family. 'The sexes drew further and further apart. No open conversation was tolerated. Evasions and concealments were sedulously practised on both sides', wrote Virginia Woolf of the Victorian age.[27]

Purveyors of embroidery patterns assured their customers that embroidery made for domestic happiness, providing the comfort that would win a husband's love and prove a wife's devotion. Magazines invented patterns for an incredible selection of male attire: German Plaid Comforter, Darned necktie, Nepaulese smoking cap, Cornucopia smoking cap, shaving-book, Shield-design Cigar case. *The Ladies Newspaper*, 1860, in their regular column 'The Worktable conducted by Mlle Roche', offered A Braided Lounging cap for 'the comfort it bestows on those gentlemen who are compelled to wear a hat the greater portion of the day'; The Hanging Whatnot which 'well deserves admission into the drawing room, not only for the sake of its ornamental character but the usefullness'; The Watchhanger 'now a necessary appendage in every sleeping apartment'; A Footmuff 'One of those useful comforts it is necessary to prepare in anticipation'; A Lapp Cap which was 'A pleasant sort of economy'.

The endless assurances that embroidered objects were necessary and useful were prompted perhaps by the guilt women felt that they found pleasure in embroidery; but also in response to critics of the art such as the anonymous author of *Girls, Wives and Mothers; A Word to the Middle Classes*, 1884, who wrote that:

> The woman not over- but mis-educated is becoming an alarmingly fruitful cause of the downward tendencies of much of our middle-class society . . . She cannot sew to any purpose. If she deign to use a needle at all, it is to embroider a smoking-cap for a lover or a pair of slippers for Papa. To sew on a button, or cut out and unite the plainest piece of male or female clothing, is not always within her powers, or at least her inclinations.[28]

Elizabeth Barrett Browning, on the other hand, saw clearly the self-defeating desperation that fuelled mid-century needlework. In *Aurora Leigh*, 1857, she writes:

> By the way,
> The works of women are symbolic.
> We sew, prick our fingers, dull our sight,
> Producing what? A pair of slippers, sir,
> To put on when you're weary – or a stool
> To stumble over and vex you . . . 'curse that
> stool!'
> Or else at best, a cushion, where you lean
> And sleep, and dream of something we are not
> But would be for your sake. Alas, alas!
> Thus hurts most, this – that, after all, we are paid
> The worth of our work, perhaps.

It was feminists like Elizabeth Barrett Browning who regarded embroidery with compassion, whereas the proponents of femininity were suspicious of the very behaviour they fostered. The insistence that it was a woman's duty to embroider for love aroused the old association of embroidery with seduction. A women's magazine of the 1850s listed the things a well-behaved young woman does not do: 'She does not read novels in bed . . . She is not perpetually embroidering mysterious braces . . . or having a Turkish slipper on hand for a mysterious foot in the guards. She does not keep her mother waiting . . . She does not take long walks.'[29]

Clearly the motives behind embroidery were many and mixed. Some stitched to elicit love, some to manifest the love they believed they ought to feel, and others embroidered to declare their love in as decorous a way as possible.

In embroidery itself is inscribed the sense of inadequacy and insecurity which prompted the work. A sampler verse of 1840 reads:

I ask not for a kinder tone, for thou wert ever kind.
I ask not for less frugal fare, my fare I do not mind.
I ask not for attire more gay, if such as I have got
Suffice to make me fair to thee, for more I murmur not.
But I would ask some share of hours that you on clubs bestow
Of knowledge which you prize so much, might I not
    something know.
Subtract from meetings amongst men, each even an hour for
    me.
Make me companion of your soul as I may safely be,
If you will read I'll sit and work, then think when you're away
Less tedious I shall find the time, dear Robert, of your stay.
A meet companion soon I'll be for e'en your studious hours
And teacher of those little ones you call your cottage flowers
And if we be not rich or great, we may be wise and kind
And as my heart can warm your heart, so may my mind, your
    mind.[30]

The sentiments the sampler verse illustrates, the desire for companionship, love, and closeness in the home, suggest that in reality the embroiderer experienced a profound lack of intimacy and intellectual deprivation. The need to believe in the domestic dream co-existed with a sharp awareness of its absence. Women blamed themselves, shouldered the entire responsibility for domestic discomfort – it was, after all, their social sphere. Mrs Ellis often warned that a wife could drive her husband from his home by the 'leaden weight of her uncompanionable society'. Obviously not every embroiderer was familiar with Sarah Ellis' strictures. Her historical importance lies in the fact that she voiced the Victorian ideology of domestic femininity. She also gave form to the fears arising from the Victorian marriage, encouraging women's tendency to blame themselves if all in the domestic sphere failed to fulfil the fantasies created by the mythology of femininity. In Sarah Ellis' words we can see where the ideal came into conflict with lived social relations – and worked to paper over the cracks.

Embroidery as an effort to create domestic 'comfort' was prompted not only by women's particular circumstances within the home; it was a symptom of a wider sense of insecurity amongst the middle class. Leonore Davidoff, Jean L'Esperance, and Howard Newby[31] argue that this shaped the physical character of the house. It was designed to create a sense of security as well as preserving inmates from rank pollution by inferiors. They point to the house's carefully guarded entrances with drives, gate and hedge, its attended portals and elaborate rituals of entrance. Inside, soft, warm, brightly coloured Berlin woolwork spread over everything: over curtains, portières, pianos, antimacassars, mantelpieces, tables, chairs, stools, screens, books, etc, providing a padding against the world outside, and emphasising how different were conditions inside where the lady of the house possessed all the virtues of domestic femininity. Virginia Woolf in her novel *Orlando* suggests that during the nineteenth century it was as if the whole of the British Isles were overhung by a great cloud, so that damp made its way into every house and accordingly 'Rugs appeared, beards were grown, trousers fastened tight under the insteps. The chill which he felt in his legs the country gentleman soon transferred to his house, furniture was muffled; walls and tables covered; nothing was left bare.'[32]

It was not enough for women to cover every available surface of the home with embroidered evidence of their presence, it was important that it be done with taste.

The concept of taste had shifted since the eighteenth century. For women it now connoted morality and spirituality, as much as class standing. Good taste was to be a 'regulating' factor in a woman's life; everything about her must convey the 'beauty of fitness'. Taste was demonstrated in the subjects she chose for her pictorial embroidery. The royal family was a popular subject which demonstrated the embroiderer's loyalty and patriotism, while associating her own home with the domestic virtues the royal family represented. Critics of upholstery stitched with portraits of royalty attacked the embroidery on moral, and aesthetic, grounds: 'The prince is subjected to the indignity of being trodden under foot', wrote Mrs Merrifield in the *Art Journal*, objecting to a footstool embroidered with the Prince of Wales. A painting by Sir Edwin Landseer of *The Macaw, Lovebirds, Terrier and Spaniel Puppies belonging to Her Majesty* was often embroidered. Animals were generally a popular subject and they, too, came under attack from Mrs Merrifield. 'The head of a dog or a fox is made to cover the front of a slipper, yet how absurd, not to say startling, is the effect produced by the head of one of these animals protruding from beneath the trousers of a sportsman!'[33]

However, no Victorian embroidery was simply gratuitous excess – every footstool and screen and pair of slippers made a statement about the family's social aspirations. Femininity was a sign of social status. The family's position was ensured and protected through the constant exercise and reinforcement of femininity embodied in embroidery. The content of embroidery, moreover, was as important as the act. The whole significance of the foxy slippers was that the wearer was most likely not to be a sportsman. Along with the rural scenes stitched and framed upon the wall, the fox evoked an idealised country life style. The businessman who returned in the evening to his urban home, slipped on the symbol of the country gentleman – he became a squire in a settled community in which everyone accepted their place. Embroidery represented the bourgeois family's ideal identity drawn from the modes of the gentry and the aristocracy.

During the nineteenth century it was taken for granted that real communities could only be found in the English countryside – there a 'natural order' persisted in the imagination of the town dweller, a stable hierarchy, virtuous, static, settled and paternalistic. The following verse, attached to an embroidered landscape, encapsulates this attitude and indicates how the young embroiderer had internalised a view of herself as the protector and preserver of Old English values:

> Will my dearest papa accept from my hand,
> A trifling estate and freehold, the land
> The buildings I raised; I planted the trees

The waters I formed for convenience and ease:
The castle looks well, and will stand many years
A pleasant retreat for you and your heirs,
When with business fatigued, or sick of the town,
The boat may attend to waft you safe down
The servants are humble, neat, cleanly, and still,
No impertinent answers disputing your will.
With pleasure I offer this picture to you.
If received with kindness, repaid is the care
Of your truly affectionate daughter
M. Eyre[34]

What appears to us as saccharine sentimentality was for the nineteenth-century middle-class embroiderer a manifestation of a crucial feminine quality, *feeling*. Taste was nothing without feeling. 'To be useful a woman must have feeling' wrote Elizabeth Sandford.[35] Her definition of feeling was 'forgetting oneself and sympathising with others'. That a woman's work should show *feeling* prompted numbers of embroidered pictures which hinged on the suffering of others. Very popular historical scenes included 'The Earl of Leicester's *Last* Interview with Amy Robsart', 'The *Last* Appeal', 'Mary Queen of Scots *Mourning* over the *Dying* Douglas at the Battle of Langside', 'Charles I *Bidding Farewell* to his Family'. All were repeatedly embroidered.

As ever with embroidery it is important to establish how far the choice of subject matter was determined by the general social, political and artistic developments of the time and how far women's specific experience and the history of embroidery dictated the needlewoman's choice. The suffering of humanity was a central subject of all the arts. Walter Houghton writes that:

The cult of benevolence took a new direction in the nineteenth century when the misery of the industrial workers became sufficiently apparent to demand redress – and all the more so because it constituted a threat to the social order. If one solution proposed . . . was a more earnest sense of social duty, another lay in quickening the moral sensibility to an acute sympathy for suffering humanity.[36]

Though scenes of suffering were common in literature and the visual arts, the expectation that embroidery would manifest

160

feminine virtues determined the particular form of suffering which women selected to stitch. Enforced separation of men and women was a dominant theme in their work. Perhaps the satisfaction attained from stitching scenes of suffering was that they suffused male/female relationships with warm sentiment, in the face of the chilly reality of a patriarchal marriage. Or perhaps the presentation of death and irrevocable parting evoked, if not the love it was their duty to feel, at least pity for the distant authoritarian male.

Another required attribute of femininity was piety – and, predictably, piety was expressed in embroidery. While it was countenanced for men to experience religious doubts prompted by Darwinism and the new sciences, a woman's faith in the scriptures had to be unquestioning. The writers on femininity made no bones about it. It was their duty to accept the authority of the word: 'It is easy to attend a few scientific lectures and return home talking of gasses . . . but it requires a totally different process of mind to bow before the conviction that all must have been created by a divine hand.'[37]

Obedience in every aspect of their lives was demanded of women from their first sampler to their last embroidered footstool but, in addition, they were expected to be a repository of traditional values in an uncertain world – thus the importance of their religious obedience. Piety was also represented to women as a source of power. 'The influence of a religious woman may extend far beyond her home,' wrote Elizabeth Sandford.[38]

Bible stories once again became the subject matter of embroidery. They had of course never been entirely abandoned, but throughout the eighteenth century pastoral and mythological scenes had dominated pictorial work. In nineteenth-century Berlin woolwork the most frequently repeated scenes were stories which turned on the paternal power of God (and man). 'The Sacrifice of Isaac' was traditionally popular with embroiderers but 'The Prodigal Son' and 'Joseph Presenting his Father to Pharoah' were new to the art. Paternal power and filial obedience were dominant themes of sampler verses:

> Be grateful to thy father for he
> gave thee life and to thy father for he
> sustained thee. Hear the words of his mouth
> for they are spoken for thy good. Give ear

> to their admonition for it proceeds
> from love. Let the bands of affection
> Unite thee with thy mother and sister
> that peace and happiness may dwell in
> thy father's house. To be good is
> to be happy
>
> *Elizabeth Haydn. Born 1828*

Another popular subject for embroidered pictures was 'Christ and The Woman of Samaria'. Jesus chose to convince the Samaritans that he was the Messiah through the agency of a woman he met at Jacob's well. It was a story guaranteed to appeal to embroiderers, so materially powerless, yet led to believe that piety would powerfully extend their influence beyond the home.[39]

At a more material level women employed needlework for pious ends by embroidering in aid of charity bazaars. Countless pincushions, caps, braces and mats were made to sell for good causes. Charlotte Brontë described an institution known as the 'Jews Basket', or 'Missionary Basket':

> Willow-repositories, of the capacity of a good-sized family clothes-basket, dedicated to the purpose of conveying from house to house a monster collection of pin-cushions, needle-books, card-racks, work-bags, articles of infant wear, etc, made by the willing or reluctant hands of the Christian ladies of the parish, and sold perforce to the heathenish gentlemen thereof, at prices unblushingly exorbitant. The proceeds of such compulsory sales are applied to the conversion of the Jews, the seeking up of the ten missing tribes, or to the regeneration of the interesting coloured population of the globe. Each lady-contributor takes it in her turn to keep the basket a month, to sew for it, and to foist off its contents on a shrinking male public.[40]

George Eliot was similarly scornful of sewing for bazaars, the usual mode of selling fancy work for charity. In *The Mill on The Floss* she describes how Lucy Deane and Maggie Tulliver prepare for a bazaar. 'Worsted flowers were growing under Lucy's fingers.' Lucy was the fair representative of femininity, while dark-haired Maggie, the representative of womanhood, is occupied with 'plain sewing'. Stephen Guest watches them work, and George Eliot observes that 'if Maggie had been the queen of coquettes she could hardly have invented a means of giving greater piquancy to her beauty in Stephen's eyes: I am not sure that the quiet admission of plain sewing would have done alone, but assisted by beauty, they made Maggie more unlike other women even than she had seemed at first.'[41] The bazaar itself represented the triumph of plain sewing and womanliness over fancy work and femininity. Maggie begs to be allowed to sell functional articles rather than 'bead mats and other elaborate products of which she had but dim understanding', and her stall was besieged by gentlemen.

But though George Eliot had no sympathy for the creations of femininity, she understood what drove women to embroider for bazaars. She conveys her attitude and analysis through Stephen Guest's words:

Here is another of the moral results of this idiotic bazaar . . . taking young ladies from the duties of the domestic hearth into scenes of dissipation among urn-rugs and embroidered reticules. I should like to know what is the proper function of women if it is not to make reasons for husbands to stay at home and still stronger reasons for bachelors to go out. If this goes on much longer the bonds of society will be dissolved.[42]

Skilfully George Eliot conveys the attraction of bazaars. They permitted women to cross the threshold into public life, to be mobile themselves instead of acting as anchors for others.

But there were other more material motivations behind bazaars. They were part of the Season's social calendar and could provide *nouveaux riches* families with an opportunity for mixing with a higher social stratum.[43] Aware that bazaars were not quite the pious, elevated events they purported to be, Lady Charlotte Neville Grenville feared that they would turn her nieces into shop women: 'I declare I do not know which I should dislike most,' she said, 'to hear of you waltzing or you selling, those who practise one would shine at the other.'[44]

Another public, pious outlet for embroidery was provided by the religious revival discussed in Chapter One. Charlotte Yonge explained why femininity made women pre-eminently suited to embroidering for the church: 'There are things . . . that can only be properly done by loving hands that spend much taste and time over them. Such are church embroideries.' In *The Family Secret*, a novel serialised in *The Englishwoman's Domestic Magazine*, one of the ladies' spiritual awakening is sardonically described: 'Little feeble touches of it she had experienced like other people, as when she brought wool and silk for that altarcloth.'[45]

Sampler verses reflected the religious changes of the times. Adherents of millenarist movements stitched samplers with words from *The Second Advent Harbinger* by the American adventist William Miller: 'Prepare to meet your God / that Heaven may be your home'.[46] Femininity was to be lived through pious, loving management of a home, and the reward for the attainment of perfect femininity was to be a heavenly home.

Within Judaism women traditionally presented their embroidery to the synagogue.[47] From the seventeenth century onwards it was received on the Sabbath with the following blessing: '. . . the One who blessed our mothers, Sarah, Rebecca, Rachel, and Leah, may He give His blessings to every daughter of Israel who makes a mantle or cloth for the honour of the Torah, may the Lord reward and remunerate her and let us say amen.' As Jews gained access to the sampler-making classes, their tradition of religious embroidery was translated into sampler making: Hebrew characters were added to the Roman lettering and Jewish religious symbols replaced Christian iconography. The public function of women's work was privatised.[48]

Embroidery was on the one hand expected to be the place where women manifested supposedly natural feminine characteristics: piety, feeling, taste, and domestic devotion; and on the other it was the instrument which enabled a woman to obliterate aspects of herself which did not conform to femininity. A passage in *Madam*, 1885, a novel by Mrs Oliphant, illustrates embroidery in its role as an instrument of repression in the production of femininity:

Her hands were like ice, her slight figure shivering with cold, yet her heart beating so that she could scarcely draw her breath. All this must disappear before the gentlemen came in . . . She felt sure that her misery, her anguish of suspense, her appalling doubts and terrors, must be written on her face; but it was not so. The emergency brought back a rush of warm blood tingling

164

78 *Florence Nightingale and her sister Parthenope,*
William White, National Portrait Gallery,
London. c 1836.
Florence Nightingale considered that embroidery
was symptomatic of the restraints imposed on
women by the feminine ideal. In *Cassandra* she
wrote, 'but suppose we were able to see a number
of men in the morning sitting round a table in
the drawing room, looking at prints, doing
worsted work, and reading little books, how we
should laugh.'

79 Sampler, Jane Bailey, Victoria and Albert
Museum, London.
The verse spells out the nineteenth-century code
of feminine behaviour.

Seek to be good but aim not to be great,
A woman's noblest station is retreat,
Her fairest virtues fly from public sight
Domestic worth still shuns too strong a light.

Jane Bailey her work ____ January 27th 1830.

NEEDLE-CRAFT. 157

together with cord run through eyelets and tied at the bottom, the ends being tipped with large plush balls. A beautiful spray of flowers in appliqué, in two parts, decorates the

fits the mantel perfectly is covered smoothly with the plush, and to it the lambrequin is secured. A few pretty ornaments on the mantel is all that is desirable, and when the

FIGURE NO. 11.—MANTEL-DRAPERY.

lambrequin. The spray is a selection from manufactured satin floral appliqués of which there is a very large variety. A board that

fire is not lighted in the grate a Japanese parasol will make a charming screen. China or India silk, Surah, cloth, crétonne, velvet,

80 Advertisement in *Needlecraft: Artistic and Practical*, Butterick, New York, 1889.
The appearance of an advertisement for a guide to etiquette in a book on embroidery indicates the extent to which the art was involved in the effort by the middle class to establish what was appropriate feminine drawing-room behaviour, as the home assumed a new role as a social centre.

81 Pattern for mantel drapery.
Purveyors of embroidery patterns emphasised their taste and elegance. They assured their customers that embroidery enhanced domestic happiness, providing the comfort that would win a husband's love and prove a wife's devotion.

83 Sampler, Bek Berta, Jewish Museum, New York. Mid-nineteenth century.
Given the long, rich history of embroidery in Jewish culture, it is not surprising to
find the tradition translated into sampler-making during the nineteenth century.
The existence of Jewish samplers indicates the pervasiveness of notions of ideal
femininity conveyed through embroidery, even when influenced by specific
cultural contexts.

82 (left) Embroidered picture, Christies, London. c 1825. Silk and chenille, 41 × 51 cm.
The embroiderer has depicted an ideal representation of family life. The father is
absent – in his sphere, the world of work and public business. The mother
embroiders in a natural but perfectly ordered, fenced off (or fenced in?) environment.
The children occupy themselves in ways considered appropriate to their sex.

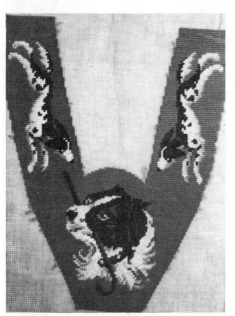

84 Slippers, unfinished, Castle Museum, Nottingham. Mid-nineteenth century. Berlin woolwork. 38.5 × 27.9 cm.

85 *The Prince of Wales*, Victoria and Albert Museum, London. c 1845. Berlin woolwork. Every pair of slippers, firescreen or footstool made a statement about the family's social aspirations. Rural motifs identified the urban home with an idealised image of country life; the Prince of Wales associated the home with the domestic virtues represented by the royal family; while the presence of embroidery in abundance asserted the femininity of the lady of the house – in itself a sign of social status.

to her fingers' ends . . . Then Rosalind took up the delicate work that lay on the table and when the gentlemen entered, was seated on a low seat within the circle of a shaded lamp, warm in the glow of the genial fireside, her pretty head bent a little over her pretty industry, her hands busy. She who had been the image of anxiety and unrest a moment before, was now the culminating point of all the soft domestic tranquility, luxury, boundless content and peace, of which this silent room was the home.[49]

Embroidery in Victorian novels is a signifier of femininity which is revealed as a mode of behaviour demanded by masculinity. Even while promoting and supporting 'pretty industry', Mrs Oliphant acknowledges that it is an artificial construct, an extraordinary act of self-repression motivated by fear. Charlotte Brontë presents the issue more critically. She deliberately reveals the curious contradictions in femininity through embroidery. In her work embroidery, and thus femininity, emerge as both self denial and self defence, as a means of establishing an inviolate female space and announcing female subservience and availability. Shirley Keeldar as the active, non-sexual, independent woman has little time for embroidery. 'She takes her sewing occasionally; but, by some fatality, she is doomed never to sit steadily at it for above five minutes at a time: her thimble is scarcely fitted on, her needle scarcely threaded when a sudden thought calls her upstairs . . . After tea Shirley reads, and she is just about as tenacious of her book as she is lax with her needle.'[50]

Once Shirley becomes aware of her love for Louis Moore all this changes. She takes up her work, 'the creation of a wreath of parma violets', and hides coyly behind it during an interview with her lover:

She suspended her work a moment . . . Mr Moore looked as if he had at last gained some footing in this difficult task . . . Mr Moore leaned back in his chair, and folded his arms across his chest; Miss Keeldar resumed her square of silk canvas, and continued the creation of parma violets . . . She smiled. She pursued her embroidery carefully and quickly; but her eyelash twinkled, and then it glittered . . .

Recalling the encounter later in his diary, Louis Moore writes

'I was near enough to count the stitches of her work, and to discern the eye of her needle.'[51]

Charlotte Brontë makes it plain that Shirley masks her own temperament, denies herself in order to appeal to Moore, protecting his masculinity and preventing him from feeling threatened by her economic power. Brontë apportions no blame and indicates that Shirley had no choice but to conform to the ideology of femininity; however she takes pleasure in demonstrating its failure. Louis Moore, far from being encouraged, is reduced to silence by the passive Shirley:

> The door unclosed; Miss Keeldar came in. The message it appeared had found her at her needle: she brought her work in her hand . . . This was no Thalastris from the fields, but a quiet domestic character from the fireside. Mr Moore had her at advantage: he should have addressed her at once in solemn accents [instead] . . . The tutor stood silent.[52]

In women's novels the crucial interview between lovers is invariably marked by the moment when the woman drops her work – with her embroidery inevitably goes her self-containment and she surrenders to her lover. Dinah M. Craik in *Agatha's Husband* allows her heroine no interval between dropping modest, maidenly femininity and adopting soothing, wifely femininity: 'She went on with her work, and he sat quietly looking at her for some little time more . . . She looked at him – saw how earnest he was, and put down her work. The softness of her manner soothed him.'[53]

Embroidery was intended to signify absolute innocence and subservience, but both Charlotte Brontë and Elizabeth Gaskell suggest it became an instrument of self defence for the subjugated sex. Charlotte Brontë described the defensive stance of femininity:

> Men rarely like such of their fellows to read their inward nature too clearly and truly. It is good for women especially, to be endowed with a soft blindness: to have mild, dim eyes, that never penetrate below the surface of things – that take all for what it seems: thousands, knowing this, keep their eyelids drooped on system; but the most downcast glance has its loophole, through which it can, on occasion, take its sentinel survey of life.[54]

In *Wives and Daughters*, 1866, Elizabeth Gaskell shows contrasting modes of using embroidery as a 'loophole' – for women to speak what they were unable to say openly. When Mrs Gibson has an unwelcome caller she demonstrates her displeasure through her worsted work: 'Mrs Gibson was at her everlasting worsted work frame when he entered; but somehow in rising to receive him, she threw down her basket of crewels, and, declining Molly's offer to help her, she would pick up all the reels herself, before she asked her visitor to sit down.' She successfully dominated her environment through the very medium that was expected to still and silence women. She counted her stitches 'aloud with great distinctness and vigour', she continually interrupted people 'with remarks about the pattern of her worsted work'. Above all she controlled the children in her care by setting them 'at piece after piece; knights kneeling to ladies; impossible flowers'.[55]

Her daughter Cynthia represents the effects of an education in femininity through embroidery. Mrs Gibson employed embroidery as a weapon; it both demonstrated her implacable domesticity and respectability and allowed her to control her immediate environment. Cynthia recapitulates her mother's behaviour but with a significant difference. Receiving the full force of her mother's aggression she fights back and the two are locked into subtle combat. Instead of refusing to embroider – a time-honoured gesture of defiance – Cynthia becomes overskilled at the art of embroidery. She cynically and brilliantly uses embroidery as a weapon, not in her mother's field of domestic femininity but in terms of sexual allure. While apparently presenting the picture of the innocent embroiderer, she projects an air of mystery and unobtainability: 'Cynthia, in obedience to her mother's summons, came into the room, and took up her work. No one could have been quieter – she hardly uttered a word; but Osborne seemed to fall under her power at once.'[56] Elizabeth Gaskell sympathises with Cynthia, acknowledging that her tactics are those of the powerless, but is nevertheless critical of the brand of femininity Cynthia so skilfully displays and deploys. Using embroidery as a signifier of femininity she contrasts Cynthia with her step-sister Molly who has none of Cynthia's skill with the needle. Molly's attitude towards embroidery represents uncorrupt, unselfconscious femininity. When she visits her friends the Hamleys, she takes her 'company worsted work' with her. Mrs Hamley remarks, 'Ah, you've got your sewing, like a good girl

. . . Now I don't sew much, I live alone a great deal, you see, both my boys are at Cambridge and the squire is out of doors all day long – so I have almost forgotten how to sew, I read a great deal.' She reads aloud to Molly who, 'As she became interested in the poem dropped her work, and listened in a manner that was after Mrs Hamley's own heart.'[57]

Although the Brontë sisters and Elizabeth Gaskell were highly critical of embroidery and its role in the creation of femininity, they nevertheless relied upon their readers' familiarity with the art, going so far as to date their stories by the kind of work the women were doing. In the *Tenant of Wildfell Hall*, 1848, Ann Brontë informs the reader that the action took place before the advent of Berlin woolwork embroidery. And Elizabeth Gaskell places *Wives and Daughters* firmly in the past by observing that 'people did worsted work in those days'.

Not only were books dated by the type of needlework then popular, but the days were described in terms of mornings or afternoons devoted to embroidery. In the regulation of social life in private homes embroidery played an ordering role. Even relations between women were ideally to be mediated through embroidery. Giving instructions on preparing a room for a friend, Sarah Ellis informed her reader that she must 'with her own hand place upon a table the favourite toilet-cushion, worked by a friend who was alike dear to herself and her guest.'[58] The habit of communicating their care for another through embroidery started early amongst women with friendship samplers:

> Dear Debby
> I love you sincerely
> My heart retains a grateful sense of your past kindness
> When will the hours of our
> Separation be at an end?
> Preserve in your bosom the remembrance
> of your affectionate
> Deborah Jane Berkin

When women called on one another they invariably worked together. Catherine Hutton, reminiscing about her early Victorian girlhood, recalls how awkward she felt when she called on two women friends empty handed: 'Miss Greves and Miss Boothby worked at their netting and embroidery, while I was an idle spectator, as I had brought no work with me.' It was a rare moment for Catherine Hutton to have no work. In her eighty-ninth year she drew up a list of her needlework:

> I have made furniture for beds, with window curtains, and chair and sofa covers; these included a complete drawing room set. I have quilted counterpanes and chest covers in fine white linen, in various patterns of my own invention. I have made patchwork beyond calculation, from seven years old to eighty-five . . . I worked embroidery on muslin, satin, and canvas, and netted upwards of 100 wallet purses, in combined colours, and in patterns of my own invention.[59]

Catherine Hutton emphasised with pride that her patterns were of her own invention, partly because of the unprecedented boom in mass-produced embroidery patterns in the early nineteenth century. Magazines, printers, and craft suppliers exploited the place of embroidery in the creation of femininity and promoted particularly lucrative styles of embroidery; lucrative in the sense that they demanded lavish materials and patterns. The first magazine to include embroidery patterns was the *Ladies Magazine or entertaining Companion for the Fair Sex*. The launching editorial in 1770 announced that the magazine intended to 'present the Sex with the most elegant patterns for the tambour, embroidery, or every kind of needlework . . . They will find in the Magazine, price only sixpence, among variety of other Copper-plates a pattern that would cost them double the money at the Haberdasher.'[60] So successful was the sales gimmick that other magazines followed suit. Patterns in magazines proliferated in the nineteenth century as women's magazines became increasingly directed towards domestic concerns.

Art equipment shops, known as repositories, began to produce their own magazines to help sales. Thus Ackerman's *The Repository of the Arts* wrote articles encouraging the embroidery that demanded the most equipment, available, of course, from Ackerman's. Writers for their magazine poured scorn on one branch of embroidery, employing all the arguments used by opponents of the art, in order to clear the reputation of another style of embroidery. In March 1810 an article condemned sampler making in favour of mixed media embroidery known as fancy work:

It is not long since needlework was considered, in our schools for young ladies, as one of the greatest accomplishments; and if a girl had gone home for the half yearly holidays without either an alphabet, a map, a flower or some wretched figure, the parents would have looked upon the system of the school as extremely deficient . . . Exclusive of the injurious effects of this branch of education on the health of children when kept for hours together stooping over one object during the whole of six, and, in a larger piece, perhaps twelve months, how was it possible that, with the vivacity of that tender age, they could be other wise than disgusted with continually looking at the same thing over and over again. Consequently nothing but force and threat on the one hand and promises of going home for the holidays on the other, could prevail upon them to apply to each tedious occupation. It is impossible to congratulate our fair country women too warmly on the revolution which has of late years taken place, when drawing and fancy work of endless variety have [replaced] that heavy, unhealthy, and stupefying occupation, needlework.[61]

Praise and ridicule are skilfully employed to encourage embroiderers to purchase the vast array of materials needed for fancy work: ribbons, spangles, silk, metal cords, feathers, beetle-wings, fish scales and aerophane (brightly-coloured silk gauze). Ackerman's was not alone in worrying about the effects of embroidery on children's health, but fancy work was no less laborious than sampler making. The writer was exploiting the ideology of 'ease' that was becoming an integral part of gentility. On the one hand embroidery was praised for the immense patience and labour it revealed – important in a culture which scorned idleness – and on the other, it was vital that an embroiderer not be seen to labour. 'Ease is the distinction of true breeding'[62] pronounced Elizabeth Sandford. Pattern publishers always stressed the 'easiness' of the pattern, assuring their customers that the 'executive part will be far from difficult'. In *Treasures of Needlework*, 1885, Mrs Warren and Mrs Pullan observed that 'To toil for those we love can never be a dull or painful task to a woman, even if the toil be great. But when it is merely the light and elegant occupation [of embroidery] . . .'[63]

Berlin woolwork was the century's most successful commercial embroidery venture for embroidery suppliers. The patterns were promoted as 'tasteful' and the embroidery as 'easy'.

Patterns printed on squares with each small square representing a stitch were developed in Germany and popularised by a Berlin printer. In 1810 Frau Wittich 'perceived the great extension of which this branch of trade was capable' and encouraged her husband's printing firm to begin producing patterns. The technique was facilitated by the invention of machine-made double-thread canvas and the new softer wools. The pattern was printed on paper with squares the same size as the canvas to be embroidered. British embroidery suppliers were quick to seize the possibilities of Berlin patterns. By 1840, 14,000 different patterns had been imported into England. One of the leading London repositories employed up to 1,200 young women to colour the patterns, paying them as little as six pence to eight pence a day and selling the early designs for £30 to £40 each.[64] Different kinds of canvas were available; English canvas varied from very fine, which allowed exact reproductions of painting, to coarse large-meshed canvas for simple designs. German woollen canvas came in shades of claret, black, white and primrose, cotton canvas had a bright yellow thread after every tenth square to help count stitches. French canvas had flattened threads. Wools were available in all thicknesses and colours. Silks, chenille thread and beads were sold for highlighting.

Berlin woolwork was both heavily promoted and constantly ridiculed. Comparing embroidery to the craze for collecting ferns – a great feature of the early 1850s – Charles Kingsley wrote that women

> find an enjoyment in it, and are more active, more cheerful, more self-forgetful over it, than they would have been over novels and gossip, crochet and Berlin-wool. At least you will confess that the abomination of 'Fancy work', that standing cloak for dreamy idleness (not to mention the injury which it does to poor starving needlewomen), has all but vanished from your drawing-room since the 'Lady Ferns' and 'Venus' hair' appeared; and that you could not help yourself looking now and then at the said 'Venus' hair', and agreeing that nature's real beauties were somewhat superior to the ghastly woollen caricatures which they had superseded.[65]

In a similar patronising and jocular vein a poem titled *The Husband's Lament* includes the following verses:

I hate the name of German wool, in all its colours bright,
Of chairs and stools in fancy work, I hate the very sight;
The shawls and slippers that I've seen, the ottomans and bags
Sooner than wear a stitch on me, I'd walk the streets in rags

The other day when I went home no dinner was for me,
I asked my wife the reason; she answered 'One, two, three'
I told her I was hungry and stamped upon the floor
She never even looked at me, but murmured 'One green more'

If any lady comes to tea, her bag is first surveyed,
And if the pattern pleases her, a copy there is made.
She stares too at the gentleman, and when I ask her why,
'Tis 'Oh my love, the pattern of his waistcoat struck my eye'

Besides the things she makes are such touch-me-not affairs
I dare not even use a screen – a stool – and as for chairs!
'Twas only yesterday I put my youngest boy on one
And until then I never knew my wife had such a tongue[66]

Unerringly, male wits from the seventeenth century onwards *needled* embroiderers where it most hurt in mocking the feminine characteristics embroidery was intended to manifest. During the eighteenth century they lampooned the embroiderer's association with nature, writing derisively of ladies 'transplanting all the Beauties of Nature into their own Dress, or raising a new Creation in their closets'. In the nineteenth century, when embroidery was intended as evidence of a woman's self-denying, loving, giving, effortless yet never idle femininity, this 'poet' represented embroidery as selfish and obsessional, leading a wife to neglect her cardinal duty: that of providing for her husband's comfort.

Another mode of mockery was to belittle embroidery itself. In the eighteenth century men sneered at the fact that embroidery was considered a creative activity by women: 'Sir, she's an Artist with her needle . . .' Could anything be more laughable than a woman claiming artistic status for her sewing? In the nineteenth century, when women had learned not to claim creative merit for embroidery but to assert that it was labour for love, men mocked it as a mere pastime, just one of many trivial occupations which filled a woman's day. In *The Husband's Lament* the wife offers her own 'defence' against the husband's accusation that all she does is embroider: 'you seem to think worsted work is all the ladies do' she says, and goes on to describe her 'full' day paying bills, hemming a duster, feeding the canary, 'practising that concerto thing, you thought so fine', writing notes to ask friends to dine, filling vases with fresh flowers, and

> After that – I will confess – I sorted out my wool.
>
> Besides to tell the truth, all the worsted work I do,
> My bag, my cushion, and my chairs are in compliment to you!
> I made a set of night shirts, and did you not declare
> That the rending of the calicoe was more than you could bear
>
> I knit some lamb's wool stockings, and you kicked up such a
>   rout
> And asked how soon my ladyship was going to have the gout!
> Enough of banter; yet believe one word before we part –
> The rest perhaps was fable; but this is from the heart, –
> The loving wife, right cheerfully obeys her husband still
> And will ever lay aside her frame to meet his lordly will[67]

Mocking, prescriptive, sentimental, *The Husband's Lament* marks a low point amongst the many laughs society has had at the expense of femininity.

Once embroidery had become an accepted tool for inculcating and manifesting femininity in the privileged classes, with missionary zeal it was taken to the working class. Teaching embroidery to the poor became an aspect of Victorian philanthropy. Writers of embroidery manuals for the middle class, Mrs Warren and Mrs Pullan, hoped that 'The work may grace the Boudoir of the Peeress, and also penetrate into the cottage of the Peasant; that while it can become a source of useful recreation to the rich, it may also prove a reliable aid to the industrious effort of the poor.'[68] The Factory Act of 1833 required employers to provide two hours' schooling a day for child workers. In girls' schools an hour and three quarters were devoted to needlework. In *The Art of Needlework*, 1840, Elizabeth Stone had nothing but praise for this allocation of time:

Any of our readers who have been accustomed, as we have, to see the domestic hearths and homes of those who, brought up from infancy in factories, have married young, borne large families and perhaps descended to the grave without ever having learned how to make a petticoat for themselves, or even a cap for their children – any who know the reality of this picture, and have seen the misery consequent on it, will join us cordially in expressing the earnest and heartfelt hope that the extension of mental tuition amongst the lower classes may not supersede, in the smallest iota, that instruction and practice in sewing which next to knowledge of their catechism, is of vital importance to the future well-doing of girls in the lower stations of life.[69]

But while embroidery was associated with goodness, meekness and obedience and thus eminently suitable in Victorian eyes for working-class girls and women, it was nevertheless dangerously suggestive of class aspirations. Differences were maintained in embroidery practised by each class, dictated both by material restrictions and by ideologies about what was appropriate or possible in the hands of working-class women. Samplers produced in institutions, orphanages or village schools were far less colourful than those of middle- or upper-class girls. Some do include improving verses and border patterns but most were simply numbers and alphabets. The symbols of privilege – the basket of flowers, the mansions, lily pots and peacocks – had no place in working-class samplers.

By 1821, government regulations ensured, for example, that functional stitchery – darning samplers – dominated the working-class child's education: 'The child to perform the work in two colours, yellow and blue, on linen that it may appear more distinctly. When a child has completed one of these darns she may practise on a small piece of muslin in which a hole has been torn.'[70]

Once a girl had become skilled in fine stitchery she might still have found work as a professional hand embroiderer during the first half of the nineteenth century. Initially industrialisation encouraged hand embroidery. The newly wealthy industrialists stimulated the market for luxury goods – when the social structure is in flux embroidery is invariably in demand as a status symbol. Not only did the market for embroidery expand, but the mechanical production of muslin and net created new and plentiful material as a base for whitework embroidery.

A series of styles and techniques of whitework was developed during the nineteenth century in response to the new machine-made nets and muslins. The new techniques could be practised without a frame, and embroiderers were thus able to work at home. Thousands of women were employed to embroider, particularly in Scotland, Ireland and in the vicinity of Nottingham, Derby and Leicester. The first whitework to supersede tamboured muslin (see Chapter Six) was called Ayrshire work. More durable than tambour work, it was initiated by Mrs Jameson of Ayrshire c. 1814, and applied until c. 1870 to a wide variety of garments from christening robes to riding habits. Ayrshire work is characterised by firmly padded satin stitch, stem stitch and beading, lightened by cut-out spaces filled with needlepoint lace.

The material with the design printed upon it was distributed to women in their homes. By 1857 it was estimated that 80,000 women in Scotland were homeworking muslin and some 400,000 in Ireland.[71] Children as young as three years old were employed as 'drawers'. With a needle they would draw out the thread which joined single widths of machine-made net. Aged nine or ten they became 'menders', tying the short broken threads in the net, or 'runners', embroidering the patterns of fine curling foliage. A group of women and children would usually work in the home of one of their number – parents had their own children work with other adults whom they believed would extract more labour from them.

The Factory Commission of 1833 and the Children's Employment Commission of 1843 reported on conditions amongst the lace runners. Not only was the work badly paid but it was physically damaging. Many embroiderers were blind by the time they were twenty, or too weakened for any other occupation. A Nottingham doctor reported that he personally had treated 10,000 cases of injured eyes in fourteen years. A lace embroiderer described her day to the 1843 commission: 'We are reckoned to begin at six; sometimes later. We keep on to ten generally. Take two hours for meals. These are longer hours than in the factory. It is not so very tiring as we sit down all day; instead of standing all day. It is a very bad trade for the eyes. Where I sit I can't see the hands and figures on the clock face a bit.'[72]

Embroiderers would splash whisky on their eyes to sharpen their vision momentarily; their bodies would become painfully misshapen, their lungs constricted from bending over the work, yet they were reported to prefer it to factory work: 'I like it better than the factory, though we can't get so much. We have our own liberty at home, and get our meals comfortable, such as they are.'[73] However, they attempted to organise to change their conditions. They considered that a major cause of their exploitation was the system of distributing material to embroiderers. Warehouses gave out the net or muslin to mistresses or agents who not only employed embroiderers but gave out material to other mistresses. So sometimes there was a hierarchy of two or three mistresses taking a percentage of the profits, and often covering their take by lying to the embroiderers about the price offered by the warehouses.

In 1840 a group of Nottingham lace embroiderers issued a circular against the distribution system. Addressing other embroiderers, they asked: 'Sisters . . . are you to be robbed of your hard-earned pittance to maintain those cormorants in idleness, and many of their husbands in drunkenness and profligacy – no wonder that misery enters our dwellings – that we are in the depth of poverty, that our children are crying for bread, while there is a swarm of locusts hovering between us and the manufacturers ready to devour one half of our hire, it is not enough that we have to compete with machines which in many cases, supersede needle-work; but we are also robbed in the manner described . . .'[74]

The committee of five women who drafted the circular concluded by calling upon embroiderers to strike and for men to support them 'as it is the cause of the poor working man as much as females'. The committee requested that manufacturers stamp the price of each piece of embroidery on the material to prevent the middlewomen from cheating them: 'It would effectively put an end to the system of which we complain. The average earning of the single woman employed in embroidery of lace does not amount to more than two shillings and six pence per week! Comment is useless, we appeal to your humanity.'[75]

The strike was a failure; the mistresses intimidated the younger women from joining it and the net manufacturers were entirely unmoved by the women's appeal to their humanity. Public concern about the lace embroiderers came only when it appeared that the conditions were threatening their behaviour as wives and mothers: 'One of the most appalling features connected with the extreme reduction that has taken place in the wages of lace runners, and the consequent long hours of labour, is that married women, having no time to attend to their families, or even to suckle their offspring, freely administer opium in some form or other to their infants.'[76] And the young women 'almost all become prostitutes'. These claims made by the Factory Commission, 1833, and the Children's Employment Commission, 1843, were dramatised by Charlotte Elizabeth Tonna in her novel about Kate Clark, a lace runner's apprentice, *Wrongs of Women*, 1844. A country girl accustomed to open air and an active life, Kate's first day as a 'drawer' is undiluted agony: 'All the livelong day to sit over a trumpery fine thing, and not to go out, not to move, not to look up, not to speak! My feet are as cold as stone, just with sitting still; and my eyes are as good as poked with part of one day's picking of those good for nothing threads.'

Looking round at the other children and women working in the dark cottage she observes 'how white they are – how thin – how crooked they look'. Slowly Kate's resistance to the conditions ebbs away: she develops a chronic sore throat, aching limbs, becomes subject to fits of hysteria and, worst of all, her 'eyes smart and burn, and are, even in the deepest darkness, constantly oppressed by the pressure of balls and sparkles of light when she tries to sleep'. The drama of the novel lies in the conflict between the embroiderers' natural femininity – instinctive motherliness, kindness and sexlessness – and the evil unfeminine behaviour forced upon them by their struggle for survival. This innate femininity is proved by their ability to produce embroidery, white and pure in the gloom and dirt of the cottage. It is the system which inexorably degrades them. When Kate's employer has a baby the mother resorts to drugging it so that she can keep working. Slowly the baby starves to death. Taking Kate with her, the mother approaches the warehouseman for an advance on her embroidery to pay for the baby's coffin. He suggests that instead they exploit Kate's charms. Finally, wrecked and unfit for any other employment, Kate does indeed turn to prostitution. Charlotte Elizabeth Tonna had no doubt where the blame belonged:

The paper covering is removed from the delicate lace on which she is tracing an intricate and elaborate pattern. Some blooming bride will probably shade her face with that costly veil, amid the sumptuous preparations for a wedding, in the prospect of luxuries the means of providing which may possibly be traced to some successful speculation on the productiveness of pauper industry.[77]

By the 1880s machines which embroidered had been perfected, and embroidery ceased to be widely manufactured by hand. Cleared of its associations with the suffering lace runners, hand embroidery could be prized and sentimentalised for its evocation of home, hearth and heart.

Professional rural hand embroidery was fostered by the Arts and Crafts Movement.[78] At one level the number of philanthropic rural craft projects was an expression of the Victorian idealisation of country life. They also provided the satisfaction of controlling small, manageable local communities in the face of the 'uncontrollable' urban growth which characterised the nineteenth century. In addition, during the 1880s rural depopulation was increasing and the idea of revitalising the countryside and consolidating the rural economy 'carried a powerful humanitarian and patriotic appeal'.[79]

For middle-class women, organising rural embroidery projects was in line with the vocation of femininity. Elizabeth Gaskell observed sardonically in *Wives and Daughters* that '. . . it was always supposed that no strangers had seen Hollingford properly, unless they had been taken to the countess' school and been duly impressed by the neat little pupils, and the still neater needlework there to be inspected.'[80]

The overt reason for fostering rural craft industries was the economic hardship of peasant women whose husband's wage could not support a family, but a mixture of moralism and practicality informed the work: a contemporary writer described a worker in a rural industry as 'one of those to whom the industry has been a real blessing, enabling her to keep her tiny home together without becoming a burden to anyone.'[81]

Embroidery was expected to improve the moral quality of the workers: craft work 'brought comfort and orderliness into many a home, whose mistress is now to be found busily engaged by her own fireside, instead of gossiping beside her neighbours.'[82] There

86 *The Charity Bazaar,* Strangers Hall Museum, Norwich.
Bazaars played an important role in the Victorian social structure. The sewn and stuffed model of a bazaar stall shows two ladies presiding over an assortment of knitted, crocheted, embroidered and fancy work objects.

87 Illustration from the *Penny Magazine,* 1843. Photo: Laurie Sparham.
The drawing shows lace runners, as the women who embroidered machine-made
net in whitework were known, at work in a cottage.

88 Ayrshire work, Victoria and Albert Museum, London. Photo: Laurie Sparham
Ayrshire work was initiated by Mrs Jameson of Ayrshire in 1814, and continued to
be used on clothing until c 1870. The work was distributed to women in their
homes, and by the 1850s thousands of women in Scotland were employed
embroidering muslin. Whitework embroiderers invariably had seriously impaired
sight by the age of twenty if they started work as small children.

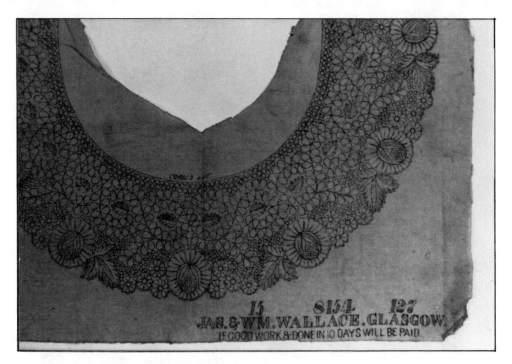

89 Pattern for Ayrshire work, Castle Museum, Nottingham. Mid-nineteenth century. 26.7 × 35.5 cm.

90 The Showroom at the Royal School of Art Needlework. Photo: Anthea Callen. The late nineteenth-century middle class emulated seventeenth-century crewel embroidery. The uniformity of style was a result of the school's credo that 'each must copy humbly and faithfully the design which should always be before her' – a mode of working in line with a feminine ideal of humility and docility.

91 Unfinished embroidery, May Morris, designed by William Morris, Victoria and Albert Museum, London.

From 1880 William Morris placed his firm's embroidery workshop in his daughter May Morris' hands. She was a skilled needleworker and designer, wrote extensively on embroidery and taught the subject at the Central School of Arts and Crafts in London.

was of course a difference maintained between the effects of embroidering in a middle-class woman's and a working-class woman's home. When a middle- or upper-class woman embroidered, it was her 'taste' which shed a moral, spiritual light; when a working-class woman embroidered the change to her surroundings came not from the woman herself but from the embroidery.

> When cottage mothers are engaged in the production of beautiful fabrics the whole family must benefit thereby, learning unconsciously to appreciate beautiful things, and also receiving a much needed training in conscientious work, no mean advantage in these days of scamping. Beauty has always a refining influence and the power of producing it markedly increases the self-respect of the maker.[83]

This was the ideology of the Arts and Crafts Movement. Its proponents believed that good design and beautiful objects would raise the moral tone of society. Good craft work and middle-class women were, in their different ways, both considered sources of moral purity and spirituality. In the midst of the social upheaval of the Industrial Revolution the angel in the house was to lead her husband's thought to higher states of existence and, in the face of an increasing division of labour, good craft work was to preserve an ideal of the dignity of labour.

The movement, which was well underway by the early 1890s, involved a range of craft workers and artists who believed that mechanisation, far from easing drudgery, meant longer hours, heavier work and the production of shoddy, ugly goods. Like its most famous member, William Morris, many members of the movement were socialists who wanted to make art available to everyone, and to unite artists, designers and craft workers. Accordingly the movement promoted the development of small workshops and countrywide organisations which taught craft skills, exhibited and marketed craft work. William Morris even envisaged a time when the sexual division within the domestic arts would vanish for ever. He anticipated the day when 'the domestic arts; the arrangement of the house in all its details, marketing, cleaning, cooking, baking and so on' would be in the hands of everyone and 'whoever was incapable of taking an interest and a share of some parts of such work would have to be considered diseased, and the existence of many diseased persons would tend to the enslavement of the weaker sex.'[84]

However, the democratic ideals of the movement soon foundered. One of the leading members, Charles Ashbee, complained, 'We have made of a great social movement a narrow and tiresome little aristocracy working for the very rich.'[85]

But what of the effects of the Arts and Crafts Movement on embroidery and its association with femininity? In itself the movement would have changed the relationship hardly at all. But it coincided with the emergence of a powerful Suffrage Movement, with campaigns in favour of wider professional and educational opportunities for women, and a growing body of feminist literature criticising the restrictions imposed in the name of femininity. Once women began to push out the boundaries of Victorian femininity, the encouragement given to embroidery by the Arts and Crafts Movement was historically responsible for profound changes within the practice of embroidery. Initially, however, all the movement did was to promote a new style of needlework.

William Morris is credited with changing the face of Victorian embroidery single-handedly. In the 1850s he did make a personal gesture towards breaking down the art's sexual division of labour. Jane Morris described how she and her husband 'studied old pieces [of crewel embroidery] and by unpicking and etc we learned much – it was uphill work, fascinating but only carried through by enormous hard work and perseverance.'[86] The implication that the Morrises alone had re-discovered the lost art of crewel embroidery is somewhat misleading. Miss Lambert's *Handbook of Needlework*, 1842, had referred to the process. Moreover, once Morris had mastered the needle, he left it to the women of his household. Anthea Callen has described the extent to which the mode of production in Morris, Marshall and Faulkner – and right across the Arts and Crafts Movement – maintained an entirely traditional sexual division of labour. Women staffed the embroidery workshop, which from 1880 William Morris placed in the hands of his daughter, May Morris.[87]

As commercial pattern producers, Morris, Marshall and Faulkner hardly deviated from established nineteenth-century traditions. The production of patterns for amateur needlewomen was the firm's most successful venture. The articles available from the firm, either as finished goods or ready traced as transfers, were the same as those offered in contemporary women's magazines: portières, billiard-table covers, wall-panels, firescreens, cushion covers, book covers, blotters, photograph frames, work bags, sachets, doilies and tea cosies. The instructions Morris issued to embroiderers to 'have nothing in your house that you do not know to be useful or believe to be beautiful'[88] echoed the way the magazines had for decades advertised their patterns as 'uniting use and beauty'. The designs provided for amateur needlewomen did however mark a move away from Berlin wool patterns. They were far more arduous. Printed on silk or linen, with a supply of specially dyed thread, a corner of the pattern was already worked as an instruction to the embroiderer. Barbara Morris in her excellent history, *Victorian Embroidery*, 1962, expressed surprise that Morris 'with his insistence on the joy of creative labour should consider that repeated patterns were suitable for embroidery'.[89] He simply transposed his designs for chintzes and wallpapers, with their repeating sinuous shapes, to embroidery patterns.

Historically William Morris was the link between the embroidery revival that began during the 1840s under the influence of mediaevalism, and the so-called 'Art Needlework' that flourished in the 1880s. In his criticism of aniline dyes, and his emphasis on the importance of carefully selecting and respecting materials, he was repeating what the proponents of mediaevalism had long preached. Morris himself had worked in the office of the architect G.E. Street who was closely associated with one of the major practitioners of the revival of mediaeval embroidered prototypes, Agnes Blencowe. Morris' involvement with mediaevalism can be seen in his early figurative embroidery designs. He designed a set of hangings based on Chaucer's *Illustrious Women*, for the Red House in Walthamstow, reviving the subject matter of heroic women so popular in the seventeenth century, and so subtly oppressive to women. Jane Morris and Elizabeth Burden stitched the illustrious women. Another vast embroidery project was conceived by Morris, in partnership with Edward Burne-Jones, for Lady Margaret Bell and her daughter Florence Johnson to stitch. Together they spent eight years embroidering the freeze from Chaucer's *Romance of the Rose*.

These two projects suggest what lay behind the apparent inconsistencies in Morris' attitude towards craft work as a whole and embroidery in particular. He believed that in the middle ages

181

designer and executor had been one, and that there had been no division between artist and craftworker. He insisted that 'The handicraftsman, left behind by the artist when the arts sundered, must come up with him, must work side by side with him.'[90] But when it came to embroidery, the idealised mediaeval image that dominated his thinking was not the collective craft workshop but the solitary stitching damsel. In Chapter One I described the particular ideological reading of the history of mediaeval embroidery provided by the Victorians. Morris was no more immune than anyone else to that image. Indeed, the Pre-Raphaelite Brotherhood, with whom he was associated, contributed to the creation of an ideal of romantic 'mediaeval' femininity.

It was the image of the mediaeval embroiderer – aristocratic, timeless, willowy, patient, natural, naive and unobtainable – that shaped Morris' advice to contemporary needlewomen. In *Some Hints for Pattern Designing*, 1881, he warns that the technical possibilities of embroidery are 'apt to lead people into a cheap naturalism'. He goes on to say that the needs of 'our material' and the nature of the craft in general demand that 'our rose and the like, however unmistakable roses, shall be quaint and naive to the last degree.' He urges embroiderers to think of their work as 'gardening with silk and gold thread' and concludes with a warning that because embroidery is 'an art which may be accused by ill-natured persons of being a superfluity of life, we must be specially careful that it shall be beautiful and not spare labour to make it sedulously elegant of form and every part of it refined in line and colour.'[91] Women and embroidery seem again to be elided; the embroiderer must be on guard to produce 'sedulously elegant', refined, natural, naive and quaint work.

Given William Morris' failure to challenge the contradictory notions of femininity associated with embroidery and expected of an embroiderer, the terms his biographer E.P. Thompson uses to criticise his poetry are poetic justice indeed. He writes 'This verse is less like music than embroidery with its repeated decorative motifs, its leisurely movement, its moody, imprecise vocabulary. Just for a moment the languorous movement of the rhythm is broken . . .'[92] Leisurely, moody, imprecise, languorous – the twentieth-century view of embroidery, or of she who embroiders?

The ideas that William Morris promoted – an admiration for seventeenth-century crewel embroidery, an emphasis on quality materials – were given form in 'Art Needlework' promoted by the Royal School of Art Needlework, founded in 1872 by Helen Welby and Lady Marion Alford. In her compendious work *Needlework as Art*, 1886, Lady Marion acknowledged the school's debt to Morris but firmly distinguished their work from his.

Only the sobriety and tenderness of his colouring, she writes, 'reconciles us to his repetitions of large vegetable forms which remind us sometimes of a kitchen-garden in tornado. For domestic decoration we should, as far as possible, adhere to reposing forms and colours. Our flowers should lie in their allotted spaces, quiet and undisturbed by elemental struggles, which have no business in our windowed and glass-protected rooms.'[93]

Lady Marion Alford stresses the domestic, feminine nature of the school's work and workers, partially to offset the school's commercial character. The Royal School provided employment and training for impoverished gentlewomen who, ideally destined only for marriage, had to support themselves. Though professional embroidery had long been one of the few respectable ways for such women to earn their keep, it was still vital for the school to stress that their embroidery was ladylike and their labour genteel.

The need for an organisation along the lines of the Royal School was demonstrated by the number of others that soon appeared. Some guaranteed a reassuring anonymity: 'Ten shillings and six pence per annum will entitle any lady to exhibit twelve articles at a time on sale at the Crystal Palace Stall. Proceeds are forwarded monthly, and strictest confidence is observed with regard to the names and addresses of the members.'[94] The Ladies Work Society obtained commissions for needlework to be stitched by members in their own homes. The society announced that it intended to 'temper the taste' of the designs offered in order to 'provide work of a useful, artistic and elevating character for ladies dependent on their own exertions.'[95] The patronising tone was prompted by the fact that it was subtly assumed to be a lady's fault if she was dependent on her own exertions: somewhere she must have strayed from the ways of virtuous femininity.

The Royal School of Needlework managed to present its work

not *as* work, but as simply the fulfilment of the vocation of femininity, by subscribing to the Arts and Crafts Movement's belief in the morally elevating effect of good design. They described their aims in terms of a crusade 'to please our public and to educate its taste. We wish to adorn and improve.'[96]

The fear of failing to be feminine even affected the mode of working at the School. It was emphasised that independence and initiative were outside the sphere of the embroiderer: 'I would impress on all, workers and superintendents too, that nothing should be left to the imagination of the stitcher, that each must copy humbly and faithfully the design which should be always placed before her.'[97]

A number of artists supplied the schools with designs, including William Morris, Sir Edward Burne-Jones, Sir Frederick Leighton and E.J. Pointer. Designers, artists and architects constantly reiterated that embroiderers were not artists. It is true that embroidery and painting are very different arts but rather than analysing the difference, theorists either aimed to keep embroiderers in their place, or to maintain embroidery as a signifier of femininity and social status. Thus Lewis F. Day, designer, wrote, 'Let her, unless she is inwardly compelled to invent, remain content to do good needlework. That is her art.'[98] The architect H.M. Baillie Scott stated,

> If it is necessary to compete with the painter, what can we achieve with the needle that cannot be achieved with the brush? There are many things. The sheen of silk, the glitter of jewels, the gleam of pearls are not the least among them . . . the essential feature is the display of the qualities of the materials.[99]

That an art work should express the character of the materials used was a tenet of art theorists opposed to *art nouveau* which gave the illusion of soft forms out of hard materials. But basically Baillie Scott is making a plea that embroidery be an object of luxury and display rather than one of aesthetic interest.

The reason why these men were so keen to keep embroiderers (and embroidery) in their place was quite simply that they were edging out of it. Fifty-odd years of campaigning by women for the recognition of needlework as art was taking effect. And whatever criticism can be levelled at the Arts and Crafts Movement in terms of sexism and elitism, it was instrumental in raising the standard of hand embroidery and allowing women to recognise the value of their work, not as mere evidence of the femininity which would enable them to attain male financial support, but as something which actually earned them money. *The Young Ladies Journal* attempted to express the profound changes that had occurred in embroidery: 'It is about seven years since embroidery once again became the favourite work of English ladies; for many years previous to that time, only the professional embroiderers dared to venture upon any work which was by most women regarded as extremely difficult.'[100]

'Art Needlework' could have done nothing more than produce a style of embroidery which evoked an ever more refined femininity. Based on seventeenth-century crewel embroidery and influenced by the aesthetic movement, irises, daffodils and cranes replaced the roses and parrots of Berlin woolwork. Predictably the embroidery soon became an object for snide ridicule: 'And what is our idea of ornament? Counterfeited down to its thorns and filmy petals, the wild rose is displayed in woolly crewels or fraying soft silks upon a piece of linen.'[101] But the development of Art Needlework coincided with the feminist challenge to the constraints of femininity. The climate was changing, it was possible for women to resist the taunts, to refuse to drop the mocked style in favour of a more 'convincing' show of femininity.

In 1894 a group of students at the Glasgow School of Art, headed by Charles Rennie Mackintosh, mounted an exhibition of furniture, metal work and embroidery – all in a very particular style. Organic forms characteristic of the style known as *art nouveau* were disposed on a geometric grid within a colour scheme of pearly-greys, silver and lilac set off by black and white. Embroidery had a place as one of a number of media contributing to the overall scheme. The woman responsible for embroidery at the Glasgow School of Art was Jessie R. Newbery, who started a needlework class in 1894 and taught there until 1908. She set forth her design principles in the *Studio* of 1898:

I believe in education consisting of seeing the best that has been done. Then, having this high standard before us, in doing what we like to do; *that* for our fathers, *this* for us.

I believe that nothing is common or unclean; that the design or decoration of a pepper pot is as important, in its degree, as

185

the conception of a cathedral.

I believe that material, space, and consequent use discover their own exigencies and as such have to be considered well.

. . . I like the opposition of straight lines to curved; of horizontal to vertical; of purple to green, of green to blue . . . I specially aim at beautifully shaped spaces and try to make them as important as the patterns.

I try to make most appearance with least effort but insist that what work is ventured on is as perfect as maybe.[102]

Anthea Callen calls this statement Newbery's artistic creed. The moral fervour of 'virtuous femininity' does indeed ring in her words, through the language and theory of her art school training. But aspects of her 'creed' completely transgress the confines of femininity. She speaks the language of desire, not that of duty, says firmly what she likes and what she wants. She believes that nothing is common or unclean. She renounces obedience and announces her independence of 'our fathers'. Not only does she reject the self-denying stance of femininity, but she views embroidery in a new light, not as something springing spontaneously from an embroiderer's natural femininity, but as an art with a history which determines but need not limit its practice. Previous theorists had seen embroidery in terms of a past that should be rejected, just as past forms of femininity were rejected as old-fashioned and 'wrong' or conversely rigidly advocated as 'right' in the face of an immoral present. And whereas other theorists wanted work to be 'perfect' in order *to improve the embroiderer,* Jessie Newbery wanted work 'as perfect as maybe' *for the sake of the design.*

Initially her class had provided an extra subject for students at the school, or for young women from Glasgow most of whom wished to become professional embroiderers. However, around 1900 the Scottish Education Department issued regulations for the further training of teachers. Embroidery was designated an important part of the normal school curriculum, and the Glasgow classes were opened to women teachers from the city and throughout the West of Scotland. Ann Macbeth who had studied at the Royal School of Needlework was put in charge of classes. She developed a way of teaching the art which still forms the basis of contemporary embroidery instruction.

If Jessie Newbery loosened the hold of femininity on

embroidery, Ann Macbeth could be said to have undermined its class connections. The silks and satins of Art Needlework were abandoned in favour of cheaper fabrics. Her basic principle was that the design should arise out of the technique employed. Students were encouraged to invent their own designs rather than obediently following patterns. Specimens of the embroidery demonstrating the technique were sent to schools throughout Britain, and women from Glasgow lectured widely on their methods. Women's Co-operative Guilds organised classes run in association with the Glasgow Art School. The face of embroidery in schools was transformed and its place in art schools far more assured.

While in no way underestimating the transformation achieved by the embroiderers at the Glasgow School of Art, their work needs to be viewed in the context of the history of women. Their innovations in embroidery coincided with women gaining access to wider areas of public life. But each new gain for women was accompanied by a new dividing line between male and female territory. While Newbery and Macbeth loosened the hold of femininity on embroidery, treating it as an art form rather than an extension of the embroiderer, simultaneously needlework in schools became institutionalised as the province of female staff and girls. The School Board for London Final Report, 1902, observed that 'The boys in the infants school were at one time taught Needlework with the girls; but this was altered in 1890, the boys now generally taking Drawing, while the girls take Needlework.'[103]

The needlework class was self-supporting; girls were expected to buy the articles they made. Items varied from practical garments – chemises, drawers, aprons, dusters – to fancy needlework including dolls' hats, pin cushions and reins. Education for girls was still a training in femininity through needlework, to the extent that boys were given books for prizes while girls were rewarded by being permitted to take home their needlework without first paying for it.[104]

School records reveal that girls did not always acquiesce to the dominance of needlework in their school lives. A Lambeth School log book entry reads: 'Commenced work this afternoon with a large attendance in consequence of having told the girls that we were going to have lessons instead of needlework.'[105]

In girls' public secondary schools, started in the late nineteenth century, teachers themselves rejected embroidery. Following a feminist tradition they supported plain sewing instead. A pupil of The North London Collegiate wrote:

> Whether Miss Buss, like my mother, had been so overdosed with it herself that she did not care to inflict it on the young, or whether she considered it a feminine and feeble pursuit, easily picked up at home, the result was joyful enough for me . . . Turning her back on the frivolities of embroidery Miss Buss encouraged plain sewing . . .[106]

However, school inspectors were vociferous in their criticism of the scant time devoted to needlework in these schools. By the turn of the century, 'accusations of unwomanliness' and 'over-pressure' led the schools, often very reluctantly, to start structured classes in needlework and embroidery.[107]

After the Education Act of 1902, the curriculum for all girls in secondary education included needlework. In state secondary schools boys did woodwork while girls did needlework. The class division which has always characterised needlework changed; for working-class girls, needlework was connected to domestic work in preparation for their future as wives, mothers or domestic servants; for middle-class girls needlework was increasingly taught as an art, following the principles established by the women at the Glasgow School of Art.

Embroidery and femininity were being transformed, but not separated.

8: A Naturally Revolutionary Art?

As we have seen, the Victorians presented the link between embroidery and women as entirely natural, thus concealing the complex social, political and economic factors that had connected the two since the middle ages. The twentieth century, receiving the full weight of Victorian literature on the subject, accepted embroidery as evidence of the naturalness of femininity. In this chapter I shall look at the legacy of nineteenth-century attitudes towards the art and women.

The range of twentieth-century embroidery is enormous. It is practised professionally by artists, dressmakers, embroiderers, teachers, and by millions of women as a 'leisure art'. Rather than attempting to encompass it all, I shall concentrate on specific instances in which embroidery became part of a move to transform the relationship of art to society, and the place of women within society. Previous chapters traced the evolution of the link between embroidery and femininity, largely through the history of British embroidery, though I have tried to show that these connections were not limited to Britain. The scope of this chapter necessarily widens, to include Western European, American and Russian radical movements.

Amédée Ozenfant in *Foundations of Modern Art*, 1931, noted the changing relationship between the so-called fine arts and applied arts, between artists and craftworkers.

> If we go on allowing the minor arts to think themselves the equal of great art, we shall soon be hail fellow to all sorts of domestic furniture, each to his place! The decorators to the big shops, the artists on the next floor up, several floors up, as high as possible, on the pinnacles, even higher. For the time being, however, they sometimes do meet on the landings, the decorators having mounted at their heels, and numerous artists having come down on their hunkers.[1]

Ozenfant's comments on the effects of the breakdown of the art hierarchy reveals a prime reason for its existence. The artist's heights of inspiration are only impressive if they can be measured against the depths of domestic furniture. Ozenfant predicts a demoralising democratisation of the arts if 'artists' and 'decorators' meet too freely on the landings. Yet that is precisely what some avant-garde art movements wanted.

The artists involved in Dada, Surrealism and Russian Constructivism believed that an end to distinctions between the fine and applied arts would create an art relevant to the lives of the masses of the people – and infinitely richer in itself. Although all three movements manifestly failed to achieve their ideals, for different historical reasons, they opened up a space for women artists. Women's particular skills and traditional areas of activity in the domestic sphere, previously thought to be beneath the concern of the fine artist, were accorded a new importance.

Not all feminist critics consider that the opportunities thus provided for women were necessarily in their best interests. Linda Nochlin voices the ambiguity:

> On the one hand for a woman artist to 'return' as it were to her traditional role in the minor arts, generally less conducive to fame and fortune than a career in painting or sculpture, can be viewed as a retrograde step. Yet from another vantage point, we can say that advanced women artists involved in the decorative arts in the early twentieth century were contributing to the most revolutionary directions – both social and aesthetic – of their time.[2]

To call their 'return' a 'retrograde step' is to confirm, and conform to, conventional distinctions between media expressed in the term 'minor arts'. Nevertheless, the effort to overthrow the hegemony of the fine arts by merging them with the applied arts tended to benefit painting rather than embroidery; to modify masculinity rather than to transform femininity. Embroidery was employed as a fine art medium because of its association with femininity and nature. It was to be a disruptive influence on the male dominated fine arts, but this was to be a one-way process. The character of embroidery was assumed to be fixed and unchanging, eternally feminine.

Take the case of the Dada movement. The movement started in Zurich during 1915. Committed to combat materialism and over-intellectualisation, the artists involved rejected oil painting for all it connoted. Sophie Tauber, a member of the group, was then teaching at the School of Applied Arts in Zurich. She introduced the painter Jean Arp to embroidery. He later wrote about their work together:

The Renaissance taught men to arrogantly exalt their reason. Modern times with their sciences and technologies have consecrated men to megalomania. The chaos of our eras is the result of that over-estimating of reason. We sought an anonymous and collective art. In 1915 Sophie Tauber and I embroidered and did collages.[3]

Jean Arp's contribution to the first issue of the magazine *Dada* in July 1917 was an embroidery, but a poem Arp wrote reveals that he valued embroidery not for its qualities as an artistic medium but for its stereotypical associations with intuition, feeling and above all with nature. The long poem called *The Spider Embroiders* ends with these lines:

Embroidery is more natural than oil painting, the swallows are embroidering the sky for thousands of centuries, there is no such thing as applied art.[4]

In other words, embroidery is seen to be timeless, mindless and simply available to be incorporated into the fine arts. With embroidery Jean Arp and Sophie Tauber believed that they had found 'new material unburdened by tradition', but it was embroidery's particular burdensome tradition, the way it was characterised as 'outside culture' and as an accomplishment, 'not work', that made it so appropriate for their intentions.

Hannah Hoch, an artist working with the Berlin Dada, did, however, evoke the particular historically determined qualities of embroidery and lace in such a way as not simply to appropriate the medium, but to highlight its gender associations. During 1922, she produced collages called 'domestic mottos'. In *Bewacht*, 1924, she disturbingly collages together a huge Chinese embroidered rose with an image of a tiny male martial figure.[5]

Embroidery has played a part in the ideological and formal concerns of twentieth-century art. It has been suggested that it was Sophie Tauber's background in applied arts that led her towards abstraction in art.[6] Similarly, the artist Sonia Terk Delaunay's work with embroidery was also, in part, responsible for her decision to work non-figuratively with colour. Her designs of tapestries and an embroidery of 1909 suggest that textile art prompted her move away from conventional use of colour and perspective, towards the development of the 'abstract' painting known as Orphism, which she initiated with her husband, Robert Delaunay, in Paris during 1913.[7]

Soon after the birth of her son in 1911, she made a patchwork blanket like those stitched by Russian peasant women. In Russia, where she was born, there had been a revival of interest in peasant needlework from the late nineteenth century. Throughout her career she continued to work simultaneously in the applied and fine arts. Committed to bringing art to a wider public and into everyday life, she designed caskets, lampshades, book covers, scarves, dresses, ballet costumes, embroidered waistcoats and embroidered coats. It has, however, been argued that, far from bringing art to a wider public, Delaunay's work was simply appropriated by the world of Parisian haute couture.

Of all the attempts to transform the relations of art to society, none was so far reaching as that which accompanied the Russian Revolution. From the October Revolution in 1917, and through the 1920s, artists and designers joined forces to 'wrench' the applied arts from the middle-class drawing rooms 'whither the old artistic culture had consigned it'.[8] A large number of women were active in the Russian avant garde, and embroidery was given a place in their innovative work.

The two factors – the number of women artists and the presence

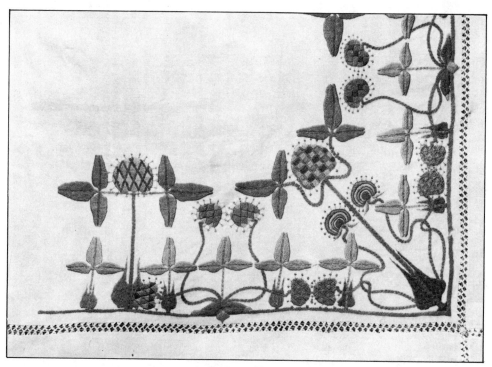

92 Embroidery designed by Jessie Newbery, worked by Edith Rowat (her mother), Glasgow School of Art, Glasgow. 1897. 66 × 259.8 cm. Photo: Anthea Callen. Jessie Newbery founded the embroidery department at the Glasgow School of Art, and from being a minor subject in the art school curriculum it soon became the most important 'craft' taught there. Whereas earlier theorists wanted embroidery to be 'perfect' in order to improve the embroiderer, Jessie Newbery wanted work 'as perfect as may be' for the sake of the design.

93 Conway School, London, 1907. Greater London Council Photo Library. Education for girls in the early years of the twentieth century still included a training in femininity through needlework. Boys were given books as school prizes, while girls were rewarded by being permitted to take home their needlework without first paying for it.

94 *Tapisserie Feuillage*, Sonia Terk Delaunay, Musée Nationale d'Art Moderne,
Paris. 1909.

95 (right) *Bewacht*, Hannah Hoch (German, b 1889), private collection,
Germany. 1925. Collage. Embroidery was an art used both figuratively and in
abstract work. Sonia Delaunay's move towards abstraction was perhaps facilitated
by her familiarity with embroidery and patchwork. Hannah Hoch in her collage
Bewacht appears more concerned with embroidery's connotations than with the
art's formal qualities: the juxtaposition of shapes and objects conjures up the class
and sexual associations of the art.

96 Embroidered bookcover, Liubov Popova (Russian, 1889–1924), c 1923–24. Silk thread on grosgrain. 45.2 × 31.5 cm. George Costakis collection.

In Russia, embroidery had a long history as a peasant art, hence during the Revolution a number of artists, including Liubov Popova and Olga Rozanova, worked with embroidery as part of their attempt to transform the relation of art to society.

97 Suffrage banner, Museum of London, London. c 1911. Paint, embroidery and appliqué.

98 Suffrage handkerchief, Janie Terreno, Museum of London, London. 1912. Embroidered signatures as gestures of solidarity and protest combined the political tradition of petition with the social tradition of embroidered signatures as mementoes to mark special occasions.

99 Suffrage banner, Museum of London, London. c 1911. Appliqué and embroidery. Banners were an established feature of political demonstrations in Britain, but whereas trades union banners were largely produced by a professional banner-making firm, the women of the Suffrage movement employed their considerable personal skills previously reserved for such objects as portières and mantel draperies. Within the Suffrage movement there was an arts and crafts society called the Suffrage Atelier.

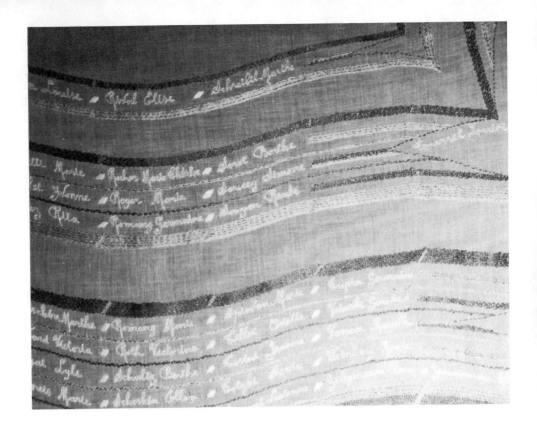

100 Table cloth, Sweden, 1945. Photo: Nappé
There is a long tradition of embroidery as testament of survival and resistance in
the face of political persecution and racial oppression – most recently in Soweto
and in Chile. In 1945 women who had survived Nazi concentration camps
embroidered a table cloth for Count Folke Bernadotte, the Swedish diplomat who
had enabled them to reach refuge in Sweden. Cornflowers, poppies and daisies are
worked in the centre and surrounded by the names of all the women who worked
on the cloth.

of embroidery – are explicable in terms of the recent history of women and the history of art in Russia. In the latter half of the nineteenth century women had been active in the intelligentsia and radical groups, setting a precedent for twentieth-century women to participate fully in the artistic avant garde. The prominence of embroidery in the work of avant-garde artists was due to the theories of the late nineteenth-century art movements in Russia. Artists in the 1870s had repudiated 'art for art's sake', wanting to make art 'useful' to society.[9] In their desire to revivify the fine arts and to create a new national culture they had turned to Russian peasant art, including embroidery. Thus, embroidery and carpentry workshops had been established as part of what is known as the Russian Neo-Nationalist movement.

Prior to the first world war, artists looked to peasant art as a means by which indigenous cultural modes could be reinforced in opposition to the dominant place given to foreign culture. The painter Natalia Goncharova wrote, 'I turn away from the West . . . for me the East means the creation of new forms, an extending and deepening of the problems of colour.'[10]

She incorporated her knowledge of peasant costume and embroidery into both painting and embroidery. Her claim that embroidery extended and deepened 'problems of colour' indicates that, as in the West, embroidery was seen as an essentially universal or intuitive medium. In 1912 Goncharova exhibited work 'in Chinese, Byzantine and Futurist styles, in the style of Russian embroidery, woodcuts and traditional tray designs'.[11]

The romantic, nationalistic use of embroidery was transformed by the Revolution of 1917. For avant-garde artists the Revolution announced the advent of a communal way of life in which the artist would be an integrated member, bringing her or his skills to industrial design and production. Declaring that easel painting was redundant, artists turned to peasant art and embroidery in their search for an art compatible with socialism and collective practice.

The Department of Fine Arts (IZO) was created in 1918 under the People's Commissariat of Enlightenment (NARKOMPROS). It organised the arts for the new Soviet Government. In the four years from 1917, artists in IZO re-organised art schools and museums all over the country. Olga Rosanova, an artist with a training in both the fine and applied arts, created the applied arts sub-section and became its head. Believing that the cultivation of a new applied art culture should grow not out of the destruction of previously existing traditions, but out of their modernisation, she organised workshops in the old centres of Russian applied arts.

Before the revolution Rosanova had been working with embroidery. For the magazine of the Suprematist artists, she prepared a design for an embroidery in three colours, declaring her determination to widen the definition of art beyond easel painting. She incorporated her embroidery designs into dress. Large patches of embroidery were placed on the dresses to accentuate the geometrical outline of the design, and to provide a sense of dynamism and rhythm.

At a State Exhibition of the Applied Arts Workshop in Moscow, 1919, peasant embroideries were exhibited after designs by Rosanova and Nadezhda Udaltsova, Kazimir Malevich and K.L. Boguslavskaya-Puni. The women peasants from Verbovka in Kiev embroidered for such objects as handbags, blotting pads, wall pockets for letters and papers, pillows, skirts and scarves. 'The embroideries were indeed amazing, shining with their coloured silk' observed Udaltsova.[12] The socialist artists appeared to accept the contradictions in designing work for the peasant women to stitch.

Embroidery gained a particular significance with the movement to develop a new Russian costume. Artists and designers collaborated in the attempt to design clothes intended for industrial mass production. At the time of the first all-Russian conference on artistic industry in 1919, however, the economic situation made it impossible for their ideas to be put into production. At the conference the dress designer Nadezhda Lamenova declared:

Art has penetrated to all spheres of our living environment, stimulating the artistic taste and sensitiveness of the masses. Dress is one of the most appropriate guidelines. Artists in the field of dress must take the initiative into their own hands, working to create from the simplest materials the simplest but beautiful types of dress, suited to the new tenor of life among the workers.[13]

Lamenova was a leading figure in the drive to design costume for the workers, to be based not on signs of social position but on the conditions of life and the requirements of health and comfort. She organised the Workshop of Contemporary Costume and the Atelier of Fashion in 1923, which produced its own magazine. The editorial elaborated their aims:

> In designing new styles one must try to achieve a blending of the existing trend in European fashion with the characteristically national features of Russian Art.

Articles included Alexander Exter, the painter, on 'Constructivist Costume' and Yevjenia Prebelskaya on 'Embroidery on Present Day Production'.[14]

Embroidery was given a place in the new costume for its beauty and for its association with peasant national costume. Yet the women artists and designers felt forced to justify its presence. Embroidery still carried overtones of bourgeois decadence. In 1918, in *Letter to the Futurists*, the artist V.E. Tatlin wrote, 'The Futurists have been too preoccupied with cafés and various embroideries for emperors and ladies. I explain this by the fact that our artistic vision has lost three-fifths of its clarity.'[15]

Prebelskaya repeatedly defended her use of embroidery:

> Work on the Constructivist phase in women's clothes has impelled the designers to take a fresh look at embroidery in relation to women's clothes, and to see it not as a separate feature or mere embellishment but as being to a certain degree a constructive and crowning element.
>
> European clothes are not without decorative features that serve no constructive purpose but a purely visual one. They are not sufficiently clear in their relationship to the garment's construction.[16]

The argument that embroidery was a 'constructive' aspect of the dress design rather than an embellishment was thin indeed. Nevertheless, Lamenova adopted a similar line of defence for her use of the art:

> What used to be called trimmings has significance for the whole garment: it can strengthen the rhythms of planes, intensify the style. . . Our New Costume will match the new quality of life

characterised by industry, dynamism and awareness of its power.[17]

Behind the women's arguments lay a more general conflict within the post-revolutionary debates on the applied arts. Some called for 'the whole decorative and embellishment aspect of costume (to be) annihilated' while others insisted that 'there is nothing inappropriate to the Proletariat in a certain degree of smartness and attractiveness.'[18] At a practical level, however, embroidery was simply not appropriate for the mass production which was the ultimate aim of the designers of the New Costume.

Tacit recognition that embroidery was unsuitable for the New Costume always existed in the organisation of the Atelier of Fashion – the 'laboratory' for revolutionary clothing. It had started in 1923, two years after the introduction of the New Economic Policy which opened up a market for consumer goods. Two types of clothing designs were produced: one for mass production and one for individual orders. Although Lamenova included embroidery in her syllabus for 'Studies in the industrial production of artistically designed clothings', by 1924 embroidery was concentrated on clothing designed for internal and external exhibition. Lamenova was put in charge of the Workshop for Folk Crafts, and in collaboration with Vera Mukhina, a sculptor, she won a prize at the Paris World Exhibition for costume based on folk art. The two incorporated Russian folk embroidery and Mukhina produced her own designs for embroidery.

Today, in Europe, Russian Constructivist clothing is greatly admired for its modernity, and the artist designers are praised for their energy and idealism:

> True daughters of the Revolution, they decided to drop art for art's sake, give up painting, and concentrate on industrial production for the masses . . . They might perhaps have been the forerunners of those gutsy, talented, young people of the Sixties who made London of the Sixties swing.[19]

Such a comparison denies the specific historical conditions which both permitted and finally frustrated their work. And it ignores the crucial fact that the artist designers were not dispensing with artistic concerns in their work. Their use of embroidery – an art form they considered appropriate for their socialist practice –

testifies to the way they were attempting to transform and fuse art and design. Later commentators, however, regard their embroidery as a shameful but natural feminine weakness which the women had tried in vain to suppress. Of the painter-designer Alexandra Exter, Meriel McCooey writes: 'Though she seldom incorporated any of these ideas into her styles for the masses, she had a secret predilection for creating extravagant fantasy dresses, richly embroidered.'[20]

Criticised by their contemporaries, misunderstood today, the revolutionary artists who advocated hand embroidery underestimated the historically determined character of the medium. Its ties with bourgois femininity were not transcended by its peasant connections. Neither could a medium which is fundamentally a 'unique' art form be employed for mass production.

For the Constructivist artists, embroidery's association with femininity was a hindrance, producing accusations of bourgeois decadence that they felt called upon to refute. For the British Women's Suffrage Movement it was a connection they believed they could use to advantage. In their hands, embroidery was employed not to transform the place and function of art, but to change ideas about women and femininity. Far from desiring to disentangle embroidery and femininity, they wanted embroidery to evoke femininity – but femininity represented as a source of strength, not as evidence of women's weakness. The movement left behind numbers of embroidered marching banners: some identifying local groups, others representing individual campaigns and professions, and a series celebrating great women of the past and present.

The tradition of banner-carrying demonstrations had grown up with the Trades Union Movement from the 1830s. Union banners were an obvious source of inspiration for the feminists. They adopted the same format of pictorial message combined with a slogan. But whereas two thirds of trades union banners, since 1837, had come from the same source – George Tuthill's banner-making business – feminist banners appear to have been varied and individual creations. Trades union banners were silken, painted, highly polished works. Suffrage banners daringly combined embroidery, paint, collage and raised work in original and equally well finished products. Their effective use of mixed media was perhaps a result of the middle-class women's lack of professionalism – a positive outcome of 'accomplishment'. Decades of skill developed for ecclesiastical banners, altarcloths, drawing-room drapery and smoking caps lie behind the banners.

Demonstrations were an important aspect of the Suffrage protest in the early years of the twentieth century. In 1906 Lady Frances Balfour described a demonstration organised by the WSPU (Women's Social and Political Union) to march on the House of Commons: 'A huge concourse of working women . . . met under the Labour Party with their own flags and carrying their own babies.'[21] The demonstration was small, however, compared with the great marches of 1908. In June of that year 13,000 non-militant Suffragists marched from the Embankment to the Albert Hall. Each trade marched under its own banner: there were actresses, artists, shop assistants, factory workers, home makers and many more. Women carried banners celebrating the achievements of well known women from Boadicea to Marie Curie. At the head of the procession a huge banner flourished the word RECTITUDE. Slogans were uniformly well designed and direct with simple, strong, instantly legible lettering. ASK WITH COURAGE; ALLIANCE AND DEFIANCE; LEARN AND LIVE; DARE TO BE FREE; COURAGE, CONSISTENCY, SUCCESS.

Ten days later a demonstration organised by the militant Suffragettes was of a size never seen before or since. *The Times* estimated that a crowd of about half a million converged on Hyde Park.

Not only banners but parasols too were embroidered in the Suffrage colours of green, purple and white with the initials WSPU, and carried on the marches. The parasol was such a quintessentially feminine object that, taken in conjunction with embroidery, it suggests that the use of the art by the movement was tactical, to counter anti-suffrage propaganda that constantly depicted feminists as 'large-handed, big-footed, flat-chested and thin-lipped'.[22] The representation of the Suffragettes as lacking in femininity might have frightened other women away from identifying with the movement; and discredited the campaign as motivated not by politics but by the personal grievances of women who had failed to achieve the supposed fruits of femininity.

There was nothing naïve in the Suffrage use of embroidery. They were familiar with methods and materials of pictorial embroidery. They understood the symbolic content of materials. In a banner depicting St George, the saint's wings are silk, his face satin, and the dragon appliquéed in linen, reminiscent of stump work from the seventeenth century.

Their excellent stitchery in the Art Needlework style (see Chapter Seven) was, to their contemporaries, evidence both of an education in the feminine virtues of selflessness and service, and of a natural feminine capacity. Their claim to femininity could, however, equally have been used against their demand for the vote, so the form and content of the banners depicted femininity not as frailty but as strength, and embroidery was presented not as women's only appropriate medium but co-existing with paint.

The banner from the Hammersmith group, for example, consists of three panels. A painted and raised depiction of hammer and horse-shoes is flanked by embroidered irises in Suffrage colours. Irises were at this time among the most popular flowers in Art Needlework, as *Needlework Monthly* observed in 1907: 'The pretty iris design is the favourite work of the season, for table covers, duchesse sets, all in unbleached linen with the design already painted, to be worked in silks.'[23]

For the Suffrage banner the irises are expertly embroidered in crewel work, the stitch taught by the Royal School of Art Needlework. The banner is reversible; backing the crewel-work irises, the same design is displayed in appliqué velvet. Paint and embroidery, and masculine and feminine symbols, share the same space and make a political point – the demand for equality, not androgyny.

The content of most of the embroidery aimed to present the Suffrage Movement as supporting equal rights – as reformist not revolutionary. Thus the Women's Tax Resistance League, created in 1909, depicted Britannia on their banner above the slogan, 'NO VOTE NO TAX', implying that, given the vote, women would work for the same ends as men. The embroidered Britannia also points to the irony in an allegorical female figure representing a nation which denied women the vote.

Similarly, amongst the banners commemorating female heroines was one dedicated to 'Queen Victoria, Queen and Mother'. The inclusion of the Queen with such women as Marie Curie, Boadicea and Elizabeth Barrett Browning demonstrated the movement's patriotism and their political astuteness. As seen in Chapter Seven, the Queen was used as a powerful affirmation of the importance of family life by embroiderers in the nineteenth century. Here, the campaigners harnessed the Queen's popularity to their cause. Acclaiming her as Queen *and* Mother countered anti-suffrage propaganda that God had ordained women to raise children, not to take part in political life.

The heroines selected for the banners and their attributes generally assert the breadth of women's capacities. The Marie Curie banner has embroidered panels radiating from the word RADIUM. Elizabeth Barrett Browning's poetry is signified by green velvet and pink silk roses and purple fleur-de-lys.

The set of heroine banners reflects the organisational ideology of the Suffrage movement, which, unlike present-day feminism with its insistence on a collective structure, set up its leaders as sources of inspiration and devotion. Thus a banner commemorating members of the WSPU who were forcibly fed in prison is embroidered with the names of Mrs Pethick Lawrence, Christabel Pankhurst, Mrs Pankhurst and Annie Kenny in *art nouveau* lettering. Below are appliquéed signatures of their followers in purple and green thread. Each woman appears to have embroidered her own name. Some were highly skilled embroiderers, others able only clumsily to follow the lines of their handwriting. This banner transformed a prison gesture of solidarity into a public statement.

Imprisoned and on hunger strike, the women embroidered handkerchiefs with their signatures, bringing together the tradition of political petition and protest with a female social tradition by which guests would embroider their signatures for their hostess to commemorate a visit. The London Museum owns two suffrage handkerchiefs: one embroidered by Janie Terreno marks the hunger strike of 1911. It bears a photograph of Mrs Pankhurst and Christabel, the signatures of those forcibly fed and some tiny embroidered violets.

Janie Terreno was a musician from Essex who took part in the mass shop-window smashing protest in March 1912. She was arrested for throwing a stone through the window of an engineering firm, Stedalls, in Oxford Street. Imprisoned in Holloway and force-fed, her letters to her husband illuminate the feelings for the Pankhursts that motivated her adulatory embroidery. The Suffragettes were forbidden to talk to their leader in Holloway, and Janie Terreno described their response: 'We fought for her and won . . . we were put into our cells by force and then broke our cell windows and everything we could . . . we only took our meal on Sunday evening after receiving her instructions that we were to eat. . . We obey her absolutely.'[24]

Elsewhere she exclaimed, 'I cannot tell you the joy it is to have our leaders with us . . . the sight of their dear faces has cheered everyone.'[25]

The other handkerchief in the London Museum is dedicated to Janie Terreno herself, and commemorates prison sentences delivered in Newcastle in 1910 and in London during 1910 and 1911.

The delicate embroidery declared that the supposed weaker sex was being subjugated to the torture of force-feeding – and resisting. They signed their names in the very medium which was considered proof of their frailty, and justification for their subjugation.

The Suffrage demand for equal rights and opportunities, and the ideology of the Arts and Crafts Movement with its insistence on the importance of creative work, combined to make considerable impact on the teaching of embroidery.

At the Glasgow School of Art, Ann Macbeth and her colleagues transformed methods of embroidery instruction, insisting that the design should arise out of the technique employed, and encouraging students to invent their own designs rather than follow patterns (see Chapter Seven).

Numbers of teachers, following those at the Glasgow School, emphasised design, colour and experiment, rather than the concentrated development of technical excellence.

Ann Macbeth encoded her ideas in *Educational Needlework*, 1913, written in collaboration with Margaret Swanson, a teacher at the Pupil Teachers Centre, Ayr, from 1899 to 1908. They believed that needlework would assist in

the development of intelligence and formation of character, . . . the imagination of the child is stirred and curiosity plays freely . . . without curiosity, no conjecture is possible – a point to be noted from the start in all experimental work. The boy or girl who uses material and needle freely in independent design ranks on a plane with the scientist who makes a hypothesis, with the artist who makes an experiment.[26]

The authors reveal the influence of feminism in that they assume both boys and girls are to develop character and curiosity, and that both can use the needle to advantage. The progressive ideas they propagated within education were still in evidence in 1928 when the National Union of Women Teachers debated a resolution at their annual conference:

> The time has come for a more equal form of education for future home life, as between boys and girls, by the giving of instruction to boys in the simple elements of domestic subjects such as needlework and cookery and the girls instruction in light woodwork.[27]

However, such attempts were continually undermined by the absolute identification of embroidery with femininity. Curriculum projects and teacher training continued to designate embroidery a girls' activity. An expanding leisure industry utilised the feminine ideal in its attempt to encourage embroidery, assisted by women's magazines.

Magazines managed to present each change in the social and political climate in terms of its implications for embroidery. Thus they represent embroidery as the means, during the economic crisis of the thirties, to manifest the feminine qualities of sensible thriftiness, and to keep up appearances. They urged their readers to create 'beauty with utility', employing embroidery techniques like cross stitch and smocking that would wash and wear.[28]

At the same time a new shift occurred in the feminine ideal. Embroidery was increasingly advocated as a means, not overtly to femininity, but to individuality. However, the concept of individuality in relation to embroiderers became subtly sex-stereotyped. The forward to Rebecca Crompton's *Modern Design and Embroidery*, 1936, suggests that embroidery 'even in its simplest form may become the expression of personal thought and feeling', as it is 'work which mirrors [a woman's] own thought and personality.'[29]

With the end of the second world war, peace – for women's magazines – meant plentiful embroidery materials. The editorial of *Embroidery* declared:

> And what a feeling of prosperity it gives to realise that once again silks, wools, fabrics and all embroidery equipment are

available in all abundance. These things can never be taken for granted again after the lean war years, when one felt guilty plying the needle for any purpose but 'make do and mend' and wools and silks were impossible to get. . . Now that every variety of material is easily and quite inexpensively available it is most encouraging to attempt any form of hitherto untried work.[30]

But the abundance of embroidery equipment was not sufficient encouragement in itself. The idea that embroidery fostered individuality was increasingly emphasised. Catherine Christopher in *The Complete Book of Embroidery and Embroidery Stitches*, 1944, observed that

few pursuits can rival embroidery for the opportunity it offers to impress her creative ability upon her surroundings and personal belongings. The things thus created may be few and far between, but they are an expression of yourself so individual and personal that they will always be cherished.[31]

In *Creative Embroidery*, 1967, Christine Risley described embroidery as 'making a personal statement'.[32] The twentieth-century writers have partially dispensed with the Victorian ideology of embroidery as selfless work for the comfort of others. Instead, embroidery has become a manifestation of the self. But the expression of personality is limited to personal thoughts and feelings. Nineteenth-century notions that to fulfil the feminine ideal an embroiderer had to manifest sensibility in her work has simply been updated – rephrased for a Freudian and post-Freudian society.

The claim that embroidery conveys the individuality and personality of the embroiderer was repeated so insistently because writers on needlework wanted embroidery accorded the status of art. In the twentieth century the personality of the artist has become all important: creativity is considered to reside in the person of the artist, not in what she or he makes. We speak of 'a David Hockney', 'a Gwen John'. Indeed, in certain art practices it is necessary for an artist only to designate an object as art for it to become so. Thus, if embroidery is to win recognition as art, it has to be stamped not with a pre-drawn pattern, but with a particular personality. But whereas the personality of a painter is expected to be eccentric and egocentric, for women embroiderers the notion of personality is still constrained by the feminine ideal. Macbeth and Swanson's conviction that embroidery allowed for the free play of the imagination, intelligence and curiosity was subsumed into a twentieth-century feminine ideal: 'Even the least skilled attempts at creating beauty reveal and help develop vitality, warmth and other desirable personality traits.'[33]

It is this categorisation of embroidery as the art of personal life outside male-dominated institutions and the world of work, that has given it a special place in counter-cultures and radical movements.

In the 1960s embroidery suddenly gained a new face. Embroidered suns rose over hip pockets, dragons curled round denim thighs, rainbows arched over backs. For the hippy era embroidery symbolised love, peace, colour, personal life and rejection of materialism. Everything in fact that embroidery and femininity had connoted since the nineteenth century. A woman reminiscing about her life in London in 1970 commented:

> In my hippy phase when I was living in a commune we all embroidered. It had various meanings: pleasure, self-indulgence with colours, a determination to make your clothes beautiful. It also functioned to establish you as a member of a tribe because all of us with our embroidered jeans knew that we were libertarians. For the men who embroidered, and wore embroidery, it signified the taking up of femininity and enjoying it.[34]

For men, long hair and embroidered clothing constituted a rebellious gesture against a hierarchical, puritanical, masculine establishment. However, this was less a subversion of sex roles than a longing for the freedom of an idealised image of childhood – mother-loved, anarchic and untouched by daddy's world.

Interestingly, one of the scenes most frequently embroidered on jeans was that of Adam and Eve in the Garden of Eden, the scene that from the sixteenth century had been so popular with embroiderers. However, as Peter Beagle in *American Denim*, 1975, points out: 'The emphasis in all the Adams and Eves is never on original sin, or even on temptation, but on the beauty of the primal couple and on a kind of wistful, original innocence in

101 Embroidered runner, Beryl Weaver, reproduced in *Spare Rib,* 1978. Taking traditional embroidery motifs, Beryl Weaver reveals the way they prescribe the feminine ideal.

102 Sampler, Kate Walker, The Gal, London. 1978.
This was one of the art works in *Feministo,* the postal art event in which a group of women in Britain exchanged art works through the post, creating a dialogue about their experience as women, artists and mothers working at home.

103 Boadicea place setting from *The Dinner Party*, Judy Chicago. 1979. Photo: Mary McNally.
In using embroidery feminists tread a difficult path. On the one hand they pay tribute to women's historic and creative relationship to the art, on the other they wish to expose the oppressive aspects of the construction of femininity which have been so closely linked with embroidery.

104 Embroidered denim jeans, private collection, London. 1970. The hippy use of embroidered jeans asserted individuality, creativity and non-conformity, but for women the ideology replaced one feminine ideal with another. Embroidery now connoted not gentility but fecundity.

105 Sampler, John Nichols Hackleton, Christies, London. 1858.
Despite the art's role in the construction of femininity since the Renaissance, there
have always been a few men and boys who practised the art for the pleasure it
provides and the artistic possibilities it offers.

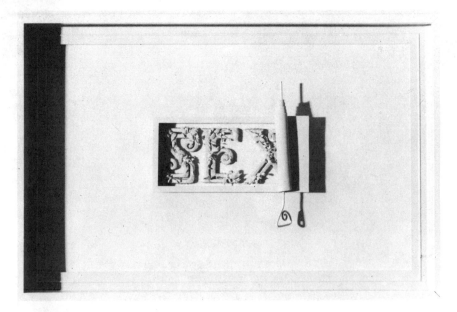

106 . . . *in a tin,* Catherine Riley, Crafts Council, London. 1978. Photo: Ed
Buziak.
Catherine Riley was trained as a textile artist but became interested in what
embroidery connoted. Here she conjures up the art's association with the
repression and containment of women's sexuality in the name of feminine purity.
The title hints at the other side of the high premium placed on women's purity –
the idea of women's bodies as commodities.

which even the serpent is a brother.'[35] But what 'freedom' for women is in this? While the man appropriated the naturalness and innocence of femininity, he referred to the woman as 'my old lady', as she sat silently stitching – an earth mother for the pre-fall Adam in his floral denim. In other words, while hippy embroidery signified loosening the constraints of masculinity for men, for women it simply replaced one feminine ideal with another. Embroidery now connoted not gentility but fecundity.

The Women's Liberation Movement in the 1970s inherited particular facets of the counter-culture: the rejection of establishment values, the refusal of rigid sex roles, and a recognition of the central importance of personal life – but all with a crucial difference. Feminists viewed these issues within a political perspective; it was an oppositional, not an alternative movement. The organisation of personal life with a strict division between the public and private, the domestic and professional, the emotional and intellectual, the masculine and the feminine, were analysed as the means by which one group maintained power over another.

The hippy love of embroidery as a gesture of defiance – one in the eye for a grey masculine world – lived on in the Women's Liberation Movement. But whereas hippies had simply celebrated the emotional and individualistic associations of embroidery, feminists in their embroidery showed that the personal was the political – that personal and domestic life is as much the product of the institutions and ideologies of our society as is public life.

Some feminists take traditional embroidery motifs which connote the domestic and feminine ideal, and reveal what the pretty stitches conceal. Beryl Weaver embroiders bouquets of flowers, ladies in crinolines amongst the hollyhocks, rustic cottages. These images, originally derived from eighteenth-century prototypes, became popular in the thirties when the rapid expansion of building in the suburbs of industrial towns had awakened the Victorian idealisation of rural life (see Chapter Seven). Today they have an added ingredient of saccharine nostalgia. Natural, rural femininity is conjured up in opposition to the brutality and artificiality of urban industrial society. Beryl Weaver subverts these images: 'I was never encouraged to create disturbing images, so my anger comes through in the pretty pictures I was brought up with.'[36]

The picturesque cottage casement is embroidered with the words 'shattered and shuttered' – Beryl Weaver's feelings about the solitary confinement of a life dedicated to domestic femininity and nothing else. She describes herself as a 'housewife drowning in suburbia'. A crinoline lady amongst the flowers has a double embroidered caption: one reads 'To women's work' in recognition of women's heritage of embroidery, and in opposition to the ideology of the embroidered convention that to be feminine is to be seen not to work, and certainly not to participate in waged labour. The second caption reads 'Two women's work', drawing attention to the assumed solitary state of both embroiderers and their embroidered lady, and to women's double burden. Often Beryl Weaver calls the images into question by a judiciously placed feminist symbol. Thus, a traditional bunch of flowers is carefully embroidered, and placed in a vase patterned with women's symbols. She attacks 'the way we are always compared to flowers: women and flowers – personal and warm – pretty but stultified. One man even went so far as to say he liked women to be independent, so he could go from one to the other, like a bee on spring flowers.'[37]

Kate Walker is an artist who has employed embroidery in a fine art and feminist context since the early 1970s. She describes how an exhibition of Polish art alerted her to the possibilities of textile art:

> They used all kinds of materials and forms which seemed to express their upheavals and dissatisfactions. I saw events, assemblages, street art using ropes, textiles and, most interesting to me, banners made of patchwork cloth in a mediaeval style. This art seemed to convey a determined respect for their own past culture, uniting it with their struggle for a better future.[38]

A year later, in 1974, she exhibited an embroidery in the first show at the Women's Arts Alliance in London called 'Sweet Sixteen and Never Been Shown'. It was a mixed media show, presenting a variety of events, performances and assemblages, with audience participation. Looking back, Kate Walker says:

> It was early in the development of the women's art movement and there was no consciously worked out programme for

insisting on equal inclusion of women's skills, but Carol McNichol showed her vegetable-like ceramics and Rose English some leather craft pieces. I sneaked in an old patchwork cushion I had made, alongside my paintings and assemblage. We automatically erased the line between function and aesthetics, between craft and art. We felt the most urgent need to be for intervention at all levels both within and without the gallery system.[39]

Kate Walker's attitude is characteristic of contemporary feminists' determination not to reject femininity but to empty the term of its negative connotations, to reclaim and refashion the category:

I have never worried that embroidery's association with femininity, sweetness, passivity and obedience may subvert my work's feminist intention. Femininity and sweetness are part of women's strength. Passivity and obedience, moreover, are the very opposites of the qualities necessary to make a sustained effort in needlework. What's required are physical and mental skills, fine aesthetic judgement in colour, texture and composition; patience during long training; and assertive individuality of design (and consequent disobedience of aesthetic convention). Quiet strength need not be mistaken for useless vulnerability.[40]

She takes the format of the sampler, but the stitched sayings are defiant not compliant, most unladylike; 'Wife is a four-letter word', 'This is a present to me', both declaring her rejection of the self-repression and submission encouraged by traditional sampler-making.

Other women have been prompted to view embroidery critically and analytically through being trained in the art.

Catharine Riley trained as a textile artist. Her embroidery evokes and subtly parodies the emotions associated with needlework – purity and chastity. In an exhibition in 1980 all the pieces on show were worked in shades of white, conjuring up and cutting across the way whitework embroidery is intended to confirm the image of women as sexless, spiritual and sensitive. In one work the word 'sex' is spelled out in bone-silk and flowers, and contained in a white sardine tin, beautifully mounted and framed in pure white.

As we have seen, the notion that femininity, and embroidery as the art of the feminine, come naturally to women has affected women of all classes but in specifically different ways. It is the relationship between embroidery and class that feminist artist Margaret Harrison explores in her work, attacking both the fine art/craft division and class divisions. She assembles examples of traditional needlecraft and contemporary doilies 'made in the factory by working-class women and sold back to them'. Her intention is to reveal the process of de-skilling working-class women since the industrial revolution.

Embroidery also has a place in the feminist effort to transform the conditions of art practice, the relationship of artist to audience and the definitions of what constitutes art. Because embroidery is an extremely popular hobby, and a skill taught in schools, it is considered by many to be a more accessible medium, reaching a wider audience, than painting. And as an art employing thread and textiles, embroidery is used to question the primacy of paint and canvas. The British feminist postal art project 'Feministo' came into being partly in opposition to established, male-dominated modes of art practice.

During 1975, women began exchanging art works through the post, setting up a visual dialogue about their lives as housewives and mothers. They utilised whatever materials they had at hand and whichever domestic skills they possessed, including embroidery. Monica Ross, a participant, summed up the ways in which 'Feministo' departed from the competitive individualism fostered by the institutions associated with fine arts:

Our creativity derives from non-prestigious folk traditions. It is diverse and integrated into our lives; it is cooked and eaten, washed and worn. Contemporary standards either ignore our creativity or rate it as second-class. We communicate, we don't compete. We share images and experiences. The posting of one piece of work from one woman to another makes ownership ambiguous. Our creativity is valid.[41]

'Feministo', with its images drawn from domestic life and its craft techniques, managed to convey a double message. Phil Goodall, an artist in the group, observed: 'Within the postal event we both celebrated the area of domestic creativity and "women's world" and exposed it for its paucity.'[42] They validated domestic art, yet drew attention to the extent to which women's time and energy has been absorbed by their massive contribution to the domestic economy.

The art works were finally collected into an exhibition. Placing the embroidered, knitted and crocheted work in an art gallery was intended to challenge the value-laden division between 'home' and 'work', 'art' and 'craft'. Similarly, by bringing work deemed to belong to personal life into a public gallery 'Feministo' affirmed the central tenet of today's Women's Liberation Movement, that the personal is political, that personal life is determined by the wider political structure. The art gallery is maintained as a special space by what is kept outside of it. 'Feministo' disrupted that structure.

Another feminist art project which carried so-called craft into the heart of the art world is *The Dinner Party*, which was first exhibited at the San Francisco Art Museum in 1979. Conceived by feminist artist Judy Chicago, it was executed by more than 400 women and men. On an open triangular table are 39 place settings, each commemorating a particular goddess or woman in Western history. The settings include a goblet, cutlery and a china-painted plate, designed to evoke each individual woman and her historical period. The plates rest upon embroidered runners. The embroideries take the work beyond hagiography. They place the women in context by being stitched in the style and technique of the woman's time. Chicago writes:

> We examined the history of needlework – as it is reflected in textiles and costumes, sculptures, myths and legends and archaeological evidence – from the point of view of what these revealed about women, the quality of their lives and their relationship to needlework.[43]

A photographer, Susan Hill, became 'Head of Needlework', after apprenticing herself to a group of traditional needleworkers. Students of textiles under her direction amassed an embroidery sampler book for Chicago to use when designing the runners: 'I would study the book endlessly,' she says, 'trying to determine how the marvellous visual qualities of these different types of embroidery could best be utilised.'[44]

The relationship between the plates and the runners is symbolic. For the place settings of the women of antiquity, the embroidery is stitched on the periphery of the runners. Slowly, over the centuries, it encroaches on the plates. In Chicago's words this is

> a metaphor for the increasing restrictions on women's power that occurred in the development of Western history. There is the same congruence between the plate and the runner that the woman experienced between her aspirations and the prevailing attitudes towards female achievement, and occasionally there is an enormous visual tension between the plate and its runner as a symbol of the woman's rebellion against the constraints of the female role.[45]

Nevertheless, given women's ambivalent relationship to embroidery, using the art to place their lives in context inevitably has its ironic moments. The plate representing seventeenth-century feminist Anna Maria von Schurman, declared enemy of needlework, is placed upon a reproduction of a Dutch sampler.

The value of *The Dinner Party* is that embroidery is used appreciatively but above all symbolically. There is no suggestion that embroidery rather than painting is women's proper art form. The piece simply states that women have and still do employ stitchery, illustrating the varied history of women and the art.

The most recent radical movement to employ embroidery is the Women's Peace Movement. Large, brightly coloured embroidered and appliquéed banners have been produced since 1978 to be carried on marches and, more recently, attached to the perimeter fence at Greenham Common air base, where women camp in protest against Cruise missiles.

The iconography of the banners combines Suffrage symbolism, traditional peace motifs and feminist political symbols. For example, the banner stitched by Thalia and Jan Campbell and Jan Higgs to celebrate the Women for Life on Earth Action for Peace, 1981 to 1982, is in the Suffragette colours, purple, green and white; and includes representations of trees, doves, a woman's sign and the anti-nuclear symbol, along with women linking hands in a circle. Groups often include specific reference to their location; thus Hastings women based their banner on the Bayeux Tapestry, and the Otley Peace Action Group's banner depicts the town.

We have seen how deeply identified embroidery has become with nature and the feminine. The peace movement women deliberately evoke the meaning of embroidery to emphasise that they are campaigning against the nuclear threat *as women*. Displayed at Greenham, the banners declare the fence a boundary between femininity and masculinity, between life and death, technology and nature. Never before has the use of embroidery so clearly demonstrated the place of the art in the splitting that structures and controls our society – and may one day destroy us.

It is crucially important to recognise how diversely women have lived and resisted the specific forms of sexual oppression operating in different cultures and classes. And embroidery continues to illustrate to this day the heterogeneity of women's work. Two comments from contemporary embroiderers provide a salutary reminder of the dramatic diversity of present-day approaches to the art:

> Starting to embroider in a fine-art context was a direct result of my activities with the Women's Liberation Movement from about 1970. At that time I had not found any application of my feminist ideas to art, but felt a strong need to make feminism literally visible. Embroidery was one technique among many which could be combined in new ways to create forms of art truer to our skills and experience.[46]

Kate Walker's utilisation of embroidery as a medium with a heritage in women's hands, and thus as more appropriate than male-associated paint for making feminist statements, co-exists with an absolutely conventional embroidery practice expressed by Lady Tavistock:

> I am always doing tapestry . . . and make about seven or eight things a year. I have completed a tremendous number of cushions, some rugs, spectacle cases and five pairs of evening slippers for my husband.[47]

Lady Tavistock could be speaking from the nineteenth century, when embroiderers stitched for home, husband and peace of mind.

Today, in the 1980s, numerous factors have again combined to encourage a revival of enthusiasm for embroidery as a 'home-craft': an economic recession co-exists with adulation of the home, the home-made, the hand-made and the natural. The production of canvas patterns is a thriving business. They sell at high prices to affirm their artistic value and social status. They are carefully designed to preserve the art's 'natural', genteel, feminine connotations. A designer for a large needlecraft shop in the United States told me that she was instructed never to include buildings in the patterns she produced: only natural scenery was permitted.

As well as the 'hobby' embroiderers there is an ever-expanding number of embroiderers who practise it as a fine-art medium. Art schools today have embroidery departments: amongst the best known is Goldsmiths' College in London. Art-school trained embroiderers consider that the medium offers 'textures and colours that would not be possible in any other medium'. Modern materials have widened the scope of the art:

> Traditional techniques like quilting, padding, couching, and the application of metal threads and glass beads are still employed, but materials such as transparent acetate are now used, and few artists produce work today that consists entirely of embroidery in the conventional sense of the word. The search for new forms and new techniques has led to a greater use of embroidery mixed with collage, where flat pieces of material are cut and sewn on to the picture surface.[48]

Embroiderers have formed numbers of exhibition groups: for example The 62 Group, The Textile Studio and the New Embroidery Movement. Possibly embroidery's connection with the tradition of craft co-operative work, rather than the fine arts which foster and expect competitive individualism, has helped to foster this tendency.

Older embroidery organisations – The Royal School of Needlework and The Embroiderers' Guild – co-exist with the new groups. The Guild has seventy-seven branches in Britain, providing instruction, organising exhibitions and maintaining a library and study group at their Hampton Court headquarters. The Royal School of Needlework, established in 1872, continues to offer classes in all forms of embroidery, in addition to a two-year apprenticeship scheme, and the restoration of old or damaged embroideries.[49]

Despite the proliferation of professional groups and the recognition of embroidery as an art form, twentieth-century feminine ideals still dominate attitudes towards the art to an amazing extent. Embroidery is still seen as an emotional gesture rather than creative work. A woman who has embroidered intermittently throughout her life, admits

> I have always embroidered for other people, for people that I was trying to woo. Initially it was my mother, and after that it has been either women or men that I have been in love with or wanting to gain favour with. I can remember quite clearly going to this man's flat, stealing his jeans and covering them with embroidery. I find it intensely pleasurable, but I have got to have the emotional inspiration, there has got to be a significant person I am embroidering for.[50]

Embroidery can also provide a vehicle for dealing with highly ambivalent, complex feelings provoked by a significant other. 'Embroidering a lover's clothes means that I am going to leave him,'[51] another woman told me. The construction of femininity inhibits the direct expression of anger. She explains her embroidery as a placatory gesture towards the man she is 'deserting', but acknowledges that the fury which fuels her departure is expressed yet safely concealed in the stabbing satin stitches.

The extent to which embroidery becomes implicated in relationships arises in part from the fact that embroidery still plays a crucial role in many women's childhood. Embroiderers I interviewed all admitted that embroidery had provided a means of gaining affirmation and attention from the adult world: 'I was the eldest of five, but a real loner. I was by myself all the time. Throughout my primary school days embroidering was the one thing I felt gave me kudos amongst adults.'[52] To embroider announced to adults that she was good and feminine, not naughty and masculine. This path to adult approval and conformity appealed because it provided a way of gaining needed love and attention; but also because, quite simply, embroidery was enjoyable:

> Did I embroider as a child? Yellow daisies round the tea-tray

cloth whiled away holiday afternoons in rainy Scarborough summers. I remember, before that even, the first sewing lessons I ever had, using thick orange silks or brown coarse 'crash cloth' were easy, a lovely feeling in the fingers, when I was five. The teacher seemed so pleased with me, always a clever, neat, teachable child. My father taught me to sew originally. He loved to make things, still does. He praised my earliest efforts, it made me want to try, it was from him I got the idea. The nuns at school gave me the skills. My feminism and friends gave me the necessity.[53]

Most embroiderers talk of the lazy-daisy tea-tray cloth still treasured by their parents: 'The Irish linen tablecloth with green embroidered shamrocks and drawn threadwork is still on the trolley at my parents' home.'[54]

However, for middle-class women embroidery usually ceases when they leave home and family, and comes to a full stop if they go to university: 'My parents were pleased with my embroidery, quite proud of it, but I stopped for a while at university because knitting, embroidery and crochet seemed like the kind of suburban things I had left behind.'[55] But above all embroidery represented the feminine, the emotional, the family, considered at odds with intellectual life. For some embroiderers the split created a deep sense of conflict:

> I am a sociologist – I cringe – never say this – why? Because it seems a lie. I care about my work, but it is not part of me as are patchwork and embroidery. Should I try to make it so, is my sewing a clinging to a dependent, passive childhood, a female stereotype, or is it truly me?[56]

The psychic disjuncture she describes is confirmed by attitudes she faces in the college where she works: 'I was doing a patchwork cushion with embroidered details one day in the staffroom and the Head of Department was entirely contemptuous. I soon learned never to tell people I embroider.'[57]

The categorical separation of femininity/embroidery from masculinity/professionalism is the outcome of the Victorian success in preserving embroidery as the demarcator of women's sphere. A comparison between Victorian and twentieth-century attitudes towards the art nevertheless reveals telling differerences.

As long as Victorian women overtly fulfilled the feminine ideal of sensitivity and service with their embroidery, stitching selflessly for home and husband, they could expect their work to be regarded with chivalrous deference. Only if they became 'selfishly' absorbed in their work did they encounter mockery.

The Victorians identified embroidery with femininity in the context of rigidly defined sex roles. Embroidery is still identified with femininity, but the framework has changed. Women have challenged the constraints of femininity and entered previously masculine preserves. On the whole women no longer embroider as a gesture of wifely or domestic duty. But the aspect of embroidery as a bond between women has lived on. Books, exhibitions, magazines and societies devoted to embroidery and dominated by women constitute a curiously autonomous female area. It is largely ignored by men. Chivalrous approval has given way to silence, unless embroidery is carried across the borders into masculine territory. An embroiderer can become a sociologist but does not bring her work out in staffroom, boardroom or pub.

The laughter provoked by embroidery practised 'out of place' illustrates the strength of sexual divisions in society. In the history of embroidery we can see both the negative and positive effects of the art's position in relation to the social structuring of sex difference and art practice. The role of embroidery in the construction of femininity has undoubtedly constricted the development of the art. What women depicted in thread became determined by notions of femininity, and the resulting femininity of embroidery defined and constructed its practitioners in its own image. However, the vicious circle has never been complete. Limited to practising art with needle and thread, women have nevertheless sewn a subversive stitch – managed to make meanings of their own in the very medium intended to inculcate self-effacement.

For women today, the contradictory and complex history of embroidery is important because it reveals that definitions of sexual difference, and the definitions of art and artist so weighted against women, are not fixed. They have shifted over the centuries, and they can be transformed in the future.

Notes

Chapter One

1 John Ezard, 'Victorian Touch to Credit Cold Britain', *The Guardian*, 6 December 1979.
2 Adrian Hopkins, 'Firm but Not Fixed in Their Ways', *The Guardian*, 30 March 1979.
3 Simone de Beauvoir, The *Second Sex*. London: Penguin Books, 1972, p 635.
4 Juliet Mitchell, *Psychoanalysis and Feminism*. London: Penguin Books, 1974, p 363.
5 Ibid.
6 Gayle Rubin, 'The Traffic in Women: Notes on the "Political Economy of Sex" ', in Rayna R. Reiter, editor, *Toward an Anthropology of Women*. New York: Monthly Review Press, 1975, p 196.
7 Millicent Fawcett, cited in Theodore Stanton, *The Woman Question in Europe*. London: 1884, p 6.
8 Rozsika Parker and Griselda Pollock, *Old Mistresses: Women, Art and Ideology*. London: Routledge & Kegan Paul, 1981.
9 Helen Black, *Notable Authors of the Day*. London: 1893, p 169.
10 Ibid. p 27.
11 Ibid. p 78.
12 May Sinclair, *The Helpmate*. London: 1907, Ch XXIX.
13 Ibid. Ch XXXI.

14 Edith Wharton, *The Age of Innocence*. London: Penguin Books, 1974, Ch V.

15 Ibid. Ch XXXI.

16 Colette, *Earthly Paradise*, London: Secker and Warburg, 1966, p 205.

17 Ibid. p 214–216.

18 Ibid.

19 Jane Gardam, 'Dead Heat', *Cosmopolitan*, July, 1981.

20 Joseph Breuer and Sigmund Freud, *Studies on Hysteria*, in James Strachey, editor, *The Complete Works of Sigmund Freud*. London: The Hogarth Press, Vol 2, p 12.

21 Olive Schreiner, *From Man to Man*. London: Virago, 1982, Ch XI.

22 Ibid. Ch IX.

23 Ibid. Ch VI.

24 Ibid. Ch IX.

25 Ruth First and Ann Scott, *Olive Schreiner*. London: André Deutsch, 1980, p 175.

Chapter Two

1 Mrs Hugo Reed, *A Plea for Women*. London: 1843, p 200. Cited in Patricia Hollis, *Women in Public: The Women's Movement 1850–1900*. London: George Allen & Unwin, 1979, p 8.

2 Elizabeth Barrett Browning, *Aurora Leigh and other poems*, introduced by Cora Kaplan. London: The Women's Press, 1979, p 9.

3 Alice Chandler, *A Dream of Order: The Mediaeval Ideal in Nineteenth Century Literature*. London: Routledge & Kegan Paul, 1971, p 195.

4 See Kate Millett, 'The Debate over Women', in Martha Vicinus, editor, *Suffer and Be Still: Women in the Victorian Age*. Bloomington: Indiana University Press, 1972, p 122.

5 T.H. Lister, 'Rights and Conditions of Women', *Edinburgh Review*, 1841, Vol 73. Cited in Patricia Hollis, op. cit. p 8.

6 A.W. Pugin, *On the Present State of Ecclesiastical Architecture in Britain*. London: Charles Dolmon, 1843, p 83.

7 C.E.M., *Hints on Ornamental Needlework as Applied to Ecclesiastical Purposes*. London: 1843. Cited in B. Morris, *Victorian Embroidery*, London: Herbert Jenkins, 1962, p 88.

8 A.W. Pugin, op. cit., p 85.

9 Sarah Ellis, *Women of England*. London: 1839.

10 Miss Lambert, *Church Needlework*. London 1844, p 7.

11 Ibid.

12 See *Needle and Bobbin Club Bulletin*, 1976, Number 59, for an article by Joan Edwards discussing the attribution of Elizabeth Stone's book to Viscountess Wilton.

13 Viscountess Wilton, *Art of Needlework*. London: 1840, p 3.

14 C.H. Hartshorne, *English Mediaeval Embroidery*. London: 1848, p 21.

15 Frances and Hugh Marshall, *Old English Embroidery: Its Technique and Symbolism*. London: 1894, p 21.

16   C.H. Hartshorne, op. cit. p 3.
17   Grace Christie, *English Mediaeval Embroidery*. Oxford: Oxford University Press, 1938, p 31.
18   Timothy Hilton, *The Pre-Raphaelites*. London: Thames and Hudson, 1979, p 65.
19   Christina Rossetti, in *From the Antique*, 28 June 1854.
20   Viscountess Wilton, op. cit. p 85.
21   Mrs Warren and Mrs Pullan, *Treasures of Needlework*. London: 1855, Introduction.
22   Miss Lambert, *The Handbook of Needlework*. New York: 1842, p 8.
23   Norman Denny and Josephine Filmer Sanker, *The Bayeux Tapestry*. London: Collins, 1970; also F. Stenton, editor, *The Bayeux Tapestry*. London: Phaidon, 1957.
24   Arnold Hauser, *The Social History of Art*. London: Routledge & Kegan Paul, 1951. Volume 1, p 17.
25   Viscountess Wilton, op. cit., p 119–120.
26   Ibid. p 138.
27   Leonore Davidoff, *The Best Circles: Society, Etiquette and The Season*. London: Croom Helm, 1973.
28   Viscountess Wilton, op. cit., p 143.
29   Ibid., p 123.
30   Eileen Power, in M.M. Postan, editor, *Mediaeval Women*. Cambridge: Cambridge University Press, 1975, p 36.
31   Meg Bogin, *The Women Troubadors*. London: Paddington Press, 1976.
32   Viscountess Wilton, op. cit., p 120.
33   John Ruskin, 'Of Queen's Gardens', in *Sesame and Lillies*. London: 1865.
34   Lady Marion Alford, *Needlework as Art*. London: Sampson Low, Marston, Searle and Rivington, 1886, p 2.
35   Ibid. p 10.
36   Ibid. p 343.
37   Meg Bogin, op. cit., p 144.
38   Gilbert French, *Practical Remarks on some of the Minor Accessories to the Services of the Church* (1844). Cited in B. Morris, op. cit. p 89.
39   Reverend T. James, *Church Work for Ladies*, a paper read to the Architectural Society of the Archdeaconry of Northampton. Published in *The Ecclesiologist*, 1855, Volume 16, p 379. Cited in B. Morris, op. cit. p 26.
40   Ladies Ecclesiastical Embroidery Society. Cited in B. Morris, op. cit., p 87.
41   Edmund Street, a paper read to the Durham Architectural Society, in *The Ecclesiologist*, 1863, Volume 21. Cited in B. Morris, op. cit. p 87.
42   Miss Lambert, *Church Needlework*. London: 1844, p 32.
43   Robert Barnes, Lumlean Lecture, *The Lancet*, 1873. Cited in Lorna Duffin, 'The Conspicuous Consumptive Woman as Invalid', Sara Delamont and Lorna Duffin, editors, *The Nineteenth Century Woman, Her Cultural and Physical World*. London: Croom Helm, 1978, p 32.

44 Anne Oakley, 'Wisewomen and Medicine Men: Changes in the Management of Childbirth', in Anne Oakley and Juliet Mitchell, editors, *The Rights and Wrongs of Women*. London: Penguin Books, 1976, p 57.

45 St Bernard cited in Mâle, Emile. *The Gothic Image*. London: Icon, 1972, p 244.

46 Lorna Duffin, op. cit. p 31.

47 May Morris, *Burlington Magazine*, July–Sept 1905, Volume 7, p 302.

Chapter Three

1 Matthew Paris, cited in Grace Christie, *English Mediaeval Embroidery*. Oxford: Oxford University Press, 1938, p 2.

2 Mary Symonds and Louisa Preece, *Needlework Through the Ages*, London: Hodder and Stoughton, 1928, pp 210–211.

3 A.F. Kendrick, *English Needlework*. London: A. & C. Black, 1967, p 40.

4 Eileen Power, *Mediaeval English Nunneries*. Cambridge: Cambridge University Press, 1922, p 257.

5 Lina Eckenstein, *Women under Monasticism*. Cambridge: Cambridge University Press, 1896.

6 The Premonstratensian Edict of 1134 expelling women from the order. Cited in F. and J. Gies, *Women in the Middle Ages*. New York: Thomas Y. Crowell, 1978, p 87.

7 Ibid. p 91.

8 *Ancren Riwle*, cited in Eileen Power, op. cit. p 258.

9 Matthew Paris, cited in F. and J. Gies, op. cit. p 91.

10 Ibid. p 93.

11 Ibid. p 93. See also Brenda M Bolton 'Vitae Matrum: A Further Aspect of the Frauenfrage' in Derek Baker, editor, *Mediaeval Women: Studies in Church History*. Oxford: Blackwell, 1978, Subsidia 1.

12 *The Book of Brother John Stone*, 1467, cited in G. Christie, op. cit. p 37.

13 'Notes on Some Mediaeval Embroideries' in *Proceedings of the Society of Antiquarians*, Second Series, 1907, Volume 12, p 389.

14 Mary Gostelow, *Embroidery*. London: Mills & Boon, 1977, p 86.

15 G. Christie, op. cit. p 18.

16 A.F. Kendrick, *English Needlework*, p 2. The catalogue introduction to an Arts Council Exhibition, *Opus Anglicanum*, 1963, is exceptional in acknowledging equal participation by both sexes in the workshops.

17 G. Christie, op. cit. p 18.

18 C.H. Hartshorne, *English Mediaeval Embroidery*. London: 1848, p 20.

19 M. Fitch, 'London Makes of Opus Anglicanum', *Transactions of the London and Middlesex Archeological Society*, 1976, Volume 27, pp 288–296.

20 R. Kent Lancaster, 'Artists, Suppliers and Clerks: the Human Factor in the Art Patronage of King Henry III', *Journal of the*

Warburg and Courtauld Institute, Volume 35, pp 81–107.

21 Calendar of Liberate Rolls 2, 3 & 4, cited in R. Kent Lancaster, op. cit.

22 Sylvia Thrupp, 'Mediaeval Industry 1000–1500', in C. Cippola, editor, *Fontana Economic History of Europe*. London: Fontana, 1972.

23 Eileen Power, in M.M. Postan, editor, *Mediaeval Women*. Cambridge: Cambridge University Press, 1975.

24 Catherine Hall, 'History of the Housewife', *Spare Rib*, Number 26, 1974, p 9.

25 Marion K. Dale, *Women in the Textile Industries and Trade of Fifteenth Century England*. Unpublished MA thesis, University of London, 1928.

26 A.H. Thomas, editor, *Calendar of Plea and Memorial Rolls 1364–1381*. Cambridge: 1929. Cited in G. Christie, op. cit., p 36.

27 Plea and Memorial Rolls A 10 m 14, A 14 m 5d. Cited in M.K. Dale, op. cit.

28 G. Christie, op. cit. p 35.

29 May Morris, 'Opus Anglicanum at the Burlington Fine Arts Club', *Burlington Magazine*, July–Sept 1905, Volume 7, p 302.

30 Eileen Power, in *Mediaeval Women* op. cit.

31 Close Rolls cited in R Kent Lancaster, op. cit.

32 Ibid.

33 Ibid.

34 Ibid.

35 Susan Mosher Stuard, editor, *Women in Mediaeval Society*. Philadelphia: University of Pennsylvania Press, 1976, p 9.

36 R.W. Southern, *Western Society and the Church in the Middle Ages*. London: Hodder and Stoughton, 1970, p 310.

37 The Decretum, cited in Julia O'Faolain and Lauro Martines, editors, *Not in God's Image*. New York: Harper & Row, 1973, p 130.

38 The Apocryphal Gospels originated in the East during the early days of Christianity. The Church officially condemned them in the sixth century.

39 The standard collection of legends of Christian saints, *The Golden Legend*, was prepared by Jacopus Voragine in the 1260s.

40 Herreus cited in Emile Mâle, *The Gothic Image*. London: Icon, 1972, p 165.

41 Merlin Stone, *The Paradise Papers*. London: Virago, 1976. See also Mary Daly, *The Church and the Second Sex*. Boston: Beacon Books, 1968.

42 Arnold Hauser, *The Social History of Art*, Volume 1. London: Routledge & Kegan Paul, 1900.

43 The scene can be found on the Brunswick Cope of the twelfth century, the Syon Cope, the Pienza Cope and the Vich Cope, all from the first half of the fourteenth century.

44 Marina Warner, *Alone of All Her Sex: The Myth and Cult of the Virgin Mary*. London: Quartet Books, 1978, p 104.

45 Ibid. pp 276–277.

46 *The Book of James* and *The Gospel According to St Thomas* were combined to form two apocryphal books, *The Gospel According to*

Pseudo Matthew and *The Story of the Nativity of Mary*

47 St Jerome Comm. in Epist. ad Ephes. 5, cited in Mary Daly, op. cit., p 210.
48 Marina Warner, op. cit.
49 Emile Mâle, op. cit.
50 Kay Lacey, *Mediaeval Women in England, Fourteenth and Fifteenth Centuries: Images and Realities.* Unpublished thesis, University College of North Wales, Bangor, 1977.
51 Adrienne Rich, *Of Woman Born: Motherhood as Institution and Experience.* London: Virago, 1977, p 105.
52 Emile Mâle, op. cit.
53 Jacopus Voragine, *The Golden Legend.* London: J.M. Dent, 1900.
54 Proceedings from the St Gertrud Symposium 'Women in the Middle Ages'. Birte Carle, Nanna Demsholt, Karen Glente et al, editors, *Aspects of Female Existence.* Copenhagen: Gyldendal, 1980.
55 Ibid.
56 Lina Eckenstein, op. cit. p 326.
57 Ibid. p 327.
58 St Thomas Aquinas, cited in Julia O'Faolain and Lauro Martines, editors, op. cit. p 131.

Chapter Four

1 W.R. Lethaby, introduction to Grace Christie, *Embroidery and Tapestry Weaving.* London: John Hogg, 1906.
2 For example, Ruth Kelso, *Doctrine for the Lady of the Renaissance.* Urbana: University of Illinois Press, 1956. Joan Kelly-Gadol, 'Did Women Have a Renaissance?', in Renate Bridenthal and Claudia Koonz, *Becoming Visible: Women in European History.* Boston: Houghton Mifflin, 1977.
3 Ian Maclean, *The Renaissance Notion of Woman.* Cambridge: Cambridge University Press, 1980.
4 Baldassare Castiglione, *The Book of the Courtier.* Venice: 1528. Translated, George Bull, Harmondsworth: Penguin Books, 1967, p 217.
5 Ibid. p 220.
6 Ibid. p 221.
7 In the ancient physiology still current in the middle ages the four cardinal humours were blood, phlegm, choler and melancholy; the variant mixtures of these humours in different people determined their 'complexions' or 'temperaments', their physical and mental qualities, their dispositions.
8 Ian Maclean, op. cit.
9 Frederigo Luigini, cited in Ruth Kelso, op. cit., p 121.
10 Leon Battista Alberti, *On the Family*, cited in Julia O'Faolain and Lauro Martines, op. cit., p 187.
11 Ruth Kelso, op. cit., p 44.
12 Baldassare Castiglione, op. cit., p 214.
13 G. Ciotti, cited in Ruth Kelso, op. cit., p 46.
14 Marina Warner, op. cit., p 182.

15 Baldassare Castiglione, op. cit., p 219.

16 Barbara Snook, *English Historical Embroidery*. London: Batsford, 1960.

17 For further information see George Unwin, *The Guilds and Companies of London*. London: Methuen, 1908; Francis Aiden Hibbert, *The Influence and Development of English Guilds*. Cambridge University Press, 1897; Toulmin Smith and L.T. Smith, *The English Guilds (1870). Oxford University Press, 1964; Christopher Holford, A Chat About The Broderers' Company*, London: George Allen, 1910. K. Abram 'Women Traders in Mediaeval London', in *The Economic Journal*, Volume 26, June 1916.

18 Calendar of Patent Rolls 1441, 6, p 496. Cited in Marion K. Dale, *Women in the Textile Industries and Trade of Fifteenth Century England*. Unpublished MA thesis, University of London, 1928.
W.R. Lethaby, 'The Broderers of London and Opus Anglicanum', *Burlington Magazine*, Volume XXIX, May, 1916.

19 Mary Gostelow, *A World of Embroidery*, London: Mills and Boon, 1975.

20 An exhibition of works of art belonging to the livery companies was held at the Victoria and Albert Museum in 1926.

21 Priory Church of St Peter, Dunstable, church guide book.

22 Cited in Kathleen Casey, 'The Cheshire Cat: Reconstructing the Experience of Mediaeval Women', in Berenice A. Carroll, editor, *Liberating Women's History*. Urbana: University of Illinois Press, 1976.

23 Ibid. p 248.

24 Christine de Pisan, cited in Ruth Kelso, op. cit., p 261.

25 Lu Emily Pearson, *Elizabethans at Home*. Stamford: Stamford University Press, 1957, p 81.

26 Edmund Harrison, cited in Mary Eirwen Jones, *A History of Western Embroidery*. London: Studio Vista, 1969, p 34.

27 Cited in A.F. Kendrick, *English Needlework*. London: A. and C. Black, 1967, p 49.

28 Cited in George Wingfield Digby, *Elizabethan Embroidery*. London: Faber and Faber, 1963, p 62.

29 Linda Nochlin and Ann Sutherland Harris, *Women Artists 1550–1950*. New York: County Museum of Art and Alfred A. Knopf, 1976, p 17.

30 George Wingfield Digby, op. cit., p 24.

31 Cited in Thomasina Beck, *Embroidered Gardens*. London: Angus and Robertson, 1979, p 21.

32 Cited in Thomasina Beck, op. cit., p 28.

33 Cited in Dorothy Gardiner, *English Girlhood at School*. Oxford: Oxford University Press, 1929, p 192–3.

34 C.S.L. Davies, *Peace, Print and Protestantism 1450–1558*. London: Paladin, 1977, p 327.

35 Baldassare Castiglione, op. cit., p 217.

36 Ralph Holinshed, William Harrison and others, *The First and Second Volumes of Chronicles, containing the Description and History of England, Ireland and Scotland (1557–1587)*.

37 Christine de Pisan, *Le Livre des Trois Vertus* 1497 (1505, 1536).

38 Erasmus of Rotterdam, *Christiani Matrimonii Institutio*, 1526. Cited in Julia O'Faolain and Lauro Martines, op. cit., p 182.
39 Louise Labe, J. Aynard, editors, *Les Poètes Lyonnais Précurseurs de la Pléiade*. Paris: 1924, p 157. Cited in Julia O'Faolain and Lauro Martines, op. cit., p 185.
40 Rosemary Freeman, *English Emblem Books*. London: Chatto and Windus, 1948, p 4.
41 Margaret Swain, *The Needlework of Mary Queen of Scots*. New York: Van Nostrand Reinhold, 1973, p 36.
42 Ibid. p 63.
43 George Wingfield Digby, op. cit., p 123.
44 Ibid.
45 See the Oxburgh Hangings and *The Shepeard Buss* at the Victoria and Albert Museum.
46 J.L. Nevinson, 'English Domestic Embroidery Patterns of the Sixteenth and Seventeenth Centuries', *The Walpole Society*, Volume 28, 1938–40, p 5.
47 Cited in M. Jourdain, *English Secular Embroidery*. London: Kegan Paul, Trench, Trubner and Co., 1910, p 56.
48 Harriet Bridgeman and Elizabeth Drury, editors, *Needlework*. London and New York: Paddington Press, 1978, p 130–134.
49 Baldassare Castiglione, op. cit., p 70.
50 Ernst Lefebure, *Embroidery and Lace*, translated and enlarged by Alan Cole. London: H. Gravel and Co., 1888, p 7.

Chapter Five

1 Mary Wollstonecraft, *The Vindication of the Rights of Women*. London: 1792. Miriam Kramnick, editor, London: Penguin Books, 1978, p 220–221.
2 Philippe Aries, *Centuries of Childhood*. London: Penguin Books, 1979.
3 Roger Thompson, *Women in Stuart England and America*. London: Routledge & Kegan Paul, 1974.
4 M Jourdain, *English Secular Embroidery*. London: Kegan Paul, Trench, Trubner and Co., p 75.
5 Dorothy Gardiner, op. cit. p 213.
6 Ann, Lady Fanshawe, *The Memoirs of Ann, Lady Fanshawe*. London: John Lane, 1907, p 22.
7 Lucy Hutchinson, editor, *Memoirs of Colonel Hutchinson*. London: John C. Nimmo, 1906, p 17.
8 Grace Sherrington, cited in Dorothy Gardiner, op. cit., p 192.
9 John Taylor, *The Needle's Excellency*, London: James Boler, 1624. Third edition by 1634.
10 William Shakespeare, *A Midsummer Night's Dream*. Act 3, Scene 1.
11 Joan Edwards, *Crewel Embroidery in England*. London: B.T. Batsford, 1975, p 40.
12 Christopher Hill, *Reformation to Industrial Revolution*. London. Penguin Books, 1967, p 40.
13 Mary Tattlewell and Joan Hit-Him-Home, *The Women's Sharpe*

Revenge. Cited in Caroll Camden, *The Elizabethan Woman 1540–1640*, p 269.

14   Hannah Smith, cited in A.F. Kendrick, *English Needlework*. London: A. and C. Black, 1967, p 129.

15   Christopher Hill, op. cit., p 98.

16   Sheila Rowbotham, *Hidden from History*. London: Pluto Press, 1973, p 8–9.

17   Jasper Mayne, cited in Averil Colby, *Samplers*. London: B.T. Batsford, 1964, p 58.

18   Thomas Milles, cited in Averil Colby, op. cit., p 155.

19   Roberta Hamilton, *The Liberation of Women*. London: George Allen and Unwin, 1978.

20   Ibid.

21   Martin Luther, *Table Talk*, 1531. Cited in Julia O'Faolain and Lauro Martines, op. cit. p 196.

22   Martin Luther, *Table Talk*, 1531. Cited in Sherrin Marshall Wyntjes, 'Women in the Reformation Era', in Renate Bridenthal and Claudia Koonz, editors, op. cit., p 174.

23   Hannah Wooley, cited in Ada Wallas, *Before the Blue Stockings*. London: George Allen and Unwin, 1923, p 33.

24   Lady Marion Alford, op. cit.

25   Alexander Pope, cited in Thomasina Beck, op. cit., p 53.

26   John Evelyn, cited in Thomasina Beck, op. cit., p 60.

27   Peter Heylin, cited in Alice Clark, *Working Women in the Seventeenth Century*. London: Cass, 1968, p 239.

28   Averil Colby, op. cit.

29   Nancy Graves Cabot, 'Pattern Sources of Scriptural Subjects in Tudor and Stuart Embroideries', in *New York Needle and Bobbin Club Bulletin*, Volume 30, Nos 1 & 2, 1946.

30   Bathsua Makin, *An Essay to Revive the Ancient Education of Gentlewomen*, London, 1693.

31   Anne Finch, Countess of Winchilsea, cited in Cora Kaplan, introduction, *Salt and Bitter and Good*. London: Paddington Press, 1975, p 62.

32   Alice Clark, op. cit., p 25.

33   Sheila Rowbotham, *Women, Resistance and Revolution*. London: Allen Lane, 1972, p 20.

34   Alice Clark, op. cit.

35   *Hic Mulier: Or the Man–Woman*, cited in Caroll Camden, op. cit., p 263.

36   John Chamberlain, cited in Caroll Camden, op. cit., p 263.

37   William Prynne, cited in Caroll Camden, op. cit., p 263.

38   Sheila Rowbotham, *Hidden from History*, p 3.

39   Cited in Doris Mary Stenton, *The English Woman in History*. London: George, Allen and Unwin, 1957, p 205.

40   Ibid. p 212–213.

41   Una Birch, *Anna Maria von Schurman: Artist, Scholar, Saint*. London: Longman's Green & Co., 1909, p 71.

42   Hannah Wooley, *The Gentlewoman's Companion*. London: 1675, p 1.

43   Ibid.

44 Bathsua Makin, cited in Mahl and Koon, op. cit., p 130.
45 Bathsua Makin, cited in Dorothy Gardiner, op. cit., p 224.
46 Cited in Christopher Hill, op. cit., p 278.
47 Bathsua Makin, op. cit., p 26.
48 Cora Kaplan, op. cit., p 14.
49 Ibid. p 29.
50 Ibid. p 61.
51 Christopher Hill, op. cit., p 96.
52 Sheila Rowbotham, *Hidden from History*, p 3.
53 Cited in Therle Hughes, *English Domestic Needlework, 1660–1860*. London: Lutterworth Press, 1961, p 122.
54 Roger Thompson, op. cit., p 204.
55 Cited in Alice Clark, op. cit., p 32.
56 David Masson, *Life of Milton*. London: Macmillan, Volume 6, p 650.
57 Doris Mary Stenton, op. cit., p 110.
58 Alice Clark, op. cit., p 235.
59 Ibid.
60 Christopher Holford, *A Chat About the Broderers' Company*, op cit.
61 Ibid.

Chapter Six

1 George Wingfield Digby, 'Lady Julia Calverley Embroideress', in *The Connoisseur*, May 1960.
2 Christopher Hill, *Reformation to Industrial Revolution*. London: Penguin Books, 1969, p 19.
3 Raymond Williams, *The Country and the City*. London: Chatto and Windus, 1973, p 21.
4 John Barrell, *The Dark Side of the Landscape: The Rural Poor in English Painting 1730–1840*. Cambridge: Cambridge University Press, 1980, p 9.
5 Margaret Swain, *Figures on Fabric, Embroidery Design Sources and Their Application*. London: A. and C. Black, 1980.
6 John Barrell, op. cit., p 12.
7 Ibid. p 15.
8 George Wingfield Digby, op. cit.
9 *The Spectator*, No. 606, 1716.
10 Ibid.
11 Ibid.
12 *The Spectator*, No. 609, 1716.
13 John Barrell, op. cit. p 52.
14 Thomasina Beck, op. cit.
15 Sheila Rowbotham, *Hidden from History*. Op. cit., p 15.
16 Patricia Branca, *Women in Europe Since 1750*. London: Croom Helm, 1978, p 89–91.
17 Lady Mary Wortley Montague, cited in Dorothy Gardiner, op. cit., p 396.
18 Samuel Richardson, *Pamela*. London: Dent Dutton 1979, p 28.
19 George Paston, *Little Memoirs of the Eighteenth Century*, cited in

M. Jourdain, *English Secular Embroidery*. London: Kegan Paul, Trench, Trubner and Co, 1910, p 3.

20 R. Parker and G. Pollock, *Old Mistresses, Women, Art and Ideology*. London: Routledge & Kegan Paul, 1981.

21 R. Walpole, *Anecdotes of Painting*. London: 1762, Volume 5.

22 Lady Llanover, editor, *The Autobiography and Correspondence of Mary Cranville, Mrs Pelany*. London: 1861, Volume 2, p 581.

23 Heckell, cited in A.F. Kendrick, *English Needlework*. London: A. and C. Black, 1967.

24 Cited in M. Jourdain, op. cit. p 107.

25 R. Walpole, cited in Ellen Clayton, *English Female Artists*. London: Tinsley Brothers, 1876, Volume 2, p 140.

26 Ruth Hayden, *Mrs Delany: Her Life and Her Flowers*. London: Colonnade Books, 1980, p 105.

27 Mary Delany's letters, cited in M. Jourdain, op. cit. p 105.

28 *Diary of Fanny Burney*, 17 July 1768. Ten volumes (with letters), Oxford University Press, 1972–82.

29 Mary Delany's letters, cited in M. Jourdain, op. cit. p 103–104.

30 Susan Moller Okin, *Women in Western Political Thought*. London: Virago, 1980.

31 Jean Jacques Rousseau, *Emile*. trans. W.H. Payne. London: Edward Arnold, 1902, Book 5, 'The Education of Warren'.

32 Ibid.

33 Ibid.

34 Ibid.

35 Mary Wollstonecraft, op. cit. p 177.

36 Margaret Swain, *Historical Needlework, A Study of Influences in Scotland and Northern England*. London: Barrie and Jenkins, 1970.

37 Rev. John Bower, cited in Margaret Swain, *The Flowerers: The Origins and History of Ayrshire Needlework*. Edinburgh: W.R. Chambers, 1955, p 22. This book was my major source of information on this subject.

38 Cited in Ivy Pinchbeck, *Women Workers and the Industrial Revolution 1750–1850*. London: Virago, 1981, p 214–215.

39 Robert Campbell, *The London Tradesman*, 1747.

40 Ibid. p 115.

41 Ibid. p 153.

42 Ibid.

43 Cited in E.A. Standen, *Working for Love and Working for Money: Some Notes on Embroiderers and Embroidereries of the Past*. New York: Metropolitan Museum of Art, 1966, pp 17, 18.

44 Jean Jacques Rousseau, *Emile*, Book 1.

45 William Buchan, *Domestic Medicine, or a Treatise on the Prevention and Care of Diseases by Regimen and Simple Medicines*, 1769.

46 Nancy Chodorow, *The Reproduction of Mothering: Psychoanalysis and the Sociology of Gender*. Berkeley: University of California Press, 1978.

47 Ibid.

48 *The Diary of Fanny Burney*, cited in M. Philips and W.S. Tomkinson, *English Women in Life and Letters*. Oxford: Oxford

University Press, 1926, p 228.

49   Isaac Watts, *Treatise on the Education of Children and Youth*, cited in Dorothy Gardiner, op. cit., p 374–375.

50   Averil Colby, *Samplers*. London: B.T. Batsford, 1964, p 171.

51   Hugh Honour, *Neo-Classicism*. London: Penguin Books, 1968, p 20.

52   Ibid. p 35.

53   Ibid. pp 35, 36.

54   Toni Flores Fratto, 'Samplers: One of the Lesser American Arts', *Feminist Art Journal*, Winter, 1976–1977.

55   Correspondence between Martha and Thomas Jefferson, cited in Mildred J. Davis, *Early American Embroidery Designs*. New Jersey, Textile Book Service, 1969, p 25.

56   Cited in Mirra Bank, *Anonymous Was a Woman*. New York: St Martin's Press, 1979. p 44.

57   Mary Wollstonecraft, op. cit. p 57.

58   Ibid. p 107.

59   Ibid.

60   Ibid. p 121.

61   Ibid. p 170.

62   Ibid. p 171.

63   William Buchan, op. cit. p 27.

64   Mary Wollstonecraft, op. cit. p 171.

65   Eliza Heywood, cited in Mary R. Mahl and Helene Koon, editors, *The Female Spectator: English Women Writers Before 1800*. Bloomington and London: Indiana University Press, 1977, p 234.

66   Mary Wollstonecraft, op. cit., p 170.

67   Ibid. p 288.

68   Ibid. p 170.

69   Ibid. p 147.

70   Hannah More, *The Practical Use of Female Knowledge with a Sketch of the Female Character and a Comparative View of the Sexes*, cited in M.R. Mahl and H. Koon, editors, op. cit.

71   Hannah More, *Remarks on the Present Mode of Educating Females*, 1794, p 48.

72   Ibid.

73   Maria Edgeworth, *Essays of Practical Education*, 1798. 1822 edition, p 375.

74   John Barrell, op. cit. p 85.

75   Cited in M. Jourdain, op. cit. p 175.

Chapter Seven

1   Sarah Ellis, *Women of England*. London: Fisher, Son and Co., 1939, pp 10, 12.

2   Ibid. p 13.

3   Florence Nightingale, 'Cassandra', cited in Ray Strachey, *The Cause*. London: Virago, 1978, p 404.

4   Walter Houghton, *The Victorian Frame of Mind*. Cambridge, Mass. and London: Yale University Press, 1957, p 54.

5   Sarah Ellis, op. cit. p 141.

6   Mary Lamb, 'On Needlework', *Miscellaneous Prose 1798–1834.* London: Methuen and Co., 1903, p 176–180.

7   Ibid.

8   Charlotte Bronte, *Shirley*, first published 1849, Chapter 23.

9   Ibid. Chapter 6.

10 Cited in Irene Danciger, *A World of Women: An Illustrated History of Women's Magazines,* London: Gill and Macmillan 1978, p 71.

11 Millicent Garrett Fawcett, 'The Education of Women of Middle and Upper Classes', *Macmillan's Magazine,* (no 17, 1865, p 511–517) cited in Carol Bauer and Lawrence Ritt, editors, *Free and Enobled: Source Readings in the Development of Victorian Feminism.* Oxford: Pergamon Press, 1979, p 120.

12 Dinah M Craik, *A Woman's Thoughts About Woman.* London: 1891, p 81.

13 Elizabeth, Dowager Queen of Romania, cited in Lolo Markevich and Heinz Kiewe, *Victorian Fancywork: Nineteenth Century Needlepoint Pattern and Design.* London: Pitman, 1975, p 169.

14 Leonore Davidoff, op. cit.

15 Richard Sennett, *The Fall of Public Man.* Cambridge: Cambridge University Press, 1977.

16 Charlotte Brontë, *Jane Eyre*, First published 1847, Chapter 10.

17 Maria and R.L. Edgeworth, *Essays on Practical Education.* London: 1822, Volume 1, p 386.

18 *Ladies Magazine*, July, 1810.

19 Sarah Ellis, op. cit. p 106.

20 Elizabeth Sandford, *Woman in Her Social and Domestic Character.* London: 1831, p 136.

21 Sarah Ellis, op. cit., p 15–16.

22 Ibid. p 18.

23 Ibid. p 20.

24 Mrs Warren and Mrs Pullan, op. cit. Introduction.

25 Sarah Ellis, op. cit., p 218.

26 G.R. Drysdale, *The Elements of Social Science.* 1854, p 357. Cited in Walter Houghton, op. cit., p 381.

27 Virginia Woolf, *Orlando.* London: Penguin Books, 1980, p 147.

28 'Girls, Wives and Mothers: A Word to the Middle Classes', *Chamber's Journal,* 1884, Volume 73, cited in Carol Bauer and Lawrence Ritt, op. cit., p 249.

29 Cited in Irene Dansiger, op. cit., p 64.

30 Cited in Averil Colby, *Samplers.* London: Batsford, 1964, p 254–255.

31 Leonore Davidoff, Jean L'Esperance and Howard Newby, 'Landscape with Figures: Home and Community in English Society', in Anne Oakley and Juliet Mitchell, editors, *The Rights and Wrongs of Women.* London: Penguin Books, 1976, p 139–175.

32 Virginia Woolf, op. cit., p 142.

33 Mrs Merrifield, 'On Design as Applied to Lady's Work', *The Art Journal,* 1851.

34 Cited in Lila Hailstone, *Illustrated Catalogue of Ancient Framed Needlework Pictures.* London: 1897.

35 Elizabeth Sandford, op. cit. p 4.
36 Walter Houghton, op. cit., p 98.
37 Sarah Ellis, op. cit., p 337.
38 Elizabeth Sandford, op. cit. p 98.
39 *Book of John*, Chapter 4, verses 7–44.
40 Charlotte Brontë, *Shirley*, Chapter 7.
41 George Eliot, *The Mill on the Floss*. First published 1860. Volume 3, Chapter 1.
42 Ibid., Chapter 6.
43 Leonore Davidoff, op. cit.
44 Lady Charlotte Nevill Grenville, cited in Duncan Crow, *The Victorian Woman*. London: George Allen and Unwin, 1971, p 19.
45 'The Family Secret', in *The Englishwoman's Domestic Magazine*, 1861, Volume 2, No. 12, p 295.
46 Millenarial movements believed in the imminent arrival of Christ on earth.
47 Cited in Anna Sebba, *Samplers: Five Centuries of a Gentle Craft*. London: Weidenfeld and Nicolson, 1979, p 127.
48 Ita Aber, *The Art of Judaic Needlework*. London: Bell and Hyman, 1979.
49 Mrs Oliphant, *Madam*, cited in Anne Oakley and Juliet Mitchell, op. cit., p 224.
50 Charlotte Brontë, *Shirley*, Chapter 22.
51 Ibid., Ch 28.
52 Ibid.
53 Dinah M. Craik, *Agatha's Husband*. London: 1853, Ch 5.
54 Charlotte Brontë, *Shirley*, Ch 19.
55 Elizabeth Gaskell, *Wives and Daughters*. London: 1886. Volume 1 Chs 20; 28; Volume 2 Ch 26; Volume 3 Ch 14.
56 Ibid., Volume 1, Ch 20.
57 Ibid., Volume 1, Ch 20.
58 Sarah Ellis, op. cit., p 195.
59 Mrs Catherine Hutton Beale, *Reminiscences of a Gentlewoman of the Last Century: Letters of Catherine Hutton*. London: 1897.
60 *The Ladies Magazine*, cited in Alison Adburgham, *Women in Print: Writing Women and Women's Magazines from the Restoration to the Accession of Victoria*. London: George Allen and Unwin, 1972, p 128.
61 Ackerman's *Repository of Arts, Literature, Commerce, Manufactures, Fashions and Politics*, March, 1810. I am grateful to Philippa Thistlethwaite for bringing this to my attention.
62 Elizabeth Sandford, op. cit. p 215.
63 Mrs Warren and Mrs Pullan, op. cit.
64 Geoffrey Warren, *A Stitch in Time*. London: David and Charles, 1976.
65 Charles Kingsley, *Glaucus: or the Wonders of the Shore*. Cambridge: 1855, p 4–5. I am grateful to Lynn Barber for bringing this to my attention.
66 M.T. Morrall, 'A History of Needlemaking', 1852, cited in Molly Proctor, *Victorian Canvas Work*. London: Batsford, 1972, p 151.

67   Ibid. p 152–3.
68   Mrs Warren and Mrs Pullan, op. cit., Introduction.
69   Viscountess Wilton, *Art of Needlework*. London: 1840, p 403.
70   Cited in Geoffrey Warren, op. cit., p 128.
71   Margaret Swain, *Historical Needlwork*. London: Barrie and Jenkins, 1970.
72   Ivy Pinchbeck, op. cit., p 236.
73   Ibid., p 237.
74   Ibid., p 213.
75   The Children's Employment Commission, 1843, cited in Ivy Pinchbeck, op. cit., p 212.
76   Ibid.
77   Charlotte Elizabeth Tonna, *Wrongs of Women*. London: 1844.
78   Anthea Callen, *Angel in the Studio: Women in the Arts and Crafts Movement 1870–1914*. London: Astragal Books, 1979.
79   Geoff Spenceley, 'The Lace Associations', *Victorian Studies*, Volume 78, 1973, p 434, 435. Cited in Anthea Callen, op. cit., p 3.
80   Elizabeth Gaskell, *Wives and Daughters*. p 38.
81   Barbara Russell, 'The Langdale Linen Industry', *Art Journal*, 1897, p 329–330, cited in Anthea Callen, op. cit., p 117.
82   Ibid.
83   Ibid.
84   William Morris, cited in E.P. Thompson, *William Morris: Romantic to Revolutionary*. London: Merlin Press, 1977, p 707.
85   Charles Ashbee, cited in Anthea Callan, op. cit., p 172.
86   Jane Morris, cited in Philip Henderson, *William Morris: His Life, Work and Friends*. London: Thames and Hudson, 1967, p 36.
87   Anthea Callen, op. cit.
88   William Morris, 'The Beauty of Life', in G.D.H. Cole, editor, *Prose, Lectures and Essays*. London: Nonesuch Library, 1934, p 561.
89   Barbara Morris, *Victorian Embroidery*. London: Herbert Jenkins, 1962, p 112.
90   William Morris, 'The Lesser Arts', in G.D.H. Cole, editor, op. cit., p 504.
91   William Morris, cited in Barbara Morris, op. cit., p 109–110.
92   E.P. Thompson, op. cit., p 152.
93   Lady Marion Alford, op. cit., p 152.
94   Cited in Barbara Morris, op. cit., p 205.
95   Cited in Anthea Callen, op. cit., p 110–111.
96   Cited in Santina Levey, *Discovering Embroidery of the Nineteenth Century*. London: Shire Publications, 1971, p 58.
97   Ibid.
98   Lewis F. Day and Mary Buckle, *Art In Needlework*. London: 1900, p 234.
99   H.M. Baillie Scott, 'Some Experiments in Embroidery', *Studio*, 1903.
100 *The Young Ladies Journal*, 1885.
101 *Magazine of Art*, 1879, cited in Barbara Morris, op. cit., p 141.
102 Jessie R Newery, cited in Anthea Callen, op. cit., p 124.
103 *The School Board for London Final Report*, 1902.

104 Annmarie Turnbull, unpublished thesis, Polytechnic of the South Bank, London.
105 Ibid.
106 Ibid.
107 Ibid.

Chapter Eight

1 Amedée Ozenfant, *The Foundations of Modern Art*, 1931. Cited in *Heresies*, Winter, 1978, p 41.
2 Ann Sutherland Harris and Linda Nochlin, *Women Artists 1550–1950*. op. cit. p 61.
3 Marcel Jean, editor, Joachim Neugroschal, translator, *Jean(Hans) Arp: Selected French Writings*. London: Calder and Boyars, 1974, p 232.
4 Ibid., p 229.
5 Will Grohman, 'The Dada-World of Hannah Hoch', *Marlborough Fine Arts*, January, 1966.
6 Ann Sutherland Harris and Linda Nochlin, op. cit., p 61.
7 Jacques Damase, *Sonia Delaunay*. London: Thames and Hudson, 1972.
8 Tatyana Strizhenova, Geoffrey Turner, translator, *The History of Soviet Costume*. Liverpool Polytechnic and Collets, 1972.
9 Camilla Gray, *The Russian Experiment in Art 1862–1922*. London: Thames and Hudson, 1962.
10 Natalia Gontcharova, in her 1913 exhibition catalogue, cited by John Bowlt in *Russian Women Artists of the Avant Garde 1910–1930*. Cologne: Gallerie Emurzynska, 1979, p 68.
11 Camilla Cray, op. cit., p 134.
12 Nadezhda Udaltsova, diary entry, cited by Larissa A Zhadora, in John Bowlt, op. cit., p 68.
13 Nadezhda Lamenova, cited in Tatyana Strizhenova, op. cit., p 7.
14 Ibid., p 15.
15 V.E. Tatlin, cited by L.A. Zhadova, in John Bowlt, op. cit., p 71.
16 Yevgenia Pribelskaya, cited in Tatyana Strizhenova, op. cit., p 28–29.
17 Nadezhda Lamenova, cited in Tatyana Strizhenova, op. cit., p 59.
18 Ibid., pp 19 and 38.
19 Meriel McCooey, 'Fashions the Russians Rejected', *Sunday Times*, 11 October, 1981.
20 Ibid.
21 Lady Frances Balfour, cited in Roger Fulford, *Votes for Women*. London: Faber and Faber, 1957, p 136.
22 Paula Harper, 'Suffrage Posters', *Spare Rib*, Number 41, 1975.
23 Constance Howard, *Twentieth-Century Embroidery in Great Britain to 1939*. London: B.T. Batsford, 1981, p 44.
24 Janie Terreno, cited in Roger Fulford, op. cit., p 250.
25 Ibid.
26 Margaret Swanson and Ann Macbeth, *Educational Needlework*. London: Longman's Green and Co., 1913, Introduction.
27 Cited in Penelope Dalton, *Issues in the Role and Status of Needle-*

craft in Secondary Schools, unpublished MA thesis, University of Sussex and Brighton Polytechnic, 1980.

28 Ibid.
29 Rebecca Crompton, *Modern Design in Embroidery*. London: B.T. Batsford, 1936
30 Cited in Penelope Dalton, op. cit.
31 Catherine Christopher, *The Complete Book of Embroidery and Embroidery Stitches*. Surrey: World's Work, 1941, p 5.
32 Christine Risley, *Creative Embroidery*. London: Studio Vista, 1969, p 7.
33 Catherine Christopher, op. cit., p 5.
34 Michèle Roberts, interview with the author, 1981.
35 Peter Beagle, *American Denim*. New York: Harry N. Abrams, 1975, p 134.
36 Anny Brackx, interview with Beryl Weaver, 'Subverting Sweetness', *Spare Rib*, Number 67, 1978.
37 Ibid.
38 Kate Walker, interview with the author, 1981.
39 Ibid.
40 Ibid.
41 Monica Ross, 'Portrait of the Postal Event', *Mama*, 1976.
42 Phil Goodall, 'Growing Points and Pains of Feministo', *Mama*, 1976.
43 Judy Chicago with Susan Hill, *The Dinner Party Needlework*. New York: Anchor Press Doubleday, 1980, p 24.
44 Ibid., p 15.
45 Ibid.
46 Kate Walker, interview with the author, 1981.
47 Interview with Lady Tavistock by Angela Levin, 'A Room of my Own', *Observer*, 12 April, 1980.
48 *Embroidered Images* exhibition catalogue, Woodlands Art Gallery, London, August–September, 1973.
49 Winefride Jackson and Elizabeth Pettifer, *The Royal School of Needlework*. Handbook, 1981.
50 Michèle Roberts, interview with the author, 1981.
51 Anonymous, interview with author, 1981.
52 Annmarie Turnbull, interview with the author, 1981.
53 Kate Walker, interview with the author, 1981.
54 Michelene Wandor, interview with the author, 1981.
55 Ibid.
56 Annmarie Turnbull, unpublished article, *Patchworking*, London, 1979.
57 Annmarie Turnbull, interview with the author, 1981.

Select Bibliography and Further Reading

Aber, I. *The Art of Judaic Needlework*. London: Bell and Hyman, 1979.

Abram, A. 'Women Traders in Mediaeval London', *Economic Journal*, volume 26, June 1916.

Adburgham, A. *Women in Print: Writing Women and Women's Magazines from the Restoration to the Accession of Victoria*. London: George Allen and Unwin, 1972.

Alford, Lady M. *Needlework as Art*. London: Sampson Low, Marston, Searle and Rivington, 1886.

Ardener, S., editor. *Defining Females*. London: Croom Helm, 1978.

Aries, P. *Centuries of Childhood*. London: Jonathan Cape, 1962, Penguin Books, 1979.

Bank, M. *Anonymous was a Woman*. New York: St Martin's Press, 1979.

Barrell, J. *The Dark Side of the Landscape: The Rural Poor in English Painting 1730–1840*. Cambridge: Cambridge University Press, 1980.

Barrett Browning, E. *Aurora Leigh*, edited and introduced by Cora Kaplan. London: The Women's Press, 1978.

Barrett, M. *Women's Oppression Today*. London: Verso, 1980.

Bauer, C. and Ritt, L., editors. *Free and Ennobled: Source Readings in the Development of Victorian Feminism*. Oxford: Pergamon Press, 1979.

de Beauvoir, S. *The Second Sex*. London: Jonathan Cape, 1963, Penguin Books, 1972.

Beck, T. *Embroidered Gardens*. London: Angus and Robertson, 1979.

Bogin, M. *The Women Troubadors*. London: Paddington Press, 1976.

Bolton, B.M. 'Vitae Matrum: A Further Aspect of Frauenfrage', in D Baker, editor, *Mediaeval Women*. Oxford: Blackwell, 1978.

Brackx, A. 'Subverting Sweetness', *Spare Rib*, February 1978.

Bridenthal, R. and Koonz, C., editors. *Becoming Visible: Women in European History*. Boston: Houghton Mifflin, 1977.

Bridgeman, H. and Drury, G., editors. *Needlework*. London and New York: Paddington Press, 1978.

Burman, S., editor. *Fit Work for Women*. London: Croom Helm, 1979.

Callen, A., *Angel in the Studio: Women in the Arts and Crafts Movement*. London: Astragal Books, 1979.

Camden, C. *The Elizabethan Woman*. Houston: The Elsevier Press, 1979.

Carroll, B.A., editor. *Liberating Women's History*. Urbana: University of Illinois Press, 1976.

Casey, K. 'The Cheshire Cat: Reconstructing the Experience of Mediaeval Women', in Carroll, op. cit.

Castiglione, B. *The Book of the Courtier*. Venice, 1528. London: Penguin Books, 1967.

Chandler, A. *A Dream of Order: The Mediaeval Ideal in Nineteenth Century Literature*. London: Routledge & Kegan Paul, London 1971.

Chicago, J., and Hill, S. *Embroidering Our Heritage: The Dinner Party Needlework*. New York: Anchor Press Doubleday, 1980.

Chodorow, N. *The Reproduction of Mothering: Psychoanalysis and the Sociology of Gender*. Berkeley: University of California Press, 1978.

Christie, G. *Samplers and Stitches*. London: Batsford, 1920.

Christie, G. *English Mediaeval Embroidery*. Oxford: Oxford University Press, 1938.

Clark, A. *Working Life of Women in the Seventeenth Century*. London: Routledge & Kegan Paul, 1982.

Colby, A. *Samplers*. London: Batsford, 1964.

Craik, D.M. *A Woman's Thoughts About Woman*. London: Hurst and Blackett, 1891.

Davidoff, L. *The Best Circles: Society, Etiquette and the Season*. London: Croom Helm, 1973.

Davidoff, L., L'Esperance, J., Newby, H. 'Landscape with Figures: Home and Community in English Society', in Oakley and Mitchell, 1976, see below.

Delamont, S., and Duffin, L., editors. *The Nineteenth Century Woman: Her Cultural and Physical World*. London: Croom Helm, 1978.

Dewhurst, C.K., MacDowell, MacDowell, M. *Artists in Aprons*. New York: E.P. Dutton, 1979.

Digby, G.W. *Elizabethan Embroidery*. London: Faber and Faber, 1963.

Dinnerstein, D. *The Mermaid and the Minotaur*. New York: Harper Colophon Books, 1977. Published as *The Rocking of the Cradle*, London: Souvenir Press, 1978.

Donnison, J. *Midwives and Medical Men*. New York: Schocken Books, 1977.

Eckenstein, L. *Women under Monasticism*. Cambridge: Cambridge University Press, 1896.

Edgeworth, M. *Essays of Practical Education*. London: 1798.

Edwards, J. *Crewel Embroidery in England*. London: Batsford, 1975.

Ehrenreich, B. and English, D. *Witches, Midwives and Nurses*. London: Writers and Readers, 1976.

Ellis, S.S. *Women of England*. London: Fisher, Son and Co, 1939.

Fanshawe, Lady A. *The Memoirs of Ann, Lady Fanshawe*. London: John Lane, 1907.

Firestone, S. *The Dialectic of Sex*. London: Jonathan Cape, 1971; The Women's Press, 1980.

Fratto, T.F. 'Samplers, One of the Lesser American Arts', *Feminist Art Journal*, Winter, 1976–1977.

Freud, S. and Breuer, J. *Studies on Hysteria*, 1883–1885, in J. and A. Strachey, editors, *The Complete Psychological Works of Sigmund Freud*, volume 2, London: The Hogarth Press, 1932-1936, Penguin Books, 1974.

Freud, S. 'Femininity', *New Introductory Lectures on Psychoanalysis',* in J. and A. Strachey, op. cit, volume 22.

Fulford, R. *Votes for Women*. London: Faber and Faber, 1957.

Gardiner, D. *English Girlhood at School*. Oxford: Oxford University Press, 1929.

Gies, F. and J. *Women in the Middle Ages*. New York: Thomas Y. Crowell, 1978.

Godfrey, E. *Home Life under the Stuarts*. London: Grant Richards, 1903.

Gostelow, M. *Blackwork*. London: Batsford, 1976.

Gostelow, M. *The Art of Embroidery*. London: Weidenfeld and Nicolson, 1979.

Gostelow, M. *Embroidery*, London: Mills and Boon, 1977.

Gray, C. *The Russian Experiment in Art 1863–1922*. London: Thames and Hudson, 1962.

Hackenbrock, Y. *English and Other Needlework, Tapestries and Textiles in the Irwin Untermeyer Collection*. London: Thames and Hudson, 1962.

Hamilton, R. *The Liberation of Women*. London: Allen and Unwin, 1978.

Hartshorne, C.H. *Mediaeval English Embroidery*. London: 1848.

Hauser, A. *The Social History of Art*. London: Routledge and Kegan Paul, 1951.

Hayden, R. *Mrs Delany, Her Life and Flowers*. London: Colonnade

Books, 1980.

Henderson, K. et al. *The Great Divide: The Sexual Division of Labour, or 'is it art?'*, Milton Keynes: The Open University, 1979.

Hill, C. *Reformation to Industrial Revolution*. London: Weidenfeld and Nicolson, 1967; Penguin Books, 1967.

Hill, G. *Women in English Life*. London: Richard Bentley and Son, 1896.

Hole, C. *English Home Life 1500–1800*. London: Batsford, 1947.

Hollis, P. *Women in Public: The Women's Movement 1830–1900*. London: George Allen and Unwin, 1979.

Houghton, W.E. *The Victorian Frame of Mind 1830–1900*. Yale University Press, 1957.

Howard, C. *Twentieth Century Embroidery in Great Britain*. London: Batsford, 1981.

Hughes, T. *English Domestic Needlework*. London: Lutterworth Press, 1961.

Huish, M. *Samplers and Tapestry Embroidery*. London: Longmans, Green and Co., 1913.

Hutchinson, L. *Memoirs of Colonel Hutchinson*. London: John C. Nimmo, 1885.

Jones, M.E. *A History of Western Embroidery*. London: Studio Vista, 1969.

Jourdain, M.A. *English Secular Embroidery*. London: Kegan Paul, Trench, Trubner and Co, 1910.

Kanner, B., editor. *The Women of England: Interpretative Bibliographical Essays*. London: Mansell, 1980.

Kaplan, C. *Salt and Bitter and Good*. London: Paddington Press, 1973.

Kelly-Gadol, J. 'Did Women Have a Renaissance', in Bridenthal and Koonz, op. cit.

Kelso, R. *Doctrine for the Lady of the Renaissance*. Urbana: University of Illinois Press, 1956.

Kendrick, A.F. *English Needlework*. London: A. and C. Black, 1933; 2nd edition, 1967.

Kent Lancaster, R. 'Artists, Suppliers and Clerks: the Human Factor in the Art Patronage of Henry III', *Journal of the Warburg and Courtauld Institute*, Volume 35.

King, D. *Samplers*. London: HMSO, 1963.

Kleinbaum, A.R. 'Women in the Age of Light', in Bridenthal and Koonz, op. cit.

Lamb, M. *Miscellaneous Prose 1798–1834*. London: Methuen and Co, 1903.

Lambert, Miss. *Church Needlework*. London: John Murray, 1844.

Lambert, Miss. *The Handbook of Needlework*. London: John Murray, 1843.

Lefebre, E. *Embroidery and Lace*. London: H. Grevel and Co, 1888.

Levey, S. *Discovering Embroidery of the Nineteenth Century*. London: Shire Publications, 1971.

Llanover, Lady, editor. *The Autobiography and Correspondence of Mary Granville, Mrs Delany*. London: 1888.

Lubbell, C. *Textile Collections of the World*. London: Studio Vista, 1976.

Maclean, I. *The Renaissance Notion of Woman*. Cambridge: Cambridge University Press, 1980.

Mahl, M.R. and Koon, H. *The Female Spectator*. Bloomington and London: Indiana University Press, 1977.

Maines, R. 'Fancywork: The Archaeology of Lives', *Feminist Art Journal*, Winter, 1974/75.

Mâle, E. *The Gothic Image*. London: E.P. Dutton, 1913; Icon Editions, 1972.

McNamara, J. and Wemple, S.F. 'Sanctity and Power: The Dual Pursuit of Mediaeval Women', in Bridenthal and Koonz, op. cit.

Millett, K. *Sexual Politics*. New York: Doubleday and Co, 1970. London: Virago, 1977.

Mitchell, J. *Psychoanalysis and Feminism*. London: Allen Lane, 1974; Penguin Books, 1974.

Moers, E. *Literary Women*. London: W.H. Allen and Co, 1977; The Women's Press 1978.

Moller Okin, S. *Women in Western Political Thought*. Princeton University Press, 1979; London: Virago, 1980.

Mosher Stuard, S., editor. *Women in Mediaeval Society*. Philadelphia: Pennsylvania Press, 1976.

Morris, B. *Victorian Embroidery*. London: Herbert Jenkins, 1962.

Morris, M. *Decorative Needlework*. London: Hughes and Co, 1893.

Morris, W. *Selected Writings and Designs*. London: Nonesuch Library, 1934; Penguin Books, 1962.

Neff, W.F. *Victorian Working Women*. London: George Allen and Unwin, 1926.

Nevinson, J.L. *Catalogue of English Domestic Embroidery*. London: Victoria and Albert Museum, 1939.

Nochlin, L. and Sutherland Harris, A. *Women Artists: 1550–1950*. New York: County Museum of Art and Alfred A. Knopf, 1976.

Oakley, A. and Mitchell, J., editors. *The Rights and Wrongs of Women*. London: Penguin Books, 1976.

Oakley, A. 'Wisewomen and Medicine Man: Changes in the Management of Childbirth', in Oakley and Mitchell, op. cit.

O'Faolain, J. and Martines, L., editors. *Not in God's Image*. New York: Harper & Row, 1973; London: Virago, 1979.

Parker, R. and Pollock, G. *Old Mistresses: Women, Art and Ideology*. London: Routledge & Kegan Paul, 1981.

Pinchbeck, I. *Women Workers and the Industrial Revolution 1750–1850*. London: Cass, 1930.

Power, E. M.M. (Postan, editor) *Mediaeval Women*. Cambridge: Cambridge University Press, 1975.

Power, E. (M.M. Postan, editor), *Mediaeval Women*. Cambridge: Cambridge University Press, 1975.

Power, E., translator. *Le Managier de Paris*. London: George Routledge and Sons, 1928.

Prochaska, F.K. *Women and Philanthropy in Nineteenth-Century England*. Oxford: Clarendon Press, 1980.

Procter, M. *Victorian Canvas Work*. London: Batsford, 1972.

Rees, B. *The Victorian Lady*. London: Gordon and Cremonesi, 1977.

Reiter, R.R. *Toward an Anthropology of Women*. New York: Monthly Review Press, 1975.

Rich, A. *Of Woman Born*, New York: W.W. Norton, 1976; London: Virago, 1977.

Rousseau, J.J., (Barbara Foxley, translator) *Emile*. London: Dent, 1911.

Rowbotham, S. *Women, Resistance and Revolution*. London: Allen Lane 1972, Penguin Books, 1974.

Rowbotham, S., *Hidden from History*. London: Pluto, 1973.

Rubin, G. 'The Traffic in Women: Notes on "Political Economy" of Sex', in Reiter, op. cit.

Sandford, E. *Woman in her Social and Domestic Character*. London: 1837.

Schuette, M. and Muller Christensen, S. *The Art of Embroidery*. London: Thames and Hudson, 1964.

Seligman, G.S. and Hughes, T. *Domestic Needlework*. London: Country Life, 1928.

Showalter, E. *A Literature of their Own*. London: Virago, 1978.

Snook, B. *English Historical Embroidery*. London: Batsford, 1978.

Standen, E.A. *Working for Love and Working for Money: Some Notes on Embroiderers and Embroideries of the Past*. New York: Metropolitan Museum of Art, 1966.

Stenton, D.M. *The Englishwoman in History*. London: George Allen and Unwin, 1950.

Strizhenova, T. (Turner, G., translator) *The History of Soviet Costume*. Liverpool: Liverpool Polytechnic, 1972.

Stone, L. *The Family, Sex and Marriage in England 1500–1800*. London: Weidenfeld and Nicolson, 1977.

Swain, M.H. *The Flowerers*. Edinburgh: W.R. Chambers, 1955.

Swain, M.H. *The Needlework of Mary Queen of Scots*. New York: Van Nostrand Reinhold Co, 1973.

Swain, M.H. *Historical Needlework*. London: Barrie and Jenkins, 1970.

Swain, M.H. *Figures on Fabric*. London: A. and C. Black, 1980.

Symonds, M. and Preece, L. *Needlework Through the Ages*. London: Hodder and Stoughton, 1928.

Vicinus, M., editor, *Suffer and Be Still: Women in the Victorian Age*. Bloomington: Indiana University Press, 1973; London: Methuen, 1973.

Vicinus, M., editor, *A Widening Sphere: Changing Roles of Victorian Women*. Bloomington: Indiana University Press, 1977; London: Methuen, 1980.

Wallas, A. *Before the Blue Stockings*. London: George Allen and Unwin, 1929.

Walpole, H. *Anecdotes of Painting in England 1760–1775*. New Haven: 1973.

Wardle, P. *Guide to English Embroidery*. London: Victoria and Albert Museum, 1970.

Warner, M. *Alone of All Her Sex: the Myth and the Cult of the Virgin Mary*. London: Weidenfield and Nicolson, 1976; Quartet Books, 1978.

Warren, G. *A Stitch in Time*. London: David and Charles, 1976.

Warren, E. and Pullan, Mrs. *Treasures of Needlework*. London: Ward and Lock, 1855.

Weyl-Carr, A-M. 'Women Artists in the Middle Ages', *Feminist Art Journal*, Volume 5, Number 1, Spring 1976.

Williams, R. *The Country and the City*. London: Chatto and Windus, 1973.

Wilton, Viscountess (Stone, E). *Art of Needlework*. London: Henry Colburn, 1840.

Wollstonecraft, M. *The Vindication of the Rights of Woman*. London: 1792; Penguin Books, 1978.

Zaretsky, E. *Capitalism, the Family and Personal Life*. London: Pluto, 1976.

GLOSSARY

Illustrated diagrams of embroidery stitches can be found in the majority of books on embroidery, and a comprehensive guide to contemporary and historical terms and techniques is available: Pamela Clabburn, *The Needleworker's Dictionary*, Morrow, New York, 1976.

Ayrshire embroidery White embroidery on fine muslin introduced into Scotland c. 1814 by Mrs Jameson, who copied the technique from a French christening robe. It is characterised by open needlepoint fillings and a floral design in satin and beading stitch. It became a major home industry in Scotland up until the middle of the nineteenth century.

Baudekyn Silk interwoven with threads of gold, it was used for ecclesiastical robings and by royalty and the nobility during the middle ages.

Beading stitch A line of small holes which are overcast.

Berlin woolwork Embroidery in wool on canvas, from patterns drawn on squared paper with each square corresponding to a square of the canvas and a stitch of the pattern. The patterns and wool were introduced into England from Germany during the early decades of the nineteenth century. The technique remained very popular until the 1880s.

Chain stitch As the name implies, it is formed of interlocking flat links.

Chenille A round fluffy thread, aptly termed chenille because it means 'caterpillar' in French. It was often used in embroidered pictures from the late eighteenth century.

Cope An ecclesiastical outer garment resembling a cloak. It is cut as a

240

semi-circle with a band known as an orphrey which runs along the straight side.

Couched stitches A form of stitch in which threads are placed on the ground fabric and secured by an extension of the same thread or others. In Opus Anglicanum a method known as underside couching was employed. The couching thread is beneath the surface and brought up only to secure the gold thread at regular intervals to form a pattern.

Crewel work Any embroidery that is made with lightly twisted, two-ply worsted yarn.

Cross stitch Crosses are formed by counting the fabric thread, usually worked diagonally from left to right.

Needle painting A method of imitating oil painting in embroidery which began in the late eighteenth century.

Needlepoint Lace made with a needle. In the United States the term refers to all canvas work.

Or nué A method of couching using coloured silks to create a shaded pattern on gold thread. It was employed in Europe during the fifteenth century and into the seventeenth century.

Satin stitch The thread is taken from one edge of the design to another to create a smooth satin-like pad. There are many different varieties of satin stitches.

Slips Individual floral motifs popular in the sixteenth and seventeenth centuries. Sometimes they were stitched separately and applied.

Split Stitch A way of working with a soft untwisted silk thread which is split with the needle.

Stump work or raised work Embroidery is given a three-dimensional effect by raising the ground with wooden moulds or pads of cotton wool.

Tambouring A form of embroidery originally made on a frame which resembled a drum. Popular for whitework between 1780 and 1850, tambouring is done with a hook which creates a continuous chain stitch.

Tester The section of a four-poster bed which stretched from behind the head to the top of the posts. It can also refer to the bed canopy, which is hung from the ceiling by chains or suspended between the posts.

Whitework Any embroidery worked in white thread on a white ground.

Worsted Fabric or yarn made from the long fibres of a sheep's fleece.

Worsted work This can refer to any embroidery made with worsted wools, and more precisely to wool embroidery with a three-dimensional effect achieved by a cut-pile surface.

Index